A Mongolian Living Buddha

D1565749

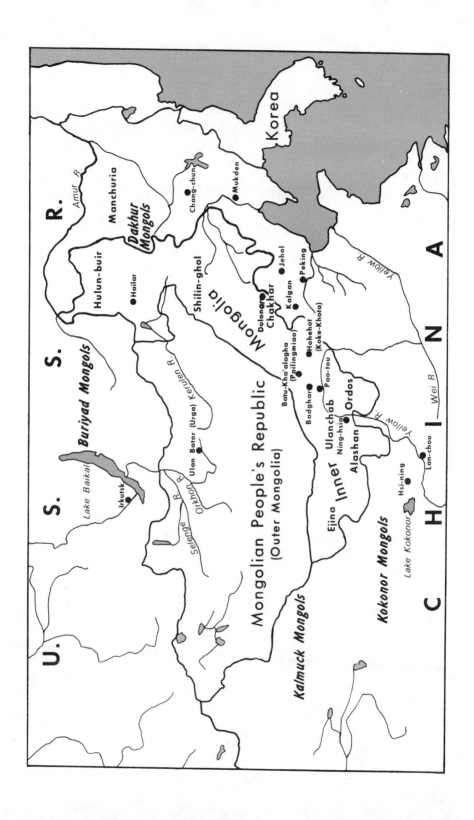

A Mongolian Living Buddha

Biography of the
Kanjurwa Khutughtu

Paul Hyer and Sechin Jagchid
BRIGHAM YOUNG UNIVERSITY

State University of New York Press

ALBANY

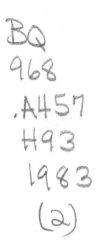

Published by State University of New York Press, Albany

Printed in the United States of America

For information, address State University of New York Press, State University Plaza, Albany, N.Y., 12246

Library of Congress Cataloging in Publication Data

Hyer, Paul.
    A Mongolian living Buddha.

    Includes index.
    1. Kanjurwa Khutughtu, 1914-1978. 2. Lamas—China—Inner Mongolia—Biography. I. Jagchid, Sechin, 1914-   . II. Title.
BQ968.A457H93   1983   294.3′923′0924[B]   83-352
ISBN 0-87395-713-X
ISBN 0-87395-714-8 (pbk.)

Contents

CONTENTS

Part Four: Politics and Religion in Inner Mongolia

Preface

This account is, to our knowledge, the first full biography in a Western language of what is popularly called a Mongolian "living Buddha (*khubilghan*)." Several such accounts have been in preparation but as yet none have been published.

One objective of the authors is to preserve an account of a key historical figure, of certain important institutions, and of a customary religious life style which was traditional in Mongolia but which now has passed into history. The Kanjurwa *khutughtu* (high-ranking transformation or reincarnate lama) was a leader in the world of Lamaist Buddhism in Inner Mongolia during the critical period from the 1920s to the end of World War II in 1945. In a broad context the reader must bear in mind that economically and politically Inner Mongolia was a sub-region of China, this to the distress of the Mongols. Within this context the Kanjurwa's life and experience span many important events and movements: the establishment of the Republic of China with Inner Mongolia subordinated to it as a special administrative region; increasing cultural change for the Mongols with more external contacts; the period of warlords in China following World War I that also greatly affected Mongolia, followed by the rise of the Nationalist Government at Nanking with its nominal unification of China in the late 1920s and early 1930s; the rise of a modern Mongolian class of intellectuals and a growing nationalistic consciousness, plus a decline in Buddhism with modern trends of secularization; the occupation of Inner Mongolia by the Japanese from 1931 to 1945; the Chinese civil war to 1950 and the Communist takeover after World War II. This account of the Kanjurwa has observations on all of these various developments.

A chronology of the life of the Kanjurwa khutughtu has been attached including additional related dates of important events. His predecessors extend back to the 1600s, contemporary with the K'ang-hsi Emperor (r.1662–1721). He was born in a Tibetan ethnic area in the Amdo region of Kokonor, on the China frontier of Inner Asia in 1914. He was educated there as a young boy in the Serkü Monastery and traveled to Inner Mongolia in 1924 at the age of ten where he was installed as the leading reincarnation, the head of Badghar Monastery located on the border between the Ulanchab League and Tümed Banner, not far from Hohhot (Köke-khota). The narrative presents observations regarding his life in a Mongolian monastery and his many travels through various parts of Inner Mongolia. Part of the Kanjurwa's life and story focuses on the monastic educational process, his experience through a series of initiations and studies, and his contact with important persons.

Certain strategic considerations are of concern in the account presented here. Inner Asia is still one of the most obscure areas of study in the world. It is large, little-known, and includes the strategic regions from Manchuria through Mongolia, Turkistan (Sinkiang), Afghanistan and Tibet. Mongolia particularly is a focal point of Russian-China confrontation. In centuries past it was the pivot of Asia—now it is a pawn in great power rivalry. The roots of contemporary problems are to be found in earlier historical experience and in the traditional culture. One important aspect of the area that requires attention is the biography of key leaders like the Kanjurwa.

Mongolia, like the other areas noted above, was long characterized as a "sacred" society, in that secularization here has been a late trend and religion traditionally permeated all phases of society and culture. From time to time Buddhist and Islamic societies experience a resurgence or revitalization of religious forces. Thus some attention should be concentrated on the nature of traditional religious institutions to more readily understand contemporary trends. For Mongolia this means a study of Lamaist Buddhism and the key institution of the khubilghan, the reincarnate lama. The Kanjurwa khutughtu of Inner Mongolia is useful as a model for understanding other such figures who had a similar role.

The fate of Mongolian Buddhism that forms the background of this biography is of concern to any person interested in the conflict between humanist as opposed to totalitarian systems. This religion has shown high qualities in the realm of ideas and the spirit. The Kanjurwa's biography sheds some light on the humanistic and cultural life of a resilient people, the Mongols, who deserve worldwide respect and admiration.

The Kanjurwa's career is a type, a pattern, or case study typical in many ways for Khalkha (Outer Mongolia) and Buriad Mongolia and to some degree for Tibet. In view of the complex pantheon of reincarnations or transformations (khubilghans) in the world of Lamaist Buddhism, it may be useful here to place the Kanjurwa in a general context. The cradle of this unique form of Buddhism, and its unrivaled focal point, was of course Tibet and more especially Lhasa. There were uppermost the famous Dalai Lama and Panchen Lama of Tibet; then, in the more limited sphere of Mongolian Lamaist Buddhism, there was the Jebtsundamba khutughtu of Urga (now Ulan Bator) in Outer Mongolia. Below him were many reincarnations, only a few of which can be mentioned. There was the high-ranking Dilowa khutughtu who left Outer Mongolia as a refugee to Inner Mongolia in the 1930s and who became an acquaintance of the Kanjurwa. There was also the Jangjia khutughtu, resident alternately in Peking, Wu-t'ai shan and Dolonor, and a well-known rival of the Kanjurwa. These three were more prominent than the Kanjurwa khutughtu. However, during the crucial periods of this narrative all of these important ecclesiastical figures were actually absent from Inner Mongolia, leaving only the Kanjurwa—the Jebtsundamba departed this world in 1924, apparently without a successor; the Dilowa left for Tibet in 1939; and the Jangjia went to south central China with the Chinese nationalists for the duration of the war. Thus, the Kanjurwa was the highest-ranking grand lama of khutughtu rank in Mongolia during much of the period of this narrative.

The high rank and official title of khutughtu was conferred on the Kanjurwa gegen (enlightened lama master) by Peking only after the establishment of the Republic of China (1912). The Kanjurwa was not one of the eight high lamas in Peking but was one of the thirteen preeminent reincarnations at the monastic center of Dolonor where he spent much time. He attracted great veneration in the Chakhar region of western Inner Mongolia and particularly in the Hulun-buir region of northeastern Inner Mongolia. His home monastery of Badghar, better known to the Chinese as Wu-tan-chao, was one of the most important monasteries in all of Inner Mongolia. It was a great academic monastery that attracted many lama-monks in recognition of its scholarly distinction.

The unique biographical account related here was quite lengthy in the writing process, and the authors should note a few items of interest the reader may wish to keep in mind. As translators, interpreters, and editors, we have avoided personal judgments of the Kanjurwa's biographical account, and we have avoided making a critique or analytical study of the information presented here. Instead of making laudatory or critical comments we have tried to set forth sympathetically a neutral record conveying the personal experiences and views of the Kangurwa gegen himself.

A note about the process of preparing the manuscript should be added. The main Mongolian language interviews with the Kanjurwa gegen were taped at his monastic residence near Taipei in 1971–1972. The interviews were then translated into English at Brigham Young University, Provo, Utah, including such explanatory insertions as seemed necessary to make the story understandable or to place the Kanjurwa's career in context. The rambling, unstructured interviews were reorganized and edited to prepare the final manuscript, maintaining the first person style, though often writing in the past tense due to what has happened to the religion since the occupation of Inner Mongolia by the Chinese Communists and the revolution of Mao Tse-tung and his "Red Guards." The authors realize that in the editing process, annotated translation becomes interpretation and have tried to avoid distortion or bias that may stem from personal viewpoints.

With great regret we note that the passing of the Kanjurwa in 1978 cut short follow-up interviews that could have greatly supplemented the information noted here. We hope his views have not been too greatly distorted but, given the problems of language and the elusive nature of certain sensitive issues involved, obviously ideal results are not possible. Some persons may have preferred a different presentation of the material included in this work, but it is impossible to please in one approach the general reader, the comparative religion specialist, and the social science behaviorist.

Regarding the monastic life discussed in the book, the reader should again bear in mind that this work is not intended as a technical, precise presentation of the complex pantheon of Buddhist deities, the intriguing art and symbolism, the important

ceremonial and ritualistic aspects of the religion, or the Buddhological philosophy involved. On these matters the specialists,
and even the general reader, must be patient. Persons who have
a special interest in religion and wish to use this work as a
reference on technical matters regarding Lamaist Buddhism should
remember that the translator-editors make no claim to be au-
thorities on all aspects concerned, and while considerable care
has been taken in the work, it is not intended for specialists
looking for a detailed analysis or presentation of the subject.

Another problem is posed by the technical terms of Lamaist
Buddhism and such institutions as the monastery, temple, or
hermitage. A general consensus dictates the use of the term
monastery rather than temple as the primary religious institution
concerned. In English this obscures or confuses such corresponding Mongolian terms as süme, küriye, keid, and juu, but even in
Mongolian society these are not carefully differentiated as to size
or function, and are often used interchangeably. This may create
a little confusion for some, and the same is the case for such
Chinese terms as miao, ssu, and chao, commonly used as coun-
terparts for the above Mongolian terms in Inner Mongolia where
Chinese influence has been so great.

In the narrative such terms as Lamaism are used instead of
consistently using Buddhism, and perhaps this usage would not
please the Kanjurwa, but it is a long-standing, common practice
in discussing the unique form of Buddhism found in Tibet and
Mongolia.

The romanized transcription of Mongolian terms from the old
Mongolian orthography presents certain problems and has been
modified by some phonetic considerations. As there is really no
standardized form, sometimes the romanized version of a term
used here favors the classical written Mongolian, sometimes the
modern spoken language. Most of the liturgical language of Mongolian Buddhism is naturally borrowed from Tibet, but the terms
are given here in the transcription or usage found in Mongolia.

Adjustments have been made in noting the age of the Kanjurwa
at various points in his career, so the traditional Mongolian custom
of considering the subject as being one year old at birth has not
been followed; dates have been adjusted to correspond to Western
conventions or usage. Care has been taken in the dates and
chronology noted, but at times it has been necessary to interpolate
from key dates in the Kanjurwa's career and to correlate or check

[xi]

these against contemporary events. Sechin Jagchid, co-author of the present work, has served as an important check on various aspects of the Kanjurwa's account. His father, Lobsanchoijur, was a lama until the age of forty-two, but left the monastery as an only son to carry on the family line. He served as an agent in Peking for the Thirteenth Dalai Lama of Tibet. Also, Jagchid's own career as an official in the Mongolian Government (Kalgan) was concurrent with the period concerned with the key time span of the Kanjurwa's own career. The authors solicit the assistance of knowledgeable readers in making corrections of fact or interpretation.

We wish to express appreciation to those who have been especially helpful in preparing the manuscript: Kerril Sue Rollins, departmental assistant; Marilyn Webb and Alison Rojas of the Brigham Young University faculty support center; the Social Science Research Council and American Council of Learned Societies for assistance to pursue research in Taiwan, China.

Selected Chronology of the Career of the Kanjurwa *khutughtu* and of Inner Mongolia

1911   Outer Mongolia declares independence. China's revolution abolishes the Manchu imperial dynasty to establish a republic.

1914   Outbreak of World War I.

Birth of the Kanjurwa *gegen*/reincarnation in Kokonor at Doloon-küree-mörin-sobrugh (seven enclosures of the horse stupa). Kanjurwa is taken from home at the age of four to be raised in a monastery.

1918   Buriad based pan-Mongolian movement fails in attempt to unite all Mongols. End of World War I.

Judba *gegen* appointed as Kanjurwa's tutor at Serkü Monastery, Amdo, Kokonor, and takes initial vows.

1920   Master Kandan-yantsan appointed as a tutor of the Kanjurwa to study special Buddhist texts.

1921   Tsambu *nom-un-khan khutughtu*, abbot of a Tibetan monastery, is invited to be a tutor of the Kanjurwa.

1924   Kanjurwa leaves Serkü Monastery, in Amdo and travels to Inner Mongolia in February. Arrives at Pao-t'ou and Hohhot (Köke-khota) in March—visits Peking for one month (age ten).

Spring—Kanjurwa takes up residence at Dolonor (Doloon-nor) monastic temple center with which his predecessors had long been associated.

Fall—journeys via Shilin-ghol and Ulanchab regions to Badghar Monastery, which became his home institution. The Kanjurwa settles at Badghar for study and training.

Death of the Eighth Jebtsundamba *khutughtu*, "living Buddha" of Urga (Ulan Bator), in Outer Mongolia and proclamation of the Mongolian People's Republic (MPR). Many Inner Mongolian youth go north and join the Mongolian People's Revolutionary Party. Civil war breaks out in China. Feng Yü-hsiang, Chinese warlord dominates western Inner Mongolia, imprisons President Ts'ao K'un and removes the abdicated Manchu emperor P'u-yi from the Forbidden City. Peking comes under Tuan Ch'i-jui's rule. First session of Sun Yat-sen's Kuomintang (KMT) congress held in Canton, several Mongolian leaders joining the KMT movement are given organization assignments in Inner Mongolia.

1925 Sun Yat-sen dies in Peking. Establishment of the Inner Mongolian People's Revolutionary Party with militant anti-feudal and anti-religious policies. The Eighth Panchen Lama arrives in Peking from Tibet and later plays a role in Mongolia. Nationalist-Communist coalition regime is established in Canton.

Spring—Kanjurwa visits the Panchen Lama in Peking after his flight from Tibet and has Dimpiral *lharamba* appointed to him as a teacher.

1926 Warlord Chang Tso-lin takes over Peking. Chiang Kai-shek leads the Northern Expedition from Canton to the Yangtze region to establish new Central Government at Nanking.

The Kanjurwa presides at special ceremonies for the installation at Badghar Monastery of the Duingkhor incarnation.

1927 Kanjurwa visits Peking—meets warlord Chang Tso-lin, Prince Gungsangnorbu, governor Ling-sheng and others; travels to Bargha in eastern Mongolia (Heilungkiang region) to visit his disciples at Kanjurwa Monastery.

Chiang Kai-shek establishes Nationalist Government at Nanking. Chang Tso-lin's power declines in eastern

Inner Mongolia, Peking and Manchuria; his assassination follows in 1928.

1928   Kanjurwa studies at Badghar to learn Buddhist texts and takes additional training in preparation to function as a high lama, an incarnation and head of the monastery.

Nationalist forces occupy Peking. Prince Gungsangnorbu resigns as head of the Mongolian Tibetan Ministry as it is reorganized. Mongolian Delegation negotiates in Nanking for Mongolian autonomy but fails. The Nationalist Government establishes four provinces in Inner Mongolia: Jehol, Chahar, Suiyüan and Ninghsia, also Chinghai Province in the Mongolian-Tibetan territory of Kokonor, and Sikang Province in the Kham region of eastern Tibet.

1930   Much suffering in Badghar Monastery region for several years due to drought, famine and locust plague. Kanjurwa has important meeting with the Tibetan Panchen Lama in Chakhar. Visits Pandita Gegen Monastery in Abakhanar Banner, Shilin-ghol League and spends the winter at Dolonor monastic center.

Mongolian Conference in Nanking passes important proposal "Law for the Organization of the Mongolian Leagues, Tribes and Banners."

1931   Spring—Kanjurwa returns to Badghar from Dolonor, by rail via Kalgan and Hohhot, experiences great plague with death of his advisor Yantson *bagshi* and many lamas.

Manchurian Incident breaks out as Japan occupies Manchuria and eastern Inner Mongolia.

1932   "Manchukuo" is established and Japan installs the Manchu imperial heir P'u-yi as head of a puppet regime. Prince De and other Mongolian leaders in visit to Nanking fail to block proposals for reformation of Mongolian traditional administrative system. Mongolian administrative district of Hsingan is established in Japan's Manchukuo with special provisions for autonomy.

Kanjurwa completes examination for and receives the monastic rank of *gebshi*.

[xv]

1933   Japanese occupy two eastern Inner Mongolian leagues,
        Josotu and Juu-uda (Jehol province), and also Dolonor
        monastic center of the Kanjurwa. The Mongolian Au-
        tonomous Movement is inaugurated at Bat-khaalagh (Pai-
        ling-miao) as a separatist movement from Chinese dom-
        ination.

        Panchen Lama visits Kanjurwa's Badghar Monastery.
        Kanjurwa comes of age and assumes full role and au-
        thority of his title.

1934   Chinese National Government recognizes Mongol de-
        mands, a compromise Mongolian Regional Autonomous
        Political Council is established. Confrontation between
        the Mongols and Chinese warlord, Fu Tso-yi, becomes
        critical. Japanese *Zenrin kyokai* (a cultural assistance
        organization) and *tokumu kikan* (military intelligence
        groups) become active in Mongolia.

        Kanjurwa resides most of the year in Gül-kökö Banner
        of Chakhar region.

1935   Chinese troops forced out of areas north of the Great
        Wall by the Japanese except in the Kalgan vicinity.
        Prince De visits Manchukuo and his contacts with the
        Japanese are strengthened.

        Kanjurwa travels to Bargha region via Shilin-ghol and
        Khaluun-arshan and visits such places in Manchuria as
        Mukden, Chin-chou and Jehol Province.

1936   Mongolian Military Government is established in West
        Sunid Banner and is soon moved to Jabsar (Te-hua).
        Japanese troops invade eastern Suiyüan Province; Fu
        Tso-yi's troops counter-attack, occupy Bat-khaalagh and
        destroy the monastery. Mongolia is threatened but as
        the Sian Incident occurs with the capture of Chiang
        Kai-shek, the crisis moderates. The Chinese Nationalist
        Government splits the Mongolian Regional Autonomous
        Political Council and establishes a rival Suiyüan Mon-
        golian Autonomous Council under General Fu Tso-yi's
        control.

        Kanjurwa spends year in Chakhar region devoted to
        medical and religious activities.

1937   Japan occupies Peking, North China and most of Inner Mongolia, Mongolian Allied Leagues Autonomous Government is established by the Mongols in Köke-khota (Hohhot). A Meng-chiang Allied Committee is established by the Japanese in Kalgan as a fore-runner of a new comprehensive political structure for the China-Mongolia border region.

Kanjurwa spends entire year in Chakhar League, Gülkökö Banner. Winter spent in Dolonor monasteries.

1938   The Kanjurwa visits Kalgan, then returns to Badghar Monastery. Receives scholarly lama Yontson of Naiman Banner, eastern Inner Mongolia as a tutor. Spends winter at Dolonor.

Prince De visits Japan. The Japanese push for a consolidation of their influence in Mongolia—the Mongols want Japan to fulfill its promises for unification and real autonomy.

1939   The Nomunkhan/Khalkha River Battle breaks out between Russian-Outer Mongolian forces and Japan-Manchukuo forces. The Mongolian United Autonomous Government is established in Kalgan as Japan takes more political control of Mongolia and unifies the Mongolian Allied League Autonomous Government with two Chinese puppet regimes, Ch'a-nan and Chin-pei.

1940   Establishment in Inner Mongolia of *khorishia*, new co-operative economic organizations to market Mongolian products.

Kanjurwa travels through Chakhar region to Dolonor and resides here through 1941. His monastery here is refurbished from its destruction during the Chinese Revolution [1911].

1941   Prince De makes second journey to Japan. The establishment of the *Mongghol öbesüben jasakhu ulus* (Mongolian Autonomous State).

1942   Kanjurwa's third visit to Bargha for special religious observances on the occasion of the completion of a thirty-six year project of building a great *loilung*, Mongolian Buddhist replica of a city of the Buddha's.

A Mongolian Development Commission is established in Kalgan, as the Japanese relax their political control over Inner Mongolia with the outbreak of the Pacific War with the United States.

1943   Kanjurwa journeys to Japan to visit Japanese Buddhist centers as leader of a group of twenty-one Mongolian Buddhist leaders. Organization of the *Lama tamagha* (office of lama affairs) with the Kanjurwa as one of the top officials.

1945   World War II ends and Soviet-MPR troops occupy areas of Inner Mongolia. The Dolonor monasteries are destroyed. The Kanjurwa *khutughtu* flees, suffers as a refugee and goes to Peking.

1946–49   Chinese civil war between the Nationalists and Communists rages in Inner Mongolia and China.

1949   Many Mongolian leaders including the Kanjurwa take refuge in Taiwan as the Chinese Communists take China.

1952   Premier Ch'en Ch'eng arranges residence for the Kanjurwa at P'u-chi Temple and he makes special preaching tour in Taiwan. He makes this circuit several times in 1950s.

1957   Kanjurwa *gegen* officiates in memorial service for Jangjia *khutughtu* at his passing. Earlier conflict between the two had been resolved. Kanjurwa serves as First Director of the Board of the Chinese Buddhist Association 1959–1962.

1958   Kanjurwa leads Chinese delegation to Bangkok to commemorate 2500th anniversary of the Buddha's birth.

1964–67   Kanjurwa makes three trips to Hong Kong to visit patrons and followers and to perform special ceremonies.

1978   Passing of Kanjurwa *khutughtu* after return from a visit to the Philippines.

PART ONE

My Origin
as an Incarnation

Birth and Selection as an Incarnation

I was born in a common family among the Tangut (Tibetan) ethnic group in the Amdo region of Kokonor (Ch. Chinghai) that was devoted to Lamaist Buddhism. But there is a tradition in our family that long ago our paternal lineage descended from a local Mongolian leader called a *t'u-ssu* by the Chinese in this region. In my native place many Mongols were assimilated to Tibetan culture rather than to the Chinese. As I look back now in my old age, I can see that my childhood world was quite Tibetan, and it was only from the age of ten that I moved into a Mongolian world. My concerns are now Mongolian, and for some reason I am uneasy if someone refers to me as a Tangut. I wonder if my life is not a little like the last great Jebtsundamba *khutughtu* (incarnate "living Buddha") of Urga in Outer Mongolia who, though a Tibetan, was the key figure there until his death in 1924 in a movement for Mongolian independence and a greater Mongolia.

The people in my native area had a nomadic tradition, but by my time they were quite settled in a semi-pastoral, semi-agricultural life. My home region was very complex ethnically, economically and politically.

In 1913, my predecessor and former incarnation left Inner Mongolia to return to his original monastery of Serku in Amdo. While there, my mother, who was suffering from serious mental distress, visited him to pay her respects and to request his blessing. She was healed, and later, when she returned to the monastery to express her gratitude, the incarnation told her, "You are to be the mother of my next *khubilghan* (reincarnation/transformation)." According to the explanation of the senior lamas, it was for this reason that I was born to this particular woman, for I did indeed become the fifth incarnation of the Kanjurwa gegen (also referred to as Kangyurwa).

My mother was also inspired in prophetic dreams about my divine calling. On a certain occasion when she went to the river to draw water for the family, my mother beheld a vision—a personage approaching in the distance, riding a reddish-yellow horse and wearing a yellow jacket with a red button of rank on his hat. It was the local protective deity of the Serkü area, who had been given special status by the Manchu emperor. Such a manifestation was fairly common in that area, and thus, my mother, wondering if perhaps an official was coming to visit the family for some reason, hurried home to greet him. No one came, however. My mother was pregnant at the time and some people interpreted this experience to mean that the birth of her child was to bring the family special distinction. That night as she slept, she had another vision—of two fireballs rolling around her. To friends and neighbors this was a sign that the birth was to be twins. My mother caught only one fireball, however, and it was a single birth. Some months following this dream, when my mother was about to give birth, she beheld another vision in which she saw many people and a yellow sedan chair coming to our home. No doubt this vision foreshadowed the day when I was to be seated in a special yellow sedan chair and confirmed as a special incarnation in the great Buddhist religion of Mongolia.

I was born in a place called Doloon-küree-morin-sobrogh (the seven enclosures of the horse stupa), in Kokonor. According to the lunar calendar it was 1914, the year of the blue tiger (the third year of the Republic of China, in which I was to spend most of my life). It was a leap year, the fifth month (horse), the twenty-third day (16 June), the day of the tiger, and the hour of the tiger (around 4:00 A.M.). Because I was born still within the fetal sack, those attending had to take great care in opening it and thus my birth was extraordinary. When only three days old, I was put on a diet of cow's milk because my mother was not able to nurse me. My mother, Rolma, and my father, Lhamujab, first named me Badmatsereng. Later I had a younger brother named Ghonchoghtsedeng.

From ancient times my home region of Amdo, Kokonor was dominated by a people of Tibetan language and Buddhist culture

[4]

which, until recent years, strongly resisted assimilation by Chinese settling in the area. From the fifteenth century on, Mongolian people from south of the Gobi began to migrate into Kokonor. Later, in the middle of the seventeenth century, an even more important migration occurred which brought the Khoshod Mongols from the T'ien-shan mountain region into Kokonor. Under Manchu administration these various Mongol peoples were organized into two separate leagues or groupings, including subdivisions of a total of twenty-nine banners, or administrative groups.

From early times Chinese influence was periodically strong in the area, as during the Han period (206 B.C.–220 A.D.), and the T'ang period (618–907). But in more recent history Chinese influence greatly increased with Chinese settlement in our area, particularly during the Ming period (1368–1644), and the Manchu-Ch'ing period (1644–1911). The main forward base or important administrative place of this Chinese influence was Hsi-ning, known to Mongols as Seleng-khota.

My home region is further complicated because it borders on the famous and important area of Chinese Turkestan (Sinkiang). During the 1800s, when rebellion and warfare seemed universal among the Moslem people, there was a great deal of destruction in all the border areas through Yünnan, Kansu, Kokonor, and western Mongolia, which was politically administered by the Chinese. Because of the Moslem rampages during this period, our Lamaist monasteries suffered greatly; many people were killed as unbelievers of Islam, and we were constantly plundered by marauding Moslem groups. As a result of the suppression of these disorders by the Manchu, a great area neighboring us was incorporated into China as a new administrative region, later known as Sinkiang or the "new dominion."

When I was a boy, I was curious about the remnants of logs used to fortify the area around the monastery where I was raised, and the old people liked to tell stories about the struggle between our Tibetan-Mongolian Buddhist people and the Moslem invaders. Even today some Buddhists here feel antagonistic toward neighboring Moslems. By my time the most powerful group in my native Kokonor was the Chinese Moslems, particularly the Ma family, which in time became the main military and political force. Their original old home was in Kansu Province, in a village called Hsiang-t'ang located in Hsia-ho *hsien* (district). From this

[5]

base the old head of the family, Ma Ch'i, expanded his influence to create a veritable warlord empire. His descendants, both infamous and powerful in this century, include Ma Fu-hsiang and his son Ma Hung-k'uei, also Ma Pu-ch'ing and his cousin Ma Pu-fang. During various periods they had great influence in the provinces of Ninghsia, Kokonor, Kansu, and even Sinkiang.

The Kokonor region was named after the famous "blue lake" there, called *Chinghai* by the Chinese. The shore of this lake was the site of the famous meetings in 1578 between Altan Khan of Mongolia and the Third Dalai Lama of Tibet. It was on this occasion that Altan Khan was converted to Buddhism and invited the Third Dalai Lama to come to Mongolia to propagate the faith. This he did, but later, after the death of Altan Khan. The greatest significance of this meeting is that it was the beginning of the process by which Tibetan Buddhism became the predominant faith of Mongolia.

At the age of two (1916), my uncle, also a lama, brought me to the monastery where I was soon to take up a monastic life and be raised by the monks. As we were traveling on horseback from my home, I, riding on his lap, lost one of the bootees my mother had made for my departure. Because I was young enough to be carried in my uncle's arms, it of course really didn't matter whether I wore bootees, but my memory of the loss is still vivid because the shoes were important to me—often we were barefooted, but more important was the fact that these things represented my mother's love.

I have often been asked how I felt as a small child of three (two by the Western calendar) when I was installed on the exalted seat in the monastery as an incarnation. I vaguely remember that when I was seated there many people came forward to offer presents in the form of a symbolic *mandala*, which I will explain later. They borrowed the holy *mandala* from the treasury of the monastery long enough to place money or some other gift on it to make an offering. These *mandalas* themselves are round or square, made of silver or brass, and are symbolic of spiritual powers. Many people came to request a blessing, or to pay respects. Being a very young child, my main recollection was of many very large, very old people gathered around me, and I felt that I too was becoming old.

My religious status brought special distinction from the beginning. While I was still a small boy, an official lama from Mongolia.

Ghombu *donir* (an official escort or retinue) visited me. When I took my first formal vow (*sakil*) as a lama, three lamas participated—myself and two others from Mongolia, one of whom was Lobsandungrub. All of us were just neophytes. The ceremonies required that I respond in a customary manner at certain times; but since I was so young and didn't know what to say, I was prompted by a lama who stood behind me. I thought it quite amusing to go through the various ceremonies of bowing and kowtowing, of standing and reciting, and so on. After receiving my first vows, I was no longer called by the name my parents had given me, but rather by a new temple name, Aghwang-lobsang-dambi-nima. These first vows were those of the *gesel* (Skt. *śrāmanera*; Ch. *sha-mi*) degree by which we, as new lamas, committed ourselves to seek the transcendental refuge of nirvana, to adopt a monastic life, and to accept the discipline, the commandments of the Buddha, foreswearing many such things as killing, sexual activity, and alcoholic drinks.

At the age of four (1918) I left home, never to return, and was taken to the Serkü Monastery in the Amdo region. (Serkü *keid*, i.e., monastery, also had a Chinese name, *Kuang-hui*, given by the emperor to distinguish it as an imperial monastery.) Here I was prepared to later assume the ecclesiastical role of the Kanjurwa incarnation in Mongolia. At this time my official title was changed from *Shasin-ig delgeren üildügchi Kanjurwa mergen nomun khan* (he who works for the development of Buddhism, Kanjurwa the enlightened king of the Law) to *Kanjurwa khutughtu* a much shorter title, though one of higher rank—for *khutughtu* is the highest rank among incarnate lamas.

Childhood Education and Training in Kokonor

People commonly feel that because an incarnation is a "living Buddha" certainly he must experience only serenity, perpetual happiness, and have no worries. Unfortunately this is not so. As a *khubilghan*, I am qualified to speak about this matter. I know the feelings of an incarnation, the hard work and long process of preparation to fill the role. While but a very young boy I was installed by the lamas in the Serkü Monastery as an incarnation and given special training. Teachers of superior ability were appointed to tutor me, and I was required to develop in discipline

[7]

and knowledge as they taught me on the basis of their experience and wisdom.

The Serkü Monastery in Kokonor where I initially resided appointed me a tutor when I was just four years old, and I took a solemn ritualistic oath that I would recognize Judba *gegen* (enlightened one), an elderly learned lama, as my venerable teacher. We called him *baghshi* (teacher). With this very binding oath, I became his *shabi* (disciple). It was from Judba *gegen* that I took the first-stage oath, *gesel sanwar*, of the Buddhist priesthood to begin the discipline of the lamas. He also taught me to read and write the Tibetan language.

Regarding the relationship between an incarnation of high rank and his teacher, there are a few customs of interest that I will relate about the Badghar Monastery where I later lived and with which I am most familiar. When an incarnation is very young, it is the responsibility of the senior lamas of the monastery to find a very capable, learned teacher to instruct him. Such respected teachers were commonly referred to as *lamakhai* (*khai* is a suffix indicating honor); thus, I usually referred to one of my beloved teachers as Sambu *lamakhai*. We young lamas were frequently in the company of our teachers and the nature of our relationship depended on each particular situation at hand. In formal situations in the great prayer hall, I, as an incarnation, was seated on an elevated seat of honor above all others. However, when my teacher came to my residence to instruct me, I was seated below him. Never did my teacher say he was "teaching" me; instead he used the phrase *nom barikh*, meaning "to explain the Law of the Buddha, to a lama superior to himself."

When I began my education at Serkü Monastery, friends and relatives came to present customary ceremonial scarfs (*khadagh*) and to congratulate me on beginning an education. Following this, because of the importance of this period of my life, my attendants made a ceremonial presentation of tea on my behalf to the large congregation of lamas in Serkü Monastery. After this presentation I began to attend daily prayer assemblies (*khural*) in the monastery, though my attendance was not strictly regular. Because of my tender age, it was necessary for someone to accompany me each time.

As a young lama leaves his family and goes to the monastery, he is first recognized as a monk novice (*khuwaragh*), and one of his first actions is to take a vow (*sanwar*), involving many restraints

[8]

and rules, that brings him to the first stage of monkhood (*gesel*). Another very early activity is the memorization of the Tibetan alphabet; when the young lama can recognize the script, his first text is the *itegel*, the creed of the Buddha. There are two forms of this *itegel* text, one in Mongolian and one in Tibetan. Generally, young monks first memorize the Mongolian *itegel* in order to clearly understand what is involved in the sacred creed. Later they memorize the Tibetan creed and then go on to study other texts. The main method of study consists of a teacher assigning the young lamas certain *ongshilagh* (readings) that are to be memorized. The memorization is not silent but takes place in a chanting fashion. There are many different types of *ongshilagh*, and it is a great task to master all of them in order to recite them at any given time. After a student is able to recite the text, only then does the teacher begin to instruct him in reading.

In 1920, at the age of six, I received another teacher, Khandan-yangtsan, with whom I began an earnest study of the Buddhist scriptures. Because this teacher had the authority to read and transmit the scriptures, I was not only taught the information they contain but also had transmitted from him to me by a special ceremony the authority to later teach them.

When I was seven years old, the head lamas of Serkü Monastery invited Tsambu *nom-un-khan khutughtu*, an abbot from a Tibetan monastery, to be yet another teacher for me. He came to stay at Serkü Monastery and my memory of the morning he arrived is still very vivid. A large group of us went out from the monastery some distance to meet and welcome him, and I was placed in a special frame on the back of a horse to make the excursion.

At the age of eight I received the *lung*—ordination or authorization from master Khandan-yangtsan to read and expound the Kanjur (Kangyur), a great body of Buddhist scripture in Tibetan. To those of us raised in the monastery who devote our lives to the religion, the term *lung* has a very special meaning as a sacred teaching, exhortation, or lecture given only by certain dignitaries of the religion. In one sense it is a special discourse intended to give those who hear it a special mandate or commission to read a certain scripture or fulfill a certain ritual. Interestingly, in the common language of the people the holy term *lung* has been popularized and is used when a person has been scolded or called to account by his superior officer in the government, at school,

[9]

or at some other such place; or, this vulgarized usage may refer to a dry, indoctrinating lecture that people do not want to hear.

That same year, 1922, while I was still at the Serkü Monastery, an *emchi gegen* (a medical doctor with the rank of an incarnation) was invited to visit. Later that same year I made a special offering for rain to Denchi Lhombu, regional deity of the place where I was born. We believed him to be the great deity of the *oboo* shrine of that place. Following my offering, it rained for eight days. I continued to study and received various ordinations or commissions to study particular scriptures in which I became accomplished.

Like all young boys, young lamas get into mischief, and sometimes it was necessary that we be punished. On such occasions our teacher would give us *khal-barikh* (an "offering" of punishment = English "Scotch blessing"). This discipline may seem a little incongruous for a *khubilghan* or a reincarnation of a monastery who is the founder, the abbot, and the "living Buddha" of the monastery in which he is installed through a series of reincarnations. Therefore, though he be but a child in his new reincarnation, even the venerable senior lamas are subordinate to him. These elderly teachers had at one time come to the monastery to become disciples of his predecessors and to give strict loyalty and obedience to the incarnation and abbot of the institution; but after the death of the incarnation, the succeeding, newly installed reincarnation was required to submit obediently to them as his teachers, for not to do so would have been contrary to the vows he had taken. Also, all know that the incarnation himself is not above the Buddha and may on occasion need to be disciplined; but before a teacher punished a young mischievous incarnation, he would first pray. He would ask for forgiveness, for support, and for approval from the Buddha on the disciplinary action he was about to take against the incarnation. Need for such punishment was, of course, uncommon.

Because problems were often created when the lamas of a monastery disciplined and taught an incarnation of their own institution, who was above them in holiness and authority, a young reincarnation was commonly sent to a distant monastery where he could be trained by other lamas and teachers not so directly involved.

Wherever I studied, my teachers would reprove me and explain that I was not an ordinary lama, that I was an exalted *gegen*, that I would someday preside over a monastery and have great power and authority, and that I must therefore make a greater effort to accomplish more than the ordinary lamas. This pressure was complicated and intensified by the fact that many of the tutors and lamas of the monasteries, especially later when I lived at Badghar and Dolonor, were extremely ambitious in wanting to expand their influence and attract as many *shabinar* (disciples) as possible. In my days of discipline and training, if my teachers hesitated to punish me, it was the responsibility of a *soibon* (steward) to administer *khal barikh*, nothing more than a common beating. I still remember with regret the beatings given me by my *soibon* for childish mistakes and inadequate efforts in study.

While I cannot complain that it was a time of suffering, still I cannot look back on my childhood as a happy time. It was a period of constant, intense learning. I was not able to play as other boys, for I was always subject to some ceremony or discipline and various related restrictions. Until I came of age and was somewhat more liberated, my world was only the four walls of the monastery. I had no knowledge of what was happening outside in Tibet, in Mongolia or China, or in other parts of the world.

The days of my youth, later, in Mongolia, were also characterized by careful attention to thrift, partly because of the wartime years of Japan's invasion of China with various military disturbances, and partly because of the resrictions and the teaching of my tutors. For long periods of time it was not possible for me even to have a new garment or to change my clothing more than once a year. No one at that time would ever suspect from my appearance that I was the incarnation of the rich and powerful Badghar Monastery (süme), the most important monastic center in western Inner Mongolia. Here it must be kept in mind that after the revolution and the establishment of the Chinese Republic (1912), North China and the frontier lapsed into warlordism. Dolonor, where I then lived, was perpetually plundered and looted by Chinese armies and bandits, and was in such difficult circumstances that men could not be sent the rather long distance from Dolonor to Badghar Monastery in Ulanchab in western Inner Mongolia to obtain assistance because of the insecurity of the countryside. In those days I was most grateful for a few cookies that some lama might bring to me. But as miserable as my suffering might have been in those days, even at its worst it did not begin to compare with the suffering of our people and the suppression

[11]

of our religion after the Chinese Communist occupation in the late 1940s, after the defeat of the Japanese who had been quite good to us.

There were many things in the monastery that surprised or interested me. For example, when I was nine or ten years old and still residing at Serku Monastery in the Amdo region, I had a friend, Monon *gegen*, two years older than I. When he died and was cremated, I observed that his *sharil* (Skt. *sārira*; a jewel-like deposit remaining after the cremation) was in the shape of an image of Yamandagha (Skt. Yamāntaka), "Conqueror of Yāma," the supreme deity of hell and the protector of Buddha's Law. This phenomenon greatly astonished me, and I bowed in veneration to it. On another similar occasion, after the cremation of a venerable lama, I beheld that on the skull of his remains were imprinted three images of the Buddha. Manjushri (Skt. Mañjuśrī; Ch., Wen-shu *p'u-sa*) was situated in the middle, with Ariyabul (the thousand handed Kuan-yin *p'u-sa* or Avalokiteśvara) on one side, and Ochir-bani (Skt., Vajrapāni; Ch. P'u-hsien *p'u-sa*) on the other. This would have been difficult for me to believe had I not seen it with my own eyes. To this day I still marvel at this miraculous occurrence.

After long study, preparation, and proper discipline, I assumed the role of an incarnation in reality, not just nominally. I was seated above all the lamas and *shabinar*, officiated in important ceremonies, and carried out the duties associated with my position. And finally I had a good feeling that I cannot really find words to describe. I was trusted and honored. Unfortunately for our religion there were those cases in which a young reincarnation was installed who was not properly trained nor wise in his actions and consequently not honored and trusted. Not only was this difficult for him; it was also an embarrassment to the lamas of the monastery and others aware of the problem. The difficulty arose from the fact that the lama had been taken from his family as a young boy, trained, and installed as an incarnation, with no provision for him to be returned to lay life if he did not succeed in his new role. While an incarnation may be exalted and have a very comfortable and honored station, he may, should he be a bad incarnation, with no provision to neutralize his divinity, become a burden and constant distress.

Mongolian Buddhism—Background

Before continuing the narrative of my life, my trip to Mongolia and career there, I should explain some of the background of our Mongolian religion, generally spoken of as "Lamaism," a subdivision of Mahayana Buddhism. After originating in India, Buddhism spread out over the Asian world, eventually developing major sects or divisions. The largest sect, Mahayana Buddhism, eventually became dominant in China, Korea, and Japan, while the second largest division, Theravada (Hinayana) Buddhism, became dominant in Sri Lanka (Ceylon), Thailand, Burma, and other parts of Southeast Asia. Known as one main stream of Mahayana Buddhism, "Lamaism" may actually be considered a unique form of Buddhism. After originating in India, as Buddhism spread through the Himalayan mountains into Tibet, Mahayana Buddhism assimilated to it the indigenous form of religion, the Shamanistic *Bon*, and eventually evolved into what is better known as Tibetan Buddhism. It has historically been associated mainly with Tibet and Mongolia and is a religion adapted to a nomadic or semi-agricultural people.

Tibetan Buddhism may also be viewed as an esoteric form of Buddhism distinct from the more outward exoteric form of Buddhism, the dominant form throughout the sedentary areas of China, Korea, and Japan. Because they have a similar culture and a similar form of religion, Mongolia and Tibet have been very intimately associated and have influenced each other greatly throughout their history. In the Western world, as well as Asia, Tibetan-Mongolian Buddhism is generally referred to as "Lamaism." The word *lama* actually means "superior one" and originally was restricted only to a few top abbots of important monasteries. Only later did it come to be widely diffused and refer to ordinary monks of Lamaist Buddhism. Among our Mongolian people and also among Tibetans we do not think of our religion as being a separate, distinct form. We speak of the monks as "lamas" and of the religion as Buddhism. We do not use any special term to distinguish it from other forms of Buddhism, but we feel it is *the* true form of religion passed down from ancient times.

Our Buddhism has a unique institution, a system of incarnations or reincarnations. Whenever a *boghda lama*, a sacred, master lama, dies, his followers search for a successor and seek to have him reincarnated as the next *boghda lama*. This system of rein-

[13]

carnations has had two functions: (1) the perpetuation of the religion and its sacred doctrines; and (2) the administration of the temporal affairs of the religion, the property and the monasteries with their numerous lamas.

In our Mongolian language *khubilghan* is the traditional term for reincarnation (*khubil*, meaning "to transform" and *ghan*, as a suffix, meaning "the person" transformed), and refers to the newly-found incarnation of the *gegen* (*gege'en* or "enlightened one"). In Chinese, the concept of *khubilghan* is expressed by the Buddhist term *pien-hua-shen* (Skt. *Nirmana-Vāyā*) "the transformed body." We Mongols feel somewhat distressed, however, when the Chinese commonly use the term *huo-fo*, literally "living Buddha," in reference to an incarnation. To us, the historical Buddha is the holy one who is above life and death, who entered *nirvana*, and thus has been liberated from the cycle of life and death. We feel it very strange for Christians to refer to their god as a living god, because to us god is neither living nor dead but eternal. The "living Buddhas" of Mongolia may be seen as a variation of the Buddhist ideal of the *bodhisattva*, an exalted lama who, by having attained great virtue, is worthy of release from this world and its distressing cycle of rebirth, but who chooses instead to remain in this life to benefit human beings.

A particular place for the installation of various incarnations and also a residence of the various lamas or monks developed in the form of temples or monastic centers. Not only do they serve as the residential centers of the sacred incarnations but also as the center for the gathering of the lamas and the followers of the religion. Originally the monasteries, the corporate, institutionalized body of the religion, were meant to be religious in nature and not involved in politics and other temporal affairs. With the development of the religion and its properties and power, however, religious affairs became closely associated with political power and the so-called "two pillars of quasifeudalism" in Mongolia were said to be the incarnations and the lay princes of Mongolia. We were aware of an antipathy towards us, the lamas and the religion, on the part of the nationalistic younger generation.

When Lamaist Buddhism was introduced from Tibet to Mongolia during the period of Altan Khan in the 1570s, an entire religious system was adopted, which meant that the institution of incarnations was adopted as well as the religious teachings. This was before large permanent monasteries were built, and originally an incarnation was installed in a special large tentlike shrine or temple of the nomadic people. In time, however, as the religion developed, numerous, powerful, and wealthy temple centers were located in fixed places and later became monasteries of stone, brick, wood, or earth. Each monastery was built either for the installation of a *gegen* or as a gift to him.

The great Mongolian emperor, Khubilai Khan, built many Buddhist temples in Peking and also the "eight white *ger (yurt)*" that had no relationship with Buddhism but which constitute an ancestral cult perpetuated by the descendants of Chinggis Khan. Khubilai's monastic temples, such as Hu-kuo *ssu* and Lung-fu *ssu*, still remain, but the most famous one, Chan-t'an *ssu* (Mong. Tsandan *juu*), was destroyed by the allied forces that occupied Peking at the time of the Boxer Rebellion in 1900. The famous Pi-yun *ssu* was originally the mansion of Yeh-lü Ch'u-ts'ai.

During the Mongolian Empire a number of important religious roles were instituted. Emperor Khubilai Khan appointed as his Imperial Tutor the famous lama Blo-gros rgyal-mtshan, known to us as Phags-pa (Tib. Phags-pa). The name *phags-pa* is actually a Tibetan term corresponding to the Mongolian *khutughtu*, "the blessed one" or "the one who blesses." Many saints and leaders of Buddhism, for example, were referred to in Tibetan as 'phags-pa. The Buddha himself was called Sanjai *phags-pa* (*sanjai*, Tib. *Sangs-rgyas*, is a Tibetan term for the Buddha).

During the Manchu rule over Mongolia and China, various terms of important religious figures were standardized. For example, *khutugktu*, the official and current translation of 'phags-pa, was restricted to the highest level of incarnations, and the title was applied to such other famous Mongolian figures as the *Jebtsundamba*, the *Jangjia*, and the *Ajia*. The proper translation of these Tibetan-Mongolian terms into Chinese should not be *huo-fo* (living Buddha), that is so commonly used, but *sheng-jen*, the sacred one. There are, of course, other terms for incarnations in Mongolian, such as *nom-un khan*, derived from the Tibetan term *choiji-jalbu*, king of the tripitaka or king of the Buddhist canon. The original Tibetan name of my first incarnation, many centuries ago, was Monoral *choiji-jalbu*, which was translated into Mongolian as Tsamba *nom-un khan*. Though the individual words have no meaning for us now, this Mongolian name is apparently a mixture of Tibetan and Mongolian elements.

[15]

As I recall from history, at the beginning of the Ch'ing Dynasty (1644–1911) the Manchu lord-emperor (ejen khan) instituted four nom-un khan incarnations and four pandita incarnations (one learned in five types of Buddhist canons). Above them in rank there were also instituted eight khutughtu. According to Ch'ing dynasty regulations these positions were carefully distinguished in three different ranks. In our Mongolian religion, however, there was no clear division among them. There was an official regulation, though, that these eight khutughtus, four panditas, and four nom-un khans had to reside in Peking periodically, if not continually. In addition to these official high-ranking, famous incarnations, there were in the nomadic areas of Mongolia many other panditas and nom-un khans and a few khutughtus.

Later, Ch'ing officials saw many problems arising from the proliferation of incarnations and advised the emperor that he must have some policy to regulate them, thus designating only certain incarnations as imperial or authorized incarnations. Other incarnations throughout Mongolia would not be recognized. As a result, when an officially recognized incarnation died, a special procedure for finding his succeeding reincarnation became an institutionalized custom carried out in the capital, Peking, through a system of the altan bomba (golden urn). This golden urn system was established in 1792 by the Emperor Ch'ien-lung. Actually, two golden bombas were established—one in Yung-ho kung, the imperial monastic temple and center of Lamaist Buddhism in Peking, and the other in Lhasa, Tibet—the purpose being to regulate and limit the number of incarnations perpetuated by Mongols and Tibetans.

Following the death of an official incarnation, it became customary for two or three successor candidates to be searched out from among the people. Their names were then sent to Peking and put into the golden urn, each name written on a separate piece of paper. After much ceremony with the chanting of Buddhist sutras, a minister of the Li-fan yüan (ministry of dependent regions) would himself draw out the piece of paper that designated which of the candidates was to become the recognized incarnation. Although the Ch'ing Dynasty came to an end, this custom continued, but then was handled by the Mongolian-Tibetan Ministry (Meng Tsang yüan). In Lhasa, where these ceremonial procedures were also carried out for Tibetan of Mongolian incarnations, they were presided over by an emissary of the emperor resident in Lhasa—the *amban*.

In the nomadic areas of Mongolia, away from the capital, there were many small monasteries with *khubilghans* or *gegens*, and various types of incarnations referred to as *shabrang*, one who is close to the foot of the Law of Buddha, but these incarnations were not selected by the "golden *bomba*" system and thus were not officially recognized. Nevertheless, they functioned much the same in the development and spread of Lamaist Buddhism.

After the great reforms in Tibet of the famous Buddhist leader Tsongkhapa (Tsong-kha-pa, ca. 1357–1419), the regulation was made that no blood relative of an abbot or head lama of a monastery could succeed him in the position of head of a monastery. The great lama Tsongkhapa himself was not reincarnated and perpetuated, though his two leading disciples were. We know them today as the *Dalai Lama* and the *Panchen Lama*. We customarily refer to the great leader Tsongkhapa as the *boghda lama*. Likewise, each very high and famous lama or incarnation also came to be known as the *boghda lama* or *gegen*, meaning the sainted, the enlightened one (the intent or meaning is close to "his holiness" as used in Christendom). Another title for these high-ranking incarnations was *degereki* (*deerki*), "the exalted one."

I have been asked many times about the difference between the Chinese and the Mongolian practice of Buddhism. Since the Chinese from ancient times have been Buddhist, there are naturally many general similarities, as well as certain distinctive differences. From my experience and observation I would judge that Mongols and Tibetans are much more inclined to have a less sophisticated, more childlike faith. They place implicit faith in the Buddha, the *Dharma* (law), and the *Sangha* (the congregation of lamas); they are not inclined to doubt and to question. They feel that the important thing is to judge according to the intent of a person's heart. The Chinese approach to Buddhism, by comparison, tends to be much more sophisticated, more intellectual, and to come less from the heart; consequently; there is much more room for doubt, for questions, for a rational approach.

Certainly we Mongols cannot cast any aspersions on the Chinese and criticize their faith, for we find such great temple centers as Wu-t'ai-shan (Shansi Province) and Pu-to-shan (an island off the coast of Chekiang Province) throughout China that confirm the

[17]

great strength of Chinese religious convictions. It seems, however, that the basis or origin of their faith is different from that of the Mongols. While a Mongol's faith may be devout and come deeply from the heart, upon leaving the great prayer-mass or *khural*, he may be found wrestling, joking, teasing, and playing. Chinese monks coming from chanting their prayers are reserved, stoic, and sober. Furthermore, most of our lamas look much like ordinary men while Chinese monks remind us of the very reserved, reflective Buddha.

I have lived most of my life among lama monks and at the same time have talked to many Chinese monks, and I have found our Mongolian lamas discuss matters in a very ordinary way and certainly have much to say about the Buddha. Chinese monks are much more inclined to use special phrases, slogans, and such formulas as *Na-mo Wo-mi-t'o-fo* (submit to the Buddha Amitabha), which they repeat often. While Mongolian lamas are concerned with inner conviction, Chinese monks are concerned with outward expression, appearance, and impressions. This is really not surprising, because Mongols and Chinese have a totally different style of life and their attitudes and behavior are thus very different. It is only natural then that this style would carry over into religious observances and views. When our Mongol people come to believe in the Buddha, they have total conviction, leaving no room for doubt, other concerns, or controversy. The Chinese, however, because their approach to religion is more intellectual, are more inclined to emphasize a particular aspect of the religion, or perhaps to change their belief to conform with some new study they have become involved in.

I have observed that when Mongolian people come to a monastery or temple to make donations, to become involved in the religious activities, or to pray, they go away with no particular thought or concern about what has been done. From my contact with the Chinese, however, I find that after they have visited the temple, they go away with much discussion, commenting on and perhaps even boasting of what they have done at the temple or in some other religious connection. In Chinese temples there are numerous carved notations of the donations people have given, the amounts so-and-so has contributed, or some other special favor someone has done for the temple. In Mongolian monasteries, however, we find no mention of who has done what. The Chinese give great attention to people who are accomplished in a particular line, or a special study, or observance. Among Mongolian lamas there is no great concern about who can do what or who is distinguished in a particular way.

All too often when comparing Lamaist Buddhism and Chinese Buddhism in terms of the faith of the people, Mongols do so to the disadvantage of the Chinese. In reality, many Chinese are very devout and greatly dedicated to the principles of Buddhism. Many things bear this out. For example, when I was still young and visited the great monastic temple center of Lamaisam, Yung-ho kung, in Peking, there was established in a prominent place there a beautiful gilded image of the famous Buddhist reformer Tsongkhapa. This image was several times larger than life-size, the construction of which was a very expensive undertaking promoted entirely by a certain Pai Lama by the name of Pu-jen. Although Pu-jen was a Mongol, all the donations and proceeds for establishing this image came from Chinese believers. Now in the 1970s, I find myself in Taiwan in a beautiful two-story building with a large impressive garden, all entirely built and maintained by Chinese disciples. Each year I have been invited to Hong Kong to participate in an elaborate ceremonial conference, my travel expenses being paid entirely by Chinese believers there. During one of these annual observances in Hong Kong, I had the misfortune of being seized by appendicitis, but again all the expenses of my hospital and recovery were taken care of by a Chinese believer living in Canada. It is rather ironic that hardly a day passes without several disciples visiting me—all of them Chinese. Only rarely am I visited by one of my Mongolian countrymen, and then they come merely to talk about Mongolian culture or history or some other such topic; never do they seek my spiritual guidance. It seems that most Mongols in Taiwan are intellectuals, government officials and many are now Christians. The only occasion for religious ceremonies is a death in a Mongolian family.

Former Incarnations of the Kanjurwa Khutughtu

It should be made clear at this point that I am the seventeenth reincarnation in a long lineage of khubilghans or incarnations, the fifth to bear the rank and title of Kanjurwa khutughtu. It would be fitting here to discuss the title and the historical back-

[19]

ground of the earlier reincarnations, my predecessors in this traditional line.

My lineage of incarnations came to be referred to as the Kanjurwa *khutughtu* because *Kanjurwa* (Kangyurwa) was the title a Manchu emperor used to designate this line of incarnations. In my long lineage the first to be recognized with title of Kanjurwa *mon-un khan* was contemporary with Emperor K'ang-hsi (r. 1662–1721) of the Ch'ing Dynasty. I am the fifth reincarnation to bear this title. The recognition of *khutughtu* rank came later in the early second decade of this century with the Fourth Kanjurwa.

We lack the records to give a complete and accurate biography of each of my sixteen previous reincarnations but included here is at least a listing, a synopsis of some useful information. The origin of the many reincarnations of the Kanjurwa line began in India, having had some link as a disciple of the Buddha. Over the centuries successive new reincarnations were discovered in Tibet and then in more recent centuries have traditionally been found in the Amdo area of Kokonor, the place of my own birth. My earlier Kokonor predecessors customarily had a retreat or hermitage on an island in the famous Kokonor Lake, known to the Chinese as Hai-hsin-shan (Mountain in the heart of the sea). They commonly travelled there to meditate in a cave on the island. Some of my former incarnations, it is reported, were miraculously blessed with knowledge without the necessity of studying.

There is no detailed information regarding my first four incarnations but the fifth, Lobsang-choidan, was an extraordinary reincarnation and showed special merit from the age of three. According to tradition it is reported that he could readily recall the career and events in the lives of his previous incarnations and, having a miraculous memory, he was able to learn the scriptures of the Buddha very rapidly by just glancing over them. This fifth reincarnation came to the attention of the Dalai Lama of Tibet and was given a special seal that we preserved in Mongolia to recent times. The Dalai Lama bestowed upon him the Tibetan title *Choiji-jalbu*, that we translate into Mongolian as Nom-un-khan (king of the Buddhist Law). When the Mongolian people were being converted to Buddhism this fifth incarnation came to Mongolia to preach. This was probably during the rule of Altan Khan (1507–1583).

[20]

I digress here to note that in Tibet many lamas recited the Kanjur (Kangyur), a great Buddhist scriptural canon, and in so doing bestowed blessings upon the people. With the conversion of the nomadic Mongolian people to Buddhism, however, there were very few Mongolian lamas capable of reciting the Tibetan Buddhist scriptures. So in attempting to propagate the faith, the Mongol lamas sent a messenger to Tibet to petition Lhasa to send a learned lama to Mongolia who could recite the Kanjur Scriptures. The messenger, a man from the Tümed Mongols, from the Saji-maidar Monastery, returned with the promise that Lhasa would send them a scholarly lama. Later, as the messenger was sitting in his yurt, a lama wearing a hood appeared at the door, carrying his luggage on his shoulders, and remarked, "You are looking for a lama who can recite the Tibetan scriptures. I am he." The messenger acknowledged the lama and then accompanied him to the Saji-maider and Ordi monasteries.

This Tibetan lama, the first in my line of incarnations to live in Mongolia, was known as the Kanjurwa *ghabji* (teacher or master). Mongolians frequently use the term *ghabji* to refer to a person who has received the lama degree of *gebshi* and who thoroughly knows the Law of the Buddha. Tibetans use the term *rambjinba* in the same way. The Tibetan lama settled down among the Tümed Mongols in the vicinity of Shujir Mountain. As people were converted his following grew and a fine monastery, Ariin-süme, was built here about thirty miles north of Hohhot (Köke-khota). The Chinese emperor later bestowed on it the name Yen-ch'ing *ssu*. The emperor also bestowed upon this fifth incarnation the title *T'ung-hui ch'an-shih* (guru or master of pervading wisdom). The documentation on these events has long been preserved in Dolonor. It is reported that this fifth reincarnation, Lobsang-choidan, lived to the advanced age of ninety-six. An academy or school was also established within this Ariin Monastery, the teaching of which was referred to as *Duingkhor datsang* (learning of the Law or kharma). Thereafter, the head of Ordi Monastery sent his disciples to the neighboring Ariin Monastery to study as a disciple of the Kanjurwa *ghabji*, and others did likewise.

Later the lamas of the Ariin Monastery sent their young disciples to Tibet to study at the *Duingkhor datsang*, to receive training in the academic field concerned with astrology, astronomy, and Tantrism. Thus, in this monastery the study of the Duingkhor discipline developed strongly, and the successors of the Tibetan

[21]

lama known as Kanjurwa *ghabji* were later reincarnated with a higher status as the Kanjurwa *nom-un khan* in the Ch'ing period (1644–1911). Finally, my preceding incarnation was elevated to the highest rank, *khutughtu*, in the beginning of the Republic of China (1912) by President Yüan Shih-k'ai. We have no noteworthy information regarding the sixth through the eleventh incarnations in the Kanjurwa line of succession. The twelfth reincarnation lived during the fall of the Chinese Ming and the rise of the Manchu-Ch'ing Dynasties—the first half of the 1600s—and was also given an imperial title and lived to the age of fifty-four. His succeeding reincarnation, the thirteenth, was not found for twenty years and was then brought from Kokonor to Inner Mongolia and was revered among the people from western Mongolia to the far northeastern regions of the Bargha and Buriad Mongols.

From the 1680s and 1690s there was a great struggle between the Manchu and the Junghar (Dzungar) Mongols led by Galdan. During his campaign against Galdan in Khalkha, Emperor K'ang-hsi came to the Ariin Monastery, and, hearing the bells of a lama reciting the scriptures, he inquired where they came from and, upon learning that they came from the Kanjurwa, requested that he be brought to him. This thirteenth Kanjurwa *ghabji* was thereupon summoned, and the Emperor was delighted with the meeting. Subsequently, an audience was held in which the emperor instructed that all the surrounding land be bestowed upon the Ariin Monastery as a token of his pleasure and as an endowment. In addition, in 1697, when the campaign into northern Mongolia was over, many of the military weapons remaining were stored in the monastery.

The Kanjurwa *ghabji*, who was to become my first incarnation as a *khutughtu*, was at that time known only as a learned, venerable teacher, not as an incarnation or *khubilghan*. During this early period the emperor was strongly influenced by advisors who were prejudiced against the Tibetan-Mongol Yellow Sect. These advisors persuaded him not to confer honors upon the Yellow Religion but rather to turn his favors to the Blue Sect monks, known by the Chinese as the *ch'ing-yi-seng* (blue-robed monks), as a means of distinguishing them from the *huang-yi-seng* (yellow-robed monks). These are the terms by which the people of Peking referred to Mongol lamas to distinguish us from the Chinese monks.

[22]

I digress to note that the term *Yellow Sect* (*Gelug-pa*) has come to mean the form of Buddhism that was strongly developed from the time of the great reformer Tsongkhapa (1357–1419). "Yellow" refers to the color of hat and robe worn by the monks of this reformed sect, and also provides a distinction between this new sect and the former old sects. The term "Red Sect" was originally restricted to the earliest Tibetan sect, *Nyingma-pa* and now is actually a popular misnomer used to refer to other sects aside from the Yellow Sects in Tibet. Red Sect used in this latter sense is a grouping of old non-reformed sects. We also commonly use the term *blue-robed sect* to refer to Chinese Buddhists who wear grey or blue robes, except for very high dignitaries. In the favorable ranking of various colors, yellow is more honorable to the Chinese than blue. Customarily all buildings that were the property of the emperor had a golden or yellow porcelain tiled roof, whereas other buildings, ordered to be built by the emperor but which were not his own personal property, had a roof of blue porcelain tiles.

Because of the competition between these two groups of lamas to gain greater favor with the emperor, a memorial or petition was sent to Peking from the Yellow Sect lamas proposing that they recite for the emperor the entire scripture of the Kanjur Canon in a special ceremony. This memorial was favorably received, and the emperor, upon conferring with the leading lama in Peking, the Jangjia *khutugtu*, accepted the proposal and also the recommendation that the high lama to be given this honor be the Kanjurwa *gegen*. The emperor stipulated, however, that the scripture must be recited from memory, not read. Thus, my former incarnation went to Peking to give the special liturgical sermon or ceremonial scriptural recitation which we speak of as a *lung*, a Tibetan word meaning a recitation of a particular liturgy by one who has been specially ordained.

In Peking, the revered Kanjurwa was received in audience and recited the holy record or Tripitaka in the presence of the Emperor. All the while he was reciting he gazed steadily into the heavens, which made the Emperor curious, and he asked Kanjurwa why he did this. Kanjurwa told him that he was reciting from the scroll of the Tripitaka held for him especially by a *choijung*, a protective deity of Lamaist Buddhism. To this, the Emperor commented, "We expect you to recite the scripture from memory. Why then are you reading it, prompted by the angel in

[23]

such a way?" It was a tense moment and this Kanjurwa Lama answered that he was aware of the order of the Emperor that he should not read, but he noted that this was a very special function and that it would be tragic if he made a mistake in the recitation; therefore, he was making a special effort to transmit the sacred record without mistake. In this difficult situation, my first incarnation prayed to the Buddha to determine what he should do and was prompted to tell the Emperor that the one turning the roll of scripture was not a man but a *choijung*, "protector of the law," and that naturally it was not possible for any common person to see these things, but that the Emperor as an exalted person could see this special being, though not those assembled with them. The Emperor was pleased with this reply.

The Emperor's ministers were not pleased, however. Shrewd and evil men, they were determined to trick my predecessor. They plotted to place a set of the Kanjur scriptures underneath the seat upon which this Kanjurwa was going to sit on some special occasion to recite the sacred scriptures and to determine if he could discern that they were there. If not, they would discredit him because Mongols would never knowingly sit over the sacred scriptures of the Buddha, for this would be a grave transgression. The plan of the ministers, a terrible trick, was carried out, and the following day, the Kanjurwa seated himself on the chair under which the sacred scriptures had been secretly installed. The Emperor then declared to him, "You are learned and capable in reciting the Buddhist texts. Do you feel yourself superior to them?" The Emperor then pointed out to my first incarnation that he was in fact seated over the sacred records and instructed his attendants to withdraw them and show them to the Kanjurwa. The attendants withdrew the volumes one by one, but they found each to be only blank paper. The Emperor then inquired excitedly about what had happened to the scriptures, and the Kanjurwa *gegen* explained to him that if the scriptures were placed back in their proper place the record would once again be there. This they did and found the writings restored to their original form. The emperor was greatly impressed by this incident and declared that he was indeed the veritable *Kanjur nom-un khan*, "the king of the canon." From this event my incarnation became known officially as Kanjurwa *mergen nom-un khan*, wise king of the Law of the Kanjur, the sacred canon or tripitaka. From that time it was customary to refer to the succession of reincarnations of this high lama as the Kanjurwa *khutughtu*, an exalted title.

The Board of Rites (*Li-pu*) confirmed upon him the full official title *Ch'eng-jen ch'an-shih Kanjurwa nom-un khan* (luminous, benevolent Kanjurwa, master of meditation, king of the Law) and thus he became the first among my many earlier *khubilghans* (reincarnations) to bear this important title. He was allowed the privilege to have under him as his staff a high lama official entitled *shangtsad-pa jasagh*. He was also given a silver seal engraved in several languages, and it was determined that he would come to the court in Peking anually for a formal audience with the emperor.

The results of this incident did not merely add to the credit of my predecessor, but also redounded to the glory of the entire Yellow Sect, which is the reason that from that time on the Tibetan-Mongolian Yellow sect was favored over the Chinese sect (Blue or Black) of Buddhism until the end of the Manchu Dynasty (1911). For example, when a prominent person in Peking died, after the initial funeral services were completed, those who accompanied the body to the tomb were arranged in a strict file by rank. In the customary procession the yellow-coated lamas of Mongolia and Tibet were the first to proceed, followed by the blue-coated Chinese Monks and then finally by the Taoist priests. Needless to say, this distinction caused the enmity already existing between the Chinese and the Mongolian monks to grow even stronger.

Because the visit of my earlier incarnation to Peking was so impressive the emperor was greatly gratified, was very complimentary and kind, and allowed him to return to Ariin Monastery. A later emperor also granted this Kanjurwa's successor a monastery at Dolonor (Doloon-nor), which had been built for an imperial princess, and it became his summer residence. In addition, Emperor K'ang-hsi conferred upon the Ariin Monastery his own personal throne which had nine dragons carved upon it. The Kanjurwa was afraid to sit upon a nine-dragon throne, however, because it was an imperial symbol, and consequently changed the center dragon to a lion, also a sacred symbol. The belief is that when one preaches the Buddhist law, it is like the sound of a roaring lion, powerful and impressive. Emperor K'ang-hsi's personal throne remained in the Ariin Monastery as a most

[25]

important historical relic for two hundred years, but I do not know whether it remains now after the communist occupation.

After Emperor K'ang-hsi returned to the capital from the war with the Junghar Mongols, he decided to have the Tibetan scriptures, the Kanjur, translated into Mongolian. He sent for the Kanjurwa gegen, commissioned him to do this work, and instructed that it was to be supervised by the noted incarnation Jangjia khutughtu, whose name was Aghwan-lobsang-choi-dong (Tib. Ngag-dbang Blo-bzang Chos-ldan). Actually, the translation was begun during the period of Lighdan Khan (r. 1604–1634), the last ruler of Mongolia, who was defeated by the Manchu just before the beginning of the Ch'ing Dynasty. Though first commissioned by Lighdan Khan, the Mongolian Tripitaka was not published until later during the Manchu reign due to the special efforts of the Jangjia khutughtu. The translation is, therefore, attributed to the Manchu rulers. The work commissioned by K'ang-hsi was thus a revision of the translation done during the time of Lighdan. At that time there was a major problem in the translation work because of the lack of standardized terminology for technical Buddhist terms; consequently, a Tibetan-Mongol dictionary titled Kabju-yin dayigh was compiled. This dictionary, a voluminous ten-volume work, greatly facilitated the revision of the earlier translation of the Tibetan scriptures. Upon completing his revision of the Kanjur, my first incarnation began a translation of the scriptures of the Duingkhor branch of Tantric Buddhism. New difficulties arose among the group of editors, however, and the Kanjurwa gegen finally requested that the emperor allow him to work on the translation alone, using only his own disciples. The authorization was given, and my predecessor was able to complete the translation.

To help him with this work, the Kanjurwa gegen used a disciple who had earlier come from the Ordi Monastery and who had studied in Tibet. In recognition of this disciple's work, the emperor bestowed upon him the title Duingkhor pandita, adopting the title from the scripture. By this name he has been known through various succeeding reincarnations. When the title Duingkhor pandita was bestowed upon this incarnation he was but a disciple, and he demurred, saying that the honor for the translation work really belonged to his teacher, the Kanjurwa, not to himself. But his modesty was of no avail and the title remained with him.

[26]

Over the centuries my incarnation has been installed in the Badghar Monastery, commonly known by the Chinese as Wu-tan *chao* (Udan *juu*). It is located in the Wu-tan Valley on the border of the Tümed and Ulanchab Leagues (two administrative regions) north of the mountain range near Pao-t'ou, and is widely known as one of the largest, and the most prestigious monastic temples in western Inner Mongolia. Over the years many Tibetans have come here and they call the monastery Badghar *choilung*, meaning "white lotus in the center of the true religion." The formal name, inscribed in Chinese on the official plaque presented by the Manchu imperial court, is Kuang-chüeh *ssu*, "the monastic temple of expansive enlightenment." The official or formal Mongolian name of the monastery, inscribed parallel to the Chinese on the official plaque over the main entrance, and having the above same meaning, was *Aghu-yeke-onoltu süme*. The official Tibetan name listed on the monastery plaque was *Jachindoghdanling*.

The Badghar Monastery had two leading incarnations who together were its founders, the Kanjurwa and the Duingkhor *pandita* lama, who later became a famous incarnation. These two incarnations, of course, enlisted the help of others in establishing this great monastery in the early Ch'ing period (1644–1911). For example, the Duingkhor *pandita* lama found in the vicinity of what is now Badghar a special type of lama known as *dayanchi lama*, one who meditates in mountain caves as a recluse, and also another outstanding lama known as a *deed lama* (literally, exalted lama). The Duingkhor *ghabji* discussed with these two men the idea of establishing a new, outstanding monastery. The main problem was financing the plan. By coincidence a powerful prince known as Tsongkhor *noyan* passed through the area on his way to see the emperor for an audience. I think he must have been from one of the Urad Banners of the Ulanchab region. The three lamas approached him, and they were able to obtain the finances necessary to begin their project. As the first undertaking, they constructed a college (*datsang*) of the Duingkhor, the beginning of the development of the great monastery Badghar-iin sume. Previous to this, a Duingkhor hall (*doghon*) had been erected at the Ariin Monastery of my first incarnation and had had bestowed upon it a memorial plaque from the emperor, conferring official recognition and patronage. It was burned by accident, however, an event that brought much grief to the lamas there. My predecessor advised them not to worry, that it was time for this hall to be moved to another place. From that time on, my incarnation, the Kanjurwa gegen, and the Duingkhor *pandita* lama both resided at the same Badghar Monastery.

Kanjurwa *ghabji* lived on into his nineties, doing much good, developing the religion, and finally passing into nirvana it seems, in the mid-1700s. When the emperor* learned of his death, he decreed that the Kanjurwa's perpetual reincarnation or *khubilgan* be established. The *shiral* (Skt. *sārīra* or a jewel-like deposit) remaining from his cremation was enshrined in a golden pagoda commissioned by the emperor and established within the Ariin Monastery.

The first incarnation of my lineage to come to Mongolia (twelfth in the Kanjurwa) took the role of a *nomchi*, a scholar. But the second of my line was educated in Tibet, not in Badghar Monastery, and took the form of an *emchi*, a medical specialist. During his career, while on a visit to Peking, and in private audience with the emperor, a supernatural event occurred. The emperor, it is reported, seemed to see a person standing behind him and inquired who it was. Turning to see for himself, this incarnation replied that the *ejen*, the spirit of the local deity of the Serkü region in Kokonor, was standing there. This pleased the emperor who then conferred upon the *ejen* a yellow jacket and a red button, headdress symbol of special rank, denoting the second rank in the hierarchy of the imperial bureaucracy. Such bestowals from an emperor were rare and greatly prized.*

Concerning the above incident it should be noted that the Chinese emperors had a tradition of performing the *feng-shan* ceremony that involved the conferring of titles and offerings upon famous mountains and rivers. This tradition was their means of demonstrating that they regarded themselves as supreme not only over local rulers but even over regional gods. The bestowal of recognition was not limited to a particular spirit but was also upon the place where the deity was customarily believed to reside. Because of this incident, my previous incarnations over the centuries were always searched for and found in this Serkü area, the Tangut region of Amdo, a Tibetan cultural area of Kokonor (Chinghai).

---

* Emperor is here no longer K'ang-hsi, but either Yung-chang (r. 1722–1735) or Ch'ien Lung (r. 1735–1795).

Former Incarnations of the Kanjurwa Khutughtu

My fifteenth Kanjurwa incarnation, third with *khutughtu* status, was found in the Serkü Monastery and was noted for his diligent study under the great Serkü lama Dobjichang and for his nine years of study on the famous island Hai-shin-shan (mountain in the heart of the sea) in Lake Kokonor (Blue Lake). Finally, after completing his preparation, this incarnation was brought to *door ghajir*, literally, "the lower land," meaning Mongolia, in contrast to the highlands of Tibet. This was probably sometime in the early 1800s. He was dedicated to building monasteries and expanding the religion, and traveled long distances to Bargha in eastern Mongolia and even to the Buriad area of Siberia. From people there he was able to enlist many patrons (*ögölig-iin ejen*) for the temple.

It is noteworthy that this Kanjurwa had conferred upon him by the Chia-ching Emperor (1796–1826) a special set of buildings in Dolonor, a former imperial residence of a princess having over two hundred rooms. As a monastery it was known as Hsin-hui *ssu*. This Kanjurwa died during the 1850s.

When in his sixties, this incarnation requested that his disciples make an offering of *usun takil*, silver or copper cups of water placed before the altar as an offering. He was also very strict in maintaining the *khural* or great prayer masses for the expounding of the Buddhist scriptures. In this incarnation's advanced years, lamas came from the Buriad areas of Mongolia requesting that he again come there to visit, but he told them he was too old, that while he could not make the journey, his next incarnation certainly would visit their temples.

Formerly in the Buriad area of Mongolia there was also another Kanjurwa *gegen*, a matter that involves an interesting story that I should relate as I have heard it. It seems that when the Kanjurwa Monastery of the Buriad was established, a young boy continually ran away from his family to the monastery; although he was repeatedly returned home, he again and again ran away. Finally the lamas of the temple sent his name to Lhasa to inquire into this matter and were told that the boy was the incarnation of the Kanjurwa lama of Dolonor. The boy's formal name was Lodon-dambi-nima, and he was installed in the Buriad monastery as its first Kanjurwa incarnation. It is of course rare for two reincarnations to arise from one original incarnation. Buriad Mongolia was never under the control of the Manchu since it was in

Siberia, so the search for new incarnations was not controlled by the "golden *bomba*" system of the Manchu court.

Among the Buriad the lay disciples of the other Kanjurwa *gegen* were organized and supervised by a *jasagh* lama. However, these *jasagh* leaders were not subject to Manchu rulers as in other areas of Mongolia. The first Kanjurwa *gegen* of the Buriad died some time prior to the Russian revolution, and his succeeding incarnation, according to the reports, was a very scholarly man. He was versed not only in the Tibetan sutras but also accomplished in the Russian language. It seems that Buriad lamas were more learned than those in most places of Mongolia. In Inner Mongolia or Outer Mongolia young boys were taken at a young age to the monastery, but Buriad young men became lamas only after they had had a certain amount of education and if they were personally inclined to become lamas. We can judge that the development of Buddhism in Buriad Mongolia was influenced by Russian culture and hence the lamas there were more literate than those in most areas of Mongolia. The reason I mention this other Kanjurwa *gegen* in distant Buriad Mongolia is that while there were two incarnations, they were paradoxically one.

My previous incarnation met the important Lodon-dambi-nima when he journeyed to Buriad Mongolia, to perform the special *Duingkhor-iin wang*, (Kālacakra) ritual, the authoritative transmission to others, through a special ordination, of the authority to chant a special sutra. There was a good deal of excitement in the Buriad area when the two Kanjurwa incarnations came together at the same time. I have been told also that when they met, each held in his hand a copy of the secret sutra *Jadongwa*, an important tantric Buddhist scripture, each grasping the sutra at the same time, demonstrating to the people the power of the Buddha in the fact that one incarnation had become two and that these two incarnations were one in mind and purpose.

I heard a rumor that following the Russian revolution the Kanjurwa *gegen* of the Buriads was taken to a special place, perhaps an academy, to translate the Kanjur sutras into Russian as they were needed. I have not yet been able to verify this rumor, however; though I heard it from a reliable source, namely the Tsonrai *jasagh*, who escaped from the Buriad area after the revolution and came to Inner Mongolia. The Buriad incarnation of the Kanjurwa ended with only two reincarnations, because of the Russian revolution (1917).

[30]

Former Incarnations of the Kanjurwa Khutughtu

All I know of the history of my various former incarnations is what has been told me by the senior lamas who were associated with them or who were knowledgeable about the tradition of the Kanjurwa line. It seems that my previous incarnations made studies and wrote commentaries on various Tibetan works and scriptures and also upon the *mani*, sacred Buddhist, Sanskrit and Tibetan formulas.

My sixteenth incarnation, the Fourth Kanjurwa *khutughtu* (1854–1913), the one just preceding myself, was born in Kokonor when there was a great turmoil among the Moslems in west China and Central Asia. Before these great disturbances began, the monastery of Serkü had over five hundred lamas studying or living within its compound (*küree*). After these disturbances subsided, the lamas built a protective wall around the compound, using massive pine logs for their materials. The Fourth Kanjurwa incarnation came to the *door ghajir* (lowlands of Mongolia) when he was fifteen years old. Since he was quite young, after his installation as a *khubilghan* he received his training in Badghar Monastery. He did not visit Tibet, but rather traveled back and forth between Kokonor and Badghar. Mainly he is remembered for his long concentration in a meditative discipline lasting from some twenty years in the Badghar Monastery. He was invited to the Bargha area of eastern Mongolia by a great lama of that area, Gendenjams *da-lama*, attracted many patrons, amassed much wealth from donations, and established a great monastic temple there known as Kanjur *süme*. After the establishment of this religious center my former incarnation ordinarily stayed at his monastery in Dolonor, partly because this center was part way between Badghar Monastery to the west and the Kanjur Monastery in northeastern Mongolia.

This Fourth Kanjurwa *khutughtu*, the sixteenth generation incarnation of my line, also journeyed to Buriad, Mongolia, to perform the special ceremony of the *Duingkhor-iin wang*. This trip was to fulfill an earlier promise of the previous incarnation who had been specially invited but unable to attend.

He lived in Dolonor through the late 1800s and the first decade of the 1900s. After the Chinese revolution of 1911 and the establishment of the Republic of China he was invited to Peking by the provisional president Yüan Shih-k'ai and had conferred upon him the title *Yüan-t'ung shan-hui Kanjurwa mergen khutughtu* (the talented and blessed one, [entitled] Tripitaka, of thoroughly pervading good and wisdom). He also had bestowed upon him a seal in the Chinese, Mongolian and Tibetan languages, stayed in Peking for one month and returned to Mongolia. He was authorized to establish three branch offices to look after his affairs and property, one in Peking, one in Dolonor, and one in Hohhot, to be supported with an annual budget or stipend furnished by the central government.

He became the head of the *Lama tamagha*, an office established by the Manchus for the supervision and control of Lamaist affairs and lay affairs having to do with the many disciples or *shabinar* of the Dolonor monastic center. From earlier times the Jangjia *khutughtu* was the supreme incarnation in the area of Dolonor. The Jangjia was officially the head of the West Temple (Baruun *süme*), also referred to as the Yellow Temple (Shira *süme*; Ch. Shan-yin *ssu*). During the first decade of this century, while this particular Jangjia was still very young, perhaps ten years old, my previous incarnation was appointed as the head of the *Lama tamagha*. This was an extremely important position, because it made him administrator for the affairs of Mongolian Buddhism in the *Öbör döchi-yesü*, the "Inner forty-nine banners."

Because the Jangjia had traditionally held this position and thus been the head lama of this entire area and also head of the aforementioned important monastic temples at Dolonor, conflict developed between the followers of the Jangjia and the followers of my previous incarnation. This struggle became very intense and complicated, and was distressing to my former incarnation. As a result, he gave up the post as head of the Lamaist affairs administration, turned it over to the Jangjia, and removed to a retreat at Juu-naiman süme, some fifty miles southwest of Dolonor. This small place of meditation was built very near the site of Khubilai Khan's summer capital, Shangdu.* He had earlier spent three years there, gathering his disciples and building up a monastery. During this time my former incarnation was killed in 1913 by the Chinese during the chaos and problems following the Chinese Revolution (1911) and as a result of the incursions from Outer Mongolia during the Mongolian independence movement, which will be discussed later.

---

* EDITOR'S NOTE: This is the famous Xanadu palace noted by the poet Coleridge.

One must understand that all of this quarreling and struggle was not between the two great lamas—the Jangjia was only about ten years old and my former incarnation was over fifty—but rather between the followers of these two great masters. Needless to say, such difficulty was shameful and disgraceful, certainly not in keeping with the teachings of the Buddha.

After his prophecy to my mother during his visit to Amdo, as related above, the Fourth Kanjurwa returned to Badghar Monastery and there performed the *sanwar*, a very important ceremony in the ordination of a new *gegen*. This was in order for the Duingkhor *pandita* to be ordained as a new and officially recognized incarnation. On this occasion the fourth incarnation performed the *Duingkhur-iin wang* and other important ceremonies. In the Badghar Monastery, it will be recalled, there were two powerful, important incarnations, The Fourth Kanjurwa *khutughtu* and the Duingkhor *pandita*.

After the completion of these ceremonies, the Fourth Kanjurwa departed for Dolonor, leaving the lamas at Badghar a message that ten years hence he should return again to Badghar Monastery. All of this took place in 1913 during what was known to the Mongolian people as the *Üker jil-iin üimeen*, "disturbance of the year of the cow," that I will now relate.

The time was just after my former incarnation, the Fourth Kanjurwa, officially handed over the seals of office of the *Lama tamagha* to the Jangjia and retired to Juu-naiman süme. Very soon after he reached this place, the Khalkha (Outer Mongolian) military forces, led by Shirun *jangjun*, (general Shirun) and Namsarai *baator* (hero Namsarai), swept into Inner Mongolia, declaring that the *Ar Boghda* (the Jebtsundamba, the holy one of northern Mongolia) was the new Boghda Khan (holy emperor). At this time, Mongols in the Khalkha areas were declaring that their purpose was to unify the people of Mongolia and oppose the Chinese. Coming into Üjümüchin, they then turned to the southwest to campaign into Chakhar, and Juu-naiman süme was directly in the path of their forces. At this time Chakhar was dominated by the governor-general Wang Hua-ch'ing.

In times past the two great Mongolian leaders mentioned had been patrons of my former incarnation, and one of their reasons for coming to this area was to pay their respects to the Fourth Kanjurwa. In this critical situation the followers of the Jangjia reported to Peking that the Kanjurwa's reason for going to Juu-naiman süme was to make common cause with invading forces from Outer Mongolia who separated from China and were struggling to unify an independent Mongolia. It seems also that governor-general Wang, stationed in Dolonor at this time, dispatched one of his officers, Kao Fu, to campaign to the north from Morin Dabaa in Chakhar to clear the invading Khalkha forces out of the region. As Kao Fu approached Juu-naiman süme, he began to fire artillery into the monastery. The Fourth Kanjurwa was unable to defend himself with only twenty or so bodyguards against many Chinese troops.

Namsarai *baator* (hero), who happened to be present during this crisis, urged the Fourth Kanjurwa to escape with him. Two horses were prepared for them, but the Kanjurwa refused to go, explaining that if he did, great damage would come to the Mongolian people in that area. Namsarai *baator* then declared that he also would remain to defend the area, and would kill every Chinese that tried to come in. He then readied his guns and began to fire on the Chinese, but the Kanjurwa grabbed these guns and ordered that there be no killing in the monastery. Namsarai *baator* was famous in those days as a sharp shooter. He never fired in vain; each shot meant a dead Chinese.

Finally, on the morning of the tenth day of the sixth lunar month, 13 July 1913, the monastery was surrounded and besieged by Chinese forces. Namsarai and his small contingent of troops were in the adjoining compound, and the Fourth Kanjurwa was on top of a two-story monastery building. The central area of the Juu-naiman süme Monastery was larger than that of the surrounding buildings, the western section being lower than the rest of it. Namsarai and his troops in the lower western section were unable to defend themselves, because their weapons had been taken away by the Kanjurwa, and consequently during the night some of them were killed, though a few managed to strike against the Chinese soldiers and escape.

The fact that the followers of the Jangjia *khutughtu* were secretly undermining the Kanjurwa *khutughtu* in reports in Peking, became known to him and his group, and the struggle between the two groups became ever more intense as the followers of the Kanjurwa fought back. During this struggle, sometime in 1913, a group of Chinese attacked and plundered Juu-naiman süme, the monastery where the Kanjurwa was living, and in the skirmish he and a number of his followers were killed. The monastic temple itself was burned and the whole incident was a tragedy.

According to later reports from his followers, just as the Fourth Kanjurwa perished a brilliant star was seen to shoot from the monastery towards the north. Chineses soldiers who were involved in the action later reported to the Mongols that they had seen him fleeing to the north on a beautiful white horse. And someone who was journeying in the night north of the monastery when it was attacked said that he met the Kanjurwa *gegen* galloping on a beautiful white horse to the north; he inquired where he was going and was told Buriad Mongolia, to join his counterpart, the Buriad Kanjurwa.

Immediately after the death of the Fourth Kanjurwa, the Chinese governor-general over Chahkar declared that *Meng-fei* (Mongol bandits) were responsible for the evil deed and that a thorough search should be made to find them. They were, of course, never found and brought to justice, and consequently there were many rumors and stories regarding this incident and its aftermath.

This tragedy was followed by a time of great turmoil and distress among the Mongolian people in that region, and they brought charges to the governor-general in Dolonor against the Chinese soldiers and their brutality. After deliberation, the governor-general took severe action against the Chinese troops who had been involved, telling them that he had given orders for them to drive out the invading Khalkha Mongolian soldiers but not orders to burn the monasteries or to kill the Kanjurwa *gegen*. He ordered the execution of the Chinese soldiers who had been involved in the incident. Ya *jasagh*, the lama who actually ran the office of the *Lama tamagha* and who supervised the lay affairs of the Kanjurwa *gegen*, also became involved in the dispute. Ya *jasagh* even traveled to Peking and brought charges against the Chinese troops and against governor-general Wang. In the meantime, however, governor-general Wang had been stationed in Dolonor and had previously developed good relations with the Jangjia *khutughtu* and his followers. Consequently, during the investigations and deliberations in the capital, the followers of the Jangjia supported Wang and opposed the followers of the Kanjurwa in their efforts to gain justice and restitution. The Chinese leaders' feeling was that whoever may be right or wrong there could be no justification for the killing of an important Mongolian incarnation,

[35]

and hence they dispatched a group of ten to make an on-the-spot investigation in Dolonor.

As one measure of compensation to the Mongols, the Peking Government financed a state funeral for the Fourth Kanjurwa gegen. The final judgment of the government was to absolve governor-general Wang and to place the blame on his subordinant officer Kao Fu, who was then relieved of his command, with the decree that he was never again to be given any position of responsibility and that he must continually wear a black arm band in mourning for the Mongolian "living Buddha" who had been killed. In addition, the government donated thirty thousand silver dollars for the reconstruction of the monastery at Juunaiman süme. The monastery was not reestablished at this place, however, possibly because the tragedy that had occurred there had made the place an inauspicious site. In fact with the coming of the Chinese warlords, the Japanese occupation, and the Communists, it was never rebuilt.

Having briefly set forth some sketchy information regarding the historical lineage of the Kanjurwa line, I will now return to my own early experience. I hope that there are not too many mistakes in what I have said above, but I have only my memory to rely on.

PART TWO

Beginning a New Life
in Mongolia

Journey to Inner Mongolia and Peking

In my ninth year, in the Western style of counting, during the eleventh day of the eleventh month (18 December, 1923 in the Western calendar), a great religious ceremony took place in the Serkü Monastery of Amdo, which Ishighawa *jasagh lama*, from *door ghajir* (Mongolia), Su *jasagh da-lama*, and many other lamas attended. The real purpose of their visit was to formally invite me to the Badghar Monastery in Inner Mongolia, a monastery reserved through generations for the line of my reincarnations. They stayed in Amdo to pass the winter.

On the second day of the first month of the following year (2 February 1924), my parents, relatives, and many friends came to the Serkü Monastery to see me off on my journey to Mongolia. I was then ten years old. On the twenty-fourth day of that lunar month (28 February), as I left Serkü at about ten A.M., accompanied by the great lamas mentioned, an impressive spectacle lay before us. The lamas of the monastery lined up on both sides of our path in long procession. When I mounted my horse for the journey, my mother was standing there to attend me. As I was leaving, the lamas performed large smoke offerings for the special *sang* ceremony which included prayers and the reading of scriptures for my good health, fortune and happiness. They also performed the ceremony of the *dallagh*, which meant that they wanted the monastery to continue to prosper and wanted me to return; the feeling was that, otherwise, my departure might drain away the blessings of the monastery.

It was with many mixed feelings that I left Serkü to travel to Mongolia. As we were mounting our horses, my mother was weeping and several people were trying to comfort her, explaining that this was a great opportunity for her who had come from a common family, an historic occasion. Other old friends standing nearby were saying the same things, though they were at the same time still sad. The people followed after me to the gate of the compound surrounding the monastery. As I and my caravan departed, I looked back to see my mother weeping and immediately said to those accompanying me that we must depart in haste in order to spare her feelings. Because this departure was a very formal affair, officials and monks of the monastery accompanied me for some ten miles, whereupon we had a final lunch. Then once again we mounted our horses and took leave of our old acquaintances and others closely associated with the monastery.

On the way we stopped at Hsi-ning, capital of our Kokonor region. As we reached the outskirts of Hsi-ning, we passed over the river Seleng *mören*; though it was flooding, a long wooden bridge had been provided for our crossing. For the first time I was seeing a bridge across a river and was rather frightened, particularly because the bridge was narrow and looked dangerous.

The name of this river, *Seleng*, is a corrupted form of the transliteration of the Chinese word *Hsi-ning*, name of this administrative center for the province of Kokonor (Chinghai). The Seleng River area has historically been the center of a struggle between the Chinese, the Mongols, and the Tibetans in their attempts over several centuries to dominate the area.

We stayed in this city for two days and then traveled to Ninghsia city (Mong. Irghai), passing through Kansu province and the Mongolian region of Alashan Banner in western Mongolia and along the border of the desert Tengger'iin *eles* (desert of heaven).

Being no ordinary desert region, Tengger-iin *eles* is particularly difficult to travel, and it was necessary for us to transfer to camels in order to make our way across it. I was quite young and unaccustomed to traveling in this manner so my attendants constructed a chair-seat of sorts. I was mounted between the backs of two camels; and as we moved along, I gained some enjoyment from playing with my two *khab* (Pekinese dogs).

In those days we of course spent much time traveling in caravans, *gösög*, generally using camels, which in Mongolia have two humps. Between the two humps are placed frames in which to carry baggage and freight. As we are preparing to load the camels for the caravan, we tug on the string laced through the camel's nostril to get the camels to kneel down, as they have been trained to do. We are then able to place the frame and the freight between the humps, always being sure to balance the load very evenly on both sides of the camel for long journeys. Camel caravans, though a traditional way to travel, and at least better than small ox carts, did have a certain disadvantage. All the camels must follow single file, one after another, and the lead camel must be very reliable, even-tempered, and carefully chosen. If it should be frightened, stampede, or cause some other trouble, all the other camels are affected. Actually, traveling in a large cart with very high wheels and a broad bed was much more comfortable than travelling on the humps of a camel.

At one point in our journey we came to a high, rather cold place in the desert area where snow was plentiful, making it possible for us to use snow instead of the water we were carrying. Here we also found an *oboo* dedicated to the Panchen *boghda*. This Tibetan incarnation was second only to the Dalai Lama in the world of Tibetan Buddhism. These two came into conflict in the 1920s and when the Panchen fled from Tibet, he passed overland through this place on the way to Peking. According to Mongolian custom *oboo* shrines always face south or southeast, but this one was an exception; it faced southwest in a symbolic welcome to the Panchen coming from Tibet. Reports describe this particular desert area as being rather unique geographically. It is the most dry and sandy desert of all Mongolia. Sand dunes pile high and travel is very slow. For this reason the Panchen *boghda*, impressed by the unique feeling of the place, established the *oboo* as he passed through in his earlier travels.

Continuing on our way, we came to Alashan *yamun*, the administrative office for the Alashan Mongolian region—this center where we stopped is called by the Chinese Ting-yüan-ying. Because there were so many of us, about thirty people in the party, we made our camp outside the city. While camping on the outskirts, I felt that if the Panchen *boghda* had established an *oboo* in his travels, I also, since I was beginning to see myself as important, should establish an *oboo* in this place, and I spent some time gathering rocks to form one. I was, I feel now, living in the imaginery world of a young nine-year-old incarnation, and what I was doing had no real meaning. Of course, no one paid any attention to my play.

[41]

Alashan, probably the most famous Mongol area in south-western Mongolia, has a unique and interesting history. This area takes its name from the Alashan *uul* (mountains), known to the Chinese as the Ho-lan mountains. For many centuries this mountain range has served as a division between the nomadic peoples to the northwest and the sedentary farming people to the southeast. Southeast of the mountains is the famous city Ninghsia, situated on the western bank of the Yellow River. Anciently this city was the capital of the Tangut (Tangghud) people who established the famous Hsia dynasty that lasted from the early part of the tenth century to 1227 with the invasion of Chinggis Khan and the spread of the Mongol Empire. Ninghsia, also known as Yin-ch'uan in the Republican period, was an important military stronghold against the Mongols during the Chinese Ming Dynasty. West of the city, along the eastern fringe of the Alashan Mountains, is a long series of tombs or tumulus of the old Tangut kings, known in Chinese as Hsia *wang fen*. Each tumulus consists of five piles of earth heaped up. A large tumulus is set in the middle with four smaller ones at each corner. There are very many of these tomb mounds and it is impossible in some cases to know which mound is the real tomb. As one comes to the top of the Alashan mountains, one can see to the northwest the red desert of Alashan and to the southeast the green fields of the fertile Yellow River valley. The Mongols conquered this entire region under Chinggis, but for some strange reason the fertile strip of farmland that was settled by the Chinese along the river was never fully taken back by the Mongols and never returned to grazing land. Just across the river to the east of Alashan is the Ordos region, long dominated by Mongolian and nomadic peoples. This fertile strip of land suggests how deeply rooted and tenacious the Chinese peasants have become and helps us realize more clearly the importance of the agricultural products from this region that feed our Mongolian people.

The capital of Alashan (Ting-yüan-ying also known as Bayanhot) is a small city that has several streams flowing near it from the Alashan (Ho-lan) mountains. On the eastern, barren side of this mountain range is Ninghsia, and on the western side, rather heavily wooded and very beautiful, is Ting-yüan-ying. It is an oasis of beautiful vegetation, particularly with its willows growing along the stream banks. Because of this fertile landscape some Chinese travelers who come into this region speak of it as the "sai-pei chiang-nan," which might be translated as the "Yangzte river beyond the northern fortress." Ting-yüan-ying is a walled city that one can walk around in less than one hour. The walls, made of stone and brick on the outside and heavy tamped mud on the inside, are so thick that a large cart can travel around the top. Still remaining are some of the large boulders used against the former invading Moslems who came to attack the city.

One reason this beautiful city was established here was that a daughter of Emperor K'ang-hsi (r. 1661–1722) was married to the Mongol prince of the Alashan Banner, and a palace of the prince was built here in a beautiful, conventional Peking style architecture. Also in the city is a fine monastic temple, built in a mixed Chinese-Tibetan architecture. Because of the earlier marriage arrangement many Manchus came to this center and settled in the vicinity outside the wall. Consequently, one visiting the area sees in the language and the manners of the people much of old Peking.

After several days' rest from our journey at Alashan, we moved on to Bayan-ghol, what soon became Teng-k'ou hsien, also a place with a rather unique history. Located near the loop of the Yellow River in the northeast corner of the Alashan region, this city has become an important port for transportation and communication, serving small river rafts and boats. Prior to the Boxer Rebellion (1900), Teng-k'ou was a rather desolate, uninhabited piece of wasteland. Earlier, it was the site of San-sheng-kung, a Chinese merchant outpost in the trade with the Mongols. Following the rebellion the Catholic missionaries obtained title to the area as reparations to the Church for its damages and losses in north China. This was partly due to the fact that during the Boxer Rebellion the Alashan Prince was opposed to the missionaries. As the land was developed the Mongols withdrew. Canals were built by Chinese land developers, and Chinese settlers were brought in as agricultural colonists. In time a rather flourishing town was established. By the time I travelled through this area, it had already become an important part of commerce and trade, as well as a link in the opium trade from the Kansu and the Ninghsia areas as opium flowed east into north China. The Chinese administrative district (hsien) of Teng-k'ou was established in the late 1920s or early 1930s.

In Teng-k'ou hsien, we heard that the region around Pao-t'ou was infested with bandits, which meant we could not travel

[43]

directly to that city. There were so many of us that we would likely attract attention and be attacked. We then devised a strategy whereby the larger group of our caravan took a wide diversion north into the Mongolian territory of Ulanchab while a smaller group, including myself, travelled down the Yellow River in a boat or raft made of inflated animal skins. After eight days on the river, we arrived at Pao-t'ou. It was already the third month (April) of 1924. We found many Chinese in the city, including a number who had branch businesses at the monastic temple of Badghar and who did business with the Mongols in the vicinity.

The name of this city, Pao-t'ou, is taken from its old Mongol name *Bout*, the meaning of which is unknown. At the time it was the western terminus of the Peking-Suiyüan Railroad. After the communist takeover, it was extended southwest to Lanchou. When I visited Pao-t'ou as a small boy, it was a very important center as the jumping-off point for caravans going west into Sinkiang, Kansu, and other places in the northwest. It was also a very important commercial center bringing together Mongolian and Chinese trade from many outlying points. When I arrived at Pao-t'ou, it was already a fairly large city inhabited by many Chinese merchants and Mongols who came there to do business, and it had attained additional importance due to the Peking-Suiyuan Railroad. Before the arrival of the railroad, it was a rather small place but still important in the trade between the Chinese and the Mongols.

Here in Pao-t'ou we stayed with one of the Chinese merchant establishments active in Mongolia named *Ting-ho-yi*. This establishment had warehouses and other facilities where we were able to stay. In those days it was very common for the Mongolian people, as they came into Pao-t'ou or other Chinese cities, to stay in the shop compound of a Mongolian *maimai*, our term for Chinese merchants with connections in Mongolia. Most of our people could not speak Chinese and they needed assistance; the merchant facilities were large and offered accommodations better than those to be gained in some other place. The Chinese merchants acted as interpreters and liaison for the Mongols in important negotiations with Chinese officialdom. Also, it was important for the Chinese to welcome and to care for Mongols with whom they did business, to wine and dine them in order to obtain additional commerce.

[44]

While our party was staying with Chinese merchants in Pao-t'ou, one of the lamas from the monastic center of Badghar made an official visit to our rooms. During the night it was decided that I should make a journey to Peking to be introduced to officialdom there and to make proper contacts before settling down to my studies and training in Mongolia. I was very young, and of course not really involved in the discussions or the decisions, so my spokesman was my administrative assistant, Ya *jasagh*, whose personal name was Aghwang-yontson, from the Tümed Banner. From Pao-t'ou we journeyed east and stopped at Hohhot (Köke-khota) where our Badghar Monastery had its own office or *shang* (Ch. *pan-shih-ch'u*).

While I was staying in Hohhot, I was visited by many princes, lamas, and other people from the surrounding Banners, along with representatives from the government in Peking. Hohhot city was first established by Altan Khan in the middle of the sixteenth century, at which time it was an important military, political and commercial center. The name Hohhot is a combination of two Mongolian words, *köke* (blue) and *khota* (city), meaning the "eternal city." Blue, the color of heaven, the traditional color of our people, symbolizes to the Mongols that which is everlasting, immortal or eternal. Here Yeke juu (Ta-chao ssu), the first great Buddhist monastery in all Inner Mongolia, was built. Altan Khan was the most powerful leader during this period, although he was nominally under the suzerainty of the "Great Khan." This monastic temple was, for a time, the most important religious center for Mongolian Buddhism and was started by the Third Dalai Lama. Large numbers of Tibetan teachers and missionaries came first to this center and then moved to all areas of Mongolia. I was greatly impressed with the large numbers of temples, monasteries, and *soborgha* (stupa shrines) in this region. When peace was finally established after the wars between the Mongols and Ming China during the rise to power of Altan Khan, the Chinese emperor gave Hohhot a new name, *Kuei-hua ch'eng*, meaning "the city which has returned to culture."

After the establishment of the Ch'ing Dynasty (1644), this city became an important base for the Manchu in handling problems among the Junghar (Dzungar) far to the northwest and in Outer Mongolia. Later, during the mid-1700s, a new city was built neighboring Kuei-hua ch'eng and given the name Suiyüan ch'eng, "the city pacifying afar." Occasionally one hears the Chinese refer to the entire area as Kuei-sui, a combination of the first part of each of the two names.

The Chinese prepared a special railroad car for my personal convenience in travelling to Peking. As our train arrived at P'ing-ti-chüan (Chi-ning) in the Chakhar Mongol area, my disciples and patrons of the four banners of the Chakhar Right Flank came to pay their respects. The Chinese name of this place is taken from the old Mongolian name, Pindinoboo. This particular place has now become the junction for the railroad coming from Ulan Bator to link into the main line between Peking and Lanchou. When we arrived at this place, a special request was made that the train stop so that we could stay for the night. There a great many people greeted me, so many that I was very surprised. We then continued on to Peking without further stops, not even at the important center of Kalgan.

We arrived at the capital at Hsi-chih men, the gate that is the Peking terminus of the railroad from Inner Mongolia. As we stepped from the train, I was almost speechless in amazement at the large number of dignitaries, a band, and a large contingent of military forces drawn up in an honor guard. I certainly was not prepared for this. I did not even know how to behave. Fortunately my advisor, Ya jasagh, was there to tell me what to say and do. At that time I knew not a single word of Chinese and only a few words of the Mongolian language; I spoke mainly the Kokonor dialect of Tibetan, and I was at a great disadvantage in communicating with the people. Ordinarily my aides would speak for me or I communicated through an interpreter. A few words spoken in the Kokonor dialect of Chinese I was able to understand, but could not understand anything at all of the Mandarin dialect. The abdicated emperor, Hsüan-t'ung (P'u-yi), the last ruler of the Manchu Dynasty, was still living in Peking at this time in the middle 1920s. The president then was Ts'ao K'un and he held an official reception for me. Among the other dignitaries assembled was the outstanding Prince Gungsangnorbu, at that time the head of the Mongolian Tibetan Ministry (Meng-Tsang yüan), and it was he who hosted me in the quarters of the Shih-chia hu-tung, the official residence attached to the Ministry.

In those days ecclesiastical politics were important among the Buddhists of Mongolia, and there were two main places for the lamas to stay as they came to Peking, sometimes on a pilgrimage, sometimes to seek political favors. Sung-chu ssu Temple was dominated primarily by the Jangjia khutughtu and his followers, and the great monastic temple Yung-ho kung was an important center for Mongols and Tibetans. As explained by Ya jasagh, it would have been rather embarrassing for us to stay at either of these places. The arch rival of Ya jasagh, a man known as Ba jasagh, whose personal name was Bayanjirghal, was influential in these monastic temples. He was from the Keshigten Banner and as a prominent disciple of the young Jangjia khutughtu, he acted as a planner and prime-mover of the master. We were indeed fortunate to stay in the official quarters of the Mongolian Tibetan Ministry. Through the good offices of Prince Gungsang-norbu, I first visited President Tsao. Then being an officially recognized lama reincarnation, so designated by the former emperor, I immediately paid my respects to Hsüan-t'ung, the former emperor, more commonly known to Westerners as P'u-yi.

When I visited Peking, though the Manchu court had lost its political power a decade earlier, the new republican government still allowed it to occupy the area of Peking known as the Forbidden City. The Presidential Office actually occupied but a small section of the area known to us as the Chung-nan-hai (southern and middle sea), and the imperial family still lived in the Forbidden City in their own little world, carrying on their courtly ceremonies. Consequently I was welcomed at a reception in their residence. This situation of the remnant of the old imperial court continued until about the year after my visit when general Feng Yü-hsiang occupied Peking and abolished this imperial farce (1925).

Being young and inexperienced, I was unaware of the political implications of the role of P'u-yi. Later when he became Japan's puppet emperor of Manchukuo, although I went to Manchuria a number of times, I never visited him. He had then become a shadowy figure in seclusion.

To enter the great compound of the imperial palace, I was given the special honor of mounting the ch'uan-ch'ao ma, a horse reserved only for high ministers and elderly dignitaries. This privilege allows one to advance into the palace area while still on horseback, rather than being forced to walk like common officials. As a result of the meeting with the abdicated emperor, I had bestowed upon me the special rank of the yellow imperial button, that authorized me from that time to travel in a specially designated yellow sedan chair. Only two or three incarnations in

[47]

all of Mongolia were given this distinction, the first was the Jebtsundamba *khutughtu*, another was the Jangjia *khutughtu*.

Soon after arriving in the capital, I was officially welcomed at the great Buddhist center of Yung-ho *kung*, where I gave an audience to all the lamas residing in this monastic temple. On this occasion in the middle 1920s, there was a great drought in North China and all of the lamas were very earnestly chanting prayers in the hall of Kuan lao-yeh, a temple within Yung-ho *kung*. The deity of this temple is Kuan Yü, a red-faced warrior known to the Chinese as Kuan lao-yeh, but known to our Mongolian people and also to the Tibetans as Geser Khan. Kuan Yü was introduced to Mongolia by Phags-pa, with the explanation that he was the incarnation of Geser. As a result of the lama's prayers, a heavy rainfall finally came to relieve the bad drought at that time.

In those days the leader of the Mongolian community in Peking was Prince Gungsangnorbu. Prince Gung petitioned President Ts'ao K'un to present me with the official title Kanjurwa *nom-un khan khutughtu*, which is why I am still called the Kanjurwa *khutughtu* today. We also visited many other important people and received many visitors in our quarters. So many people were introduced to be by Ya *jasagh* that I cannot begin to remember them. I only remember that I was required to continually be dressed in a long formal yellow robe. It was an uncomfortable, tense time for me. At that time I was fortunate to meet Mendel *gegen*, also from my original monastery of Serkü *keid*, who had come to Peking just one year earlier. At Serkü I had seen Mendel *gegen* off on his journey to Peking, and now I was able to see him again in the capital, the only man I knew there. His visit was a great comfort to me. Mendel *gegen* left Serkü Monastery in 1923 and I in 1924. In Peking I stayed two nights with him.

I and my aides of course had to make official visits or courtesy calls in Peking to the Jangjia *khutughtu*, at Sung-chu *ssu* (temple). During this first visit to Peking, a formal reception was given me by the Jangjia *khutughtu* at Sung-chu *ssu*. The most interesting part of this program for me was the magicians. Prior to this I had not seen a Chinese magician. While we were thus engaged in watching them, Ya *jasagh* quietly approached me, tugged on my arm, and prompted me to talk to the Jangjia and extend him a special invitation to my reception on the morrow. I thus invited him to a reception hosted by me at the Kuang-te *lo* opera house, where we saw a Chinese opera. Though I was the host, all the protocol and formalities were very new to me. While we were dining, there were in our group, in addition to the Jangjia, Ya *jasagh* and Ba *jasagh*. These latter two maintained a very polite, proper attitude towards each other, though actually they were rather bitter enemies in the ecclesiastical hierarchy. The Jangjia, whatever his real attitude may have been, gave the impression that he was entirely above all petty religious politics. Of course, I was but a boy and had no real understanding then about what was going on between these various ecclesiastical dignitaries and their struggle for power in the world of Lamaist Buddhism.

Later, I became aware of the important and interesting connections between Chinese merchants and Mongol customers in the cities of China. For example, in Peking of the old days there were two very important merchant headquarters, *li-kuan* and *wai-kuan*. The first was near the legation quarters of the foreign nations, in the vicinity of Morrison Street (Wang-fu ching). The *li-kuan* semi-official hostel district, with connections mainly in Inner Mongolia, eventually disappeared after the Boxer Rebellion when the legations expanded to take over the *li-kuan* area. Earlier, all Mongolian *maimai* who did business in Inner Mongolia were concentrated in this section of the city. As people from Inner Mongolia came to Peking, they stayed in this area. In those days the term *kuan* meant an official residence or quarters where Mongol dignitaries could stay and do official business through the Chinese merchants with the *Li-fan yüan* also called the Ministry of Dependencies (it later was replaced by the Ministry of Mongolian and Tibetan Affairs).

Wai-kuan, a section on the outskirts of Peking, just outside of An-ting gate, also was a semi-official quarter where princes and others from Outer Mongolia resided as they came to Peking for their annual visits or on other occasions. They also had quarters assigned to them by the *Li-fan yüan*.

Eventually, the Inner Mongolian princes and dignitaries established their own mansions or homes in other parts of the city and as a result the *li-kuan* district eventually lost its importance. After it was completely taken over by the city people, there was no "li-kuan" to accommodate the Mongols. The *wai-kuan* district continued to be important until the 1920s, when it also began to change after Outer Mongolian independence. The *li-kuan*, semi-official hostel, was gone by the time I first arrived in 1924, and

[49]

the *wai-kuan* district was rapidly losing importance. Contact with Mongols in the early days was virtually a monopoly of the Chinese merchants in these quarters, even the special business of the Peking ministries themselves was carried on through the mediation of Chinese merchants.

Altogether I stayed in Peking for about one month in the spring of 1924, and from there journeyed to Kalgan on my way to Dolonor to continue my training. On arriving at Kalgan station, I was met by the governor-general (*tu-t'ung*) of Chakhar Province, who was accompanied by two of the important *ambans* of the Chakhar Mongol regions, namely Jodbajab and Sarondongrub. With them was Nima-odsor, a popular leader, regarded in those days as the "spirit of Jodbajab," which meant that he was really his right-hand man and key advisor. Later Nima-odsor became an *amban* and then was assassinated in the early months of 1936 by the Japanese because of his nationalistic tendencies and suspicion of Japanese expansionist schemes.

Following the welcoming ceremonies at the train station I was driven in a procession to the official residence of the governor-general. We traveled in cars, a very rare thing in the Chakhar of those days. At the hotel there was prepared for me a most delicious banquet and reception, attended by many important officials, both Chinese and Mongolian. By this time the Chinese were pushing far into Mongolia and dominated economic and political life. On this occasion, Ya *jasagh* told me quietly and very kindly that I must eat "only a half-stomach full." By this he meant that I must show refinement, not behave like a hungry common boy. He also instructed me in a few words of Chinese, my first attempt at understanding this language. The phrases he taught me on that occasion were how to thank my host and how to ask to be excused early so that I could return to read the Buddhist scriptures.

Following this official reception our group made a short trip to Dolonor. At this time I was also accompanied by the three Mongolian dignitaries just mentioned. Nima-odsor had a green car, both Jodbajab and Sarondongrub had black cars. I travelled in the car of Jodbajab because he was the senior of the three Mongolian leaders. Also in our car were Ya *jasagh* and Tübshinbayar *soibon* (a personal attendant). Our procession formed quite a spectacle as we made the trip in heavy rain. Upon our arrival at Malaghtai Monastery we were welcomed to a formal lunch. From Malaghtai we traveled to my monastery at a place known as Juu-naiman süme, making the trip in one day. Here we learned that we could not continue our journey to Dolonor because the Shangdu River (Ch. Shan-tien *ho*) had flooded. This necessitated our staying in Juu-naiman süme for a time.

Located nearby was the site of the ancient Mongol capital Shangdu (Ch. Shang-tu), which was destroyed by the Chinese General Ch'ang Yü-ch'un after the fall of the Mongol Empire (1368). Shangdu seems to have been built within five concentric walls, one wall within the other, expanding the site as one of the great centers of all Mongolia. Surrounding the city were the tops of a thousand hills. It seems that the old outer wall was an earthen wall and within it considered to be the first wall was a moat called the "wall of water." The fourth inner wall was of stone, and within it was another wall of brick. Within this brick wall, located in the northeastern section, were three magnificent palace buildings. According to my observation, the eight monasteries or temples formerly located without the city walls, were built of large stones. All the buildings had been demolished years before my visit, mainly in the battles between Mongols and Chinese in Mongolia's struggle for independence in 1913.

There is an old legend regarding the original establishment of these temples. Karma *baghshi*, a lama famous for his customary garb of a Buddhist ceremonial white shawl that passes over one shoulder, came into the area when it was dominated by a *shimnüs*, an evil spirit. A power struggle ensued since each was determined to be supreme. The *shimnüs* declared it would erect one hundred and eight great piles of stone and earth, and Karma *baghshi* declared he would construct one hundred and eight temples. It should be kept in mind that one hundred and eight is a key number in Lamaist Buddhism; there are one hundred and eight volumes to the Kanjur canon of scripture. Each was to begin work at midnight and complete by dawn. As dawn came, there were indeed one hundred and eight great piles of earth set up by the *shimnüs*, but not a single temple. Just as the *shimnüs* was about to declare a victory, one hundred and eight temples miraculously appeared through the power of Karma *baghshi*. So according to the legend, the area has always been known as Juu-naiman süme (one hundred and eight temples). It seems that only eight temples were actually established, and accordingly some people called the area Naiman-süme (eight temples). The fact is

[51]

that the name is not to be taken literally, it is also said that the area is called Juu-naiman süme because it was about one hundred "örtöö (stages or stations) from the Bargha area where there was located a related monastic temple.

Though the story just related is legendary, there was an actual historical figure named Karma *baghshi* who was the head of the Karma-pa sect of Tibetan Buddhism, which in that period was equal in power to the famous Sakya-pa sect. An important master of the Sakya-pa sect during the Yüan dynasty was Phags-pa who became the Imperial Tutor of Khubilai Khan, and Karma *baghshi* was a contemporary of Phags-pa. In Mongolian chronicles Karma *baghshi* is very famous for his many miracles. In the vicinity or surrounding area of the historic ruins at Juu-naiman süme are numerous rockpiles that the local people point out as those originally established by the *shimnüs* or evil spirit of ancient times.

I greatly enjoyed searching through these ruins and admiring the fine stone carvings still remaining. After the temples collapsed, numerous interesting and valuable objects were obtainable by excavation. Now, however, it is taboo among the local people for anyone to dig in the ruins. It is said that those who do are struck by an illness, death, or a bolt of lightning. My former incarnation was very fond of this particular area and built a monastery there, utilizing old stones from the former ancient buildings. This monastery, as mentioned, was destroyed at the time of China's Republican Revolution and Mongolia's push for independence.

Also in the vicinity of Juu-naiman süme is a lake named Chaghan-nor (white lake). On the north side of the lake is an *oboo* that was established by or belongs to the *shang*, or treasury, of the temple. According to the folklore of the common people in the region, the center of Changhan-nor Lake is bottomless and coins thrown into it will reach clear to the Serkü Monastery in Kokonor. The Shangdu River is also a feature of this area. Because this river is winding and crooked in its course, it is also called "stubborn Shangdu" (ergü Shangdu) by the local people. It comprises the head waters of the Luan River, in North China, that flows into the Po-hai Gulf. It is also said that in this general region are one hundred and eight water springs. The area is rich in water and grass for the herds, and it is evident why Emperor Khubilai chose it for his summer capital. One of his favorite places to hunt with falcons was in the vicinity of Chaghan-nor.

Though it was said that there were one hundred and eight springs, they did not all flow at the same time. The local people said that if they did so, certainly a great flood would ensue. It does seem that in 1939 there was a great deal of rainfall, which increased the flow from the springs to such a degree that the people found it difficult or impossible to ford the Shangdu River. While many of these tales are really products of the people's imagination, there is nevertheless some basis for their imaginings.

In the region of Juu-naiman süme are also a number of famous *oboo*, shrines, for example, the Jibkhulangtu, the Chaghan khad, the Kholostai, and the Manitai. According to the local people, the Manitai *oboo* was established over the top of five *bolsh* (buried treasure, the burial place of ancient royalty, or the covered ruins of a famous place). These particular *bolsh* are said to be very rich. Some distance from these *oboo* is a place called Dushiin Khairkhan where there is a large stone monument said to have been established in the time of Chinggis Khan. Some time ago Chinese merchants at Dolonor tried to move this stone monument to the city of Dolonor with a special large cart drawn by eight horses. The cart was broken, however, and the monument remained unmoved. When I left the area, it was still at Dushiin Khairkhan.

I recall an interesting story about another *oboo*, Khonghor *oboo*, in that region. According to this legend, the Mongols anciently buried their documents underneath Khonghor *oboo*, but to my knowledge no one as yet has tried to unearth them. Just bordering Juu-naiman süme in the Chakhar area, enroute to the Taipus Banner (Ch. *Tai-p'u ssu*), was an imperial grazing area placed under the jurisdiction of the Manchu court. Today in that region there is a rather large site of the ruins of an ancient city, but no one seems to know anything about it. The Chinese there call it Ssu-lang ch'eng (city of Yang Ssu-lang) in honor of the legendary Chinese general who fought against the Kitan founders of the Liao Dynasty and finally surrendered to them.

The people of Juu-naiman süme provided us with special large, beautiful yurts that had been prepared years earlier for my previous incarnation. One was yellow, and the others were white and blue. The yurt given to me was lined entirely on the inside with Tibetan textiles and cloth. I had never seen one so magnificent and marvelled at this fine structure.

During our stay here the Seiwa *da-lama* came from the head monastery in Dolonor to welcome us. Earlier, while I was staying at Serkü Monastery in Kokonor, I had been invited to the monastic center at Dolonor. This invitation was brought to me by Ishighawa *da-lama*, head of the Dolonor center. When I arrived there, however, Ishighawa had gone to Tibet for a pilgrimage and it was Seiwa *da-lama*, the new administrator of the monastery, who greeted me. Juu-naiman süme was a major center for my previous incarnations, and thus upon my arrival I was given a fine reception, complete with a lama band playing traditional Mongolian and Tibetan instruments. I found it difficult to communicate with the people at this time, because I could speak only a few words of Mongolian.

The day following the reception the flood of the river had subsided, and we were able to cross on a wooden raft and continue our journey to Dolonor in three cars. When we arrived at a way station called Bayan-uul, I was instructed by Ya *jasagh* to put on my formal embroidered jacket (*kürüm*). Upon our arrival at the monastic center, I experienced the very impressive occasion of my first meeting with my disciples. We were received very formally by a long reception line on both sides of the path to the monastery. This line included Chinese officials from the local *hsien* (district), the military dignitaries of the region, and all the many lamas of the two monasteries of Köke and Shira. As I was arriving, the Chinese band played their brass instruments, making the whole reception very impressive. After alighting from the car, I was seated on a ceremonial sedan chair and taken by the bearers down the long reception line of the various lama dignitaries to the seat of honor in the main hall of the monastery. Part of the ceremony was the presentation to me, on behalf of the lamas, of an impressive *mandala* made of jewels, coins, and other precious items, all placed on a silver plate symbolic of the capital of the Buddhist world or the holy land of Shambhala. After this the lamas came in a long procession to pay their respects, to receive a blessing, and to present ceremonial *khadagh* scarfs.

Visit and Training at Dolonor

I stayed at Dolonor for several months in the spring of 1924 and learned what an important historical place it is. The name

Dolonor comes from the seven lakes (*doloon-nor*) which anciently existed in the area. Lakes are still there, although there are no longer seven of them. This place is best known to people in the West as the site of an exotic capital of Khubilai Khan, Shang-tu (Mong. Shangdu). As Khubilai's summer capital, the term Shang-tu meant literally "upper capital," to distinguish it from Peking.

The city was destroyed by a Ming Chinese general, Ch'ang Yü-ch'un with the collapse of the Yüan Dynasty. Later, in the 1680s during the great battles between the Junghar Mongols and the Khalkha Mongols, the Khalkha, being hard pressed by the Junghar, fled to the south of the Gobi for refuge, and at Dolonor, the Holy One of Khalkha, the First Jebtsundamba *khutughtu*, together with many of the great princes of Khalkha, met with the Emperor K'ang-hsi to recognize his suzerainty and gain his protection from their enemies. As a result of this turning point in our people's history, many great monastic temples were built under the patronage of the emperor and given special designation, and thus Dolonor became the single most important center of Mongolian Buddhism in southern Mongolia. Because of the many monasteries or temples built in the region of Dolonor, the Chinese commonly referred to the place as La-ma miao (lama temples).

As a Buddhist administrative center, Dolonor overshadowed all other places in Inner Mongolia, but in strictly academic Buddhist studies, our Badghar Monastery was still the preeminent center for Buddhist studies. Badghar did not have any designation as an imperial monastic center, however, nor was its administrative function important in terms of the broader scope of Mongolian Buddhism.

While it has long been important as a Buddhist center, as noted, it is also an important administrative center, and also as a commercial center. Dolonor is geographically located near the center of Inner Mongolia from east to west, and thus many people from all the various banners come here to trade. Because of its prestige as an imperial temple center, merchants were not allowed to come within the monastery compounds to carry on business, so the real commercial center was some four miles removed to the southeast. With the growing population and activity in this area, the Manchu established the administrative office of Tuo-lun t'ing (the office at Dolonor) in 1732. In 1912, at the beginning of the Republican period, the city was upgraded administratively and organized as a *hsien* (district). Of course, in terms of political administration there were more important centers in Mongolia. Each Banner area had its political center and these were grouped into six leagues or regions that each had its political center. Then we could not ignore such important places as Hohhot (Kuei-sui) and Kalgan in the west, and Wangiin süme (Wang-yeh miao), Mukden (Shengyang), Chichikhar and Harbin in the east. By my day, these had become Chinese-dominated administrative centers with great influence in Mongolian areas; of course, they came under Japanese domination in the 1930s.

After taking up residence at Dolonor for a few months in the late spring of 1924, several hundred lamas and two of my disciples from Badghar Monastery participated in a welcoming reception in my honor and presented a toghlom—an entertainment in the form of a skit or play. Actually it was not entertainment or amusement to me but rather a dialogue (choyir), a debate by two lamas in which they discussed the profound doctrines of Buddhism.

After these ceremonies and presentations, I was escorted to my quarters in a separate compound within the monastic complex that we call ordo in Mongolian and labrang in Tibetan. It consisted of seven large rooms adjoining each other in a line, with a nice flower garden in the front yard. Here in my separate residence I was again honored with another reception consisting mainly of the presentation of tea on a ceremonial khadagh/scarf. After everything had settled down, Ya jasagh informed me that my official staff offices would be in this compound that had belonged to my former incarnation, and that my private quarters would be in an adjoining building to the rear, known as the Green Palace (Noghon Ordo). I was also told that many of the personal effects of my former incarnations were still preserved there, and if I desired to read some particular scriptures they would be brought to me from a different place. Ten lamas were appointed as my personal attendants.

I soon became acquainted with Lobsang-oirob, also known as the khural-iin lama, the lama of the prayer mass who took the lead in conducting the great prayer masses held daily. This very scholarly monk was in charge of the academic affairs of the monastery in which I was residing and studying. Always within the main temple compound was the da-lama who was the head administrator of the temple. His deputy, known as ded-lama, was in this case Lobsang-oirob.

Another important lama in the affairs of the monastery, whom I met the following day, was Ghajir-oirol, who held the rank of doctor (gebshi). He informed me that it was time for guntseg (originally a Tibetan word reserved as an honorary term for the banquet of a high lama, never even used as a reference to the meal of a Mongol prince). This special meal consisted of many different dishes spread out on a square table with a setting for only one person where it was intended I should sit to eat. I took a little from each of the dishes and the attendants brought me a large rump of mutton. During the meal about ten people stood around to wait on me. The special task of slicing the meat from the rump of the mutton was done by my jama (Tibetan for cook). After he sliced it, two servers (deberchi) served the meat to me.

From day to day I customarily received many visitors who I received in my private quarters to the rear of the Green Palace. However, if my visitor was a prince or some other dignitary, I met him in the more formal outer hall (ordo). In both the inner quarters and the outer offices the walls were lined with gilded images of the Buddha and with choijung, "protectors of the law," all of which we call shüteen, objects of worship. Also displayed in the hall was a ceremonial spear (jida) used by the protectors of the Buddhist Law when they descended to make a revelation to a particular person. As part of the revelation process they thrust the sword through the person, but this was never fatal or even harmful in its consequences. Each monastic temple has such a ritual spear.

Displayed in my formal quarters was a sword with seven golden stars on it, the property of my previous incarnation. Among the Chinese from ancient times, such a ceremonial sword has been regarded as having mystical powers and is believed to have been used in supernatural ways by Chu-ke Liang, a famous statesman and marshal of the Three Kingdoms period (220–265), who has been deified. Also preserved in our monastery was a fine, beautiful sword in the shape of a crescent with impressive silver work designs all along the blade. This relic had anciently come from the Khalkha Mongol areas to the north. This type of ceremonial sword was worn by the bodyguards or attendants (kiya) of my previous incarnation whenever he attended a formal function. Because I was not so concerned with such status and display, my attendants did not bear the ceremonial swords in the customary manner.

[57]

In Dolonor there are two important monastic temples, Köke *süme* and Shira *süme*, established by order of the Manchu emperors. Koke (Blue) Monastery, (Ch. Hui-tsung *ssu*), the main temple of the region, was built by the Khalka Mongolian lords as a memorial to Emperor K'ang-hsi for his favorable policies towards them. This monastery was located where K'ang-hsi met the Khalkha leaders in 1691. Shira (Yellow) Monastery (Ch. Shan-yin *ssu*), smaller and to the west of Köke *süme*, established by Emperor Yung-cheng (r. 1723–1735), was discussed earlier. There were also here thirteen administrative offices, one each for the important incarnations in residence.

During my time, in the 1930s and 1940s, there was at Dolonor a population of over 20,000 persons, including lamas and their *shabinar* disciples associated with the various monasteries, the merchant population and the administrative staff of the civil government. The Jangia *khutughtu* was in residence there, always as the supreme reincarnation among the thirteen *khutughtus* at Dolonor, all usually living at Köke *süme*.

A branch office of the *lama tamagha* (Ch. *la-ma yin-wu ch'u*), Office of Lamaist Affairs, was located in Shira *süme*. Also the main printing office was in this monastery. From its beginning in the early Manchu period, lamas came to these monasteries from all banners of both Inner and Outer Mongolia. This meant also that many different banners sustained the monasteries by sending herds of animals for its support.

When I first arrived in Dolonor, I was visited by each of the important incarnations and this of course necessitated my making a return ceremonial visit to them. In each of these formal visits, I would ride on my sedan chair and be accompanied by an entourage of ten or twenty lamas. In this manner we exchanged many feasts and ceremonial visits. One noteworthy incarnation with whom I visited was the Shireetü *gegen*, also titled Ganden Shireetü, which meant that his previous incarnation had been honored by being seated at a special honorary table in Ganden Monastery in Lhasa, Tibet.

Not long after I arrived in Dolonor it was the season for the *cham*, a religious dance festival, mistakenly called by the Chinese *t'iao-kuei*, "devil-dance." Held in the sixth month of the lunar calendar this was an important occasion, and people gathered from many miles around to participate in the entertainment, the prayers, and a flourishing exchange of goods in the bazaar that sprang up. Together with two incarnations of Dolonor, Shireetü gegen and Mendel gegen, I attended the cham celebration of each of the two monasteries, Köke and Shira.

All religious observances at Köke Monastery are performed in the Mongolian manner, very similar to the Khalkha style at Dolonor. The prayers and ceremonies at Shira Monastery, in contrast, are performed in the Lhasa style. Following the celebration of the cham dances, special prayer ceremonies (mani khural) were held. On one occasion, as we visited one of the monasteries, the Shireetü gegen and I conducted a prayer mass.

This same month I gave instructions that the oboo or shrine of the monastery be repaired and that prayer offerings be made. The courtyard of my residence in Dolonor was very large, including three main prayer halls, one arranged behind the other. As we entered from the main gate, each hall had two large wings extending out from the sides. To the side of the courtyard and attached was a separate area in which was situated the shang, administrative office and the treasury of the monastery. Situated in another separate area was my personal residence and the office of my personal administrative assistants, and my personal treasury, also attached to the shang. All of these areas totalled nearly four hundred separate rooms.

After my stay and the various celebrations at Dolonor, I journeyed once again to Juu-naiman süme. Because the monastery there was in ruins, my followers and attendants erected a fine cloth enclosure in which they set up a beautiful yellow yurt and an eight-sided yurt, one for my personal accommodations and the other for guests. It was said that these yurts were placed on the site where the ancient khans had established their headquarter pavilion in former days.

The season had arrived for offerings to the oboo shrine, and I participated for the first time in these ceremonies. This we know is really not a pure Buddhist ritual, for it comes mostly from the Shamanistic Bon religion. At such times, because they were not conventional Buddhist occasions, I did not wear my usual Buddhist prayer robes, but rather a yellow official jacket (kürüm) adorned with a beautiful ceremonial knife and a ceremonial flint that my previous incarnation had left me. I rode a specially trained and gaited old white horse to the ceremonies, a horse I was informed had borne my previous incarnation. On the occasion of making offerings to the oboo I almost always took my pet Pekinese

[59]

dogs (khab). Sometimes I travelled by horse and other times by a four-wheeled horse-drawn carriage. Ya jasagh always took care of the travel details. We camped for a few days in the area of Juu-naiman süme and then returned to Dolonor.

In the seventh lunar month it was time for the performance of the dallagh, ceremonial prayers for wealth for the temple and its disciples, and I carried these out with the assistance of Ya jasagh and the other lamas. The dallagh, a religious ceremony to "beckon wealth," derives from an old practice of the shamans (boe) that has been taken into the ceremonies of Mongolian Buddhism. This ritual involves an arrow from the feathered end of which is hung many colored ribbon streamers and khadagh (scarves). An elder of a monastery or a family takes the arrow outside and with a background of sutra chanting, he waves the arrow overhead in a wide counter-clockwise circle while repeating the words "khurai, khurai, khurai . . ." ("gather together, gather together . . ."). This is an expression of both gratitude and hope to the deity of wealth for bounteous blessings and wealth for the monastery or family. On special occasions we travelled from Dolonor to the "northern treasury" (ar-shang)—estates and properties or grazing areas held by the monastery in this area. Here we had special prayer ceremonies from time to time. Each year on special occasions at various places and particularly at Juu-naiman süme, we performed ceremonial prayers in commemoration of the Kanjur (a collection of Buddhist scriptures). These always took place in the eighth lunar month.

Journey West to Badghar Monastery

In the last part of the ninth lunar month (October), in the fall of 1924, we decided to journey west to Badghar Monastery where I would settle down for serious study and training. Ya jasagh suggested that because of the disturbances and civil rebellions in the Chinese areas, it would be dangerous to travel by railroad through the Chinese districts, and that it would be better for us to travel northwest through the Mongolian areas of Shilin-ghol and Ulanchab. This was the distressing period of the Chinese warlords' domination.

While we were discussing the preparation and the route for this journey, Ma Chi, the Chinese commanding general in the

Suiyuan area, visited us in Dolonor and confirmed the advice of Ya *jasagh*, saying that there were indeed disturbances in the Chinese areas and that it would be better to travel through Mongol regions. This Ma Chi was the founder of the powerful Moslem Chinese Ma family, including Ma Pu-fang, Ma Pu Ch'ing, and Ma Hung-k'uei, who were important warlord governors of the northwest provinces of Kansu, Ninghsia and Chinghai.

This was the first time I had taken leave to make a major journey since my official installation as an incarnation at Dolonor, and the lamas and the dignitaries of the monastery made a special arrangement for us to travel in three stages. Every ten miles a group of tents were set up that provided a rest station (*ortoo*) at which ceremonial tea was served. A large blue tent with beautiful white Mongolian designs was set up buttressed by a temporary wall or wind break erected from blue cloth with white designs.

The evening of the first day of our journey we were hosted at the branch properties, or outlying monastic areas, of Mendel *gegen* who gave me a white horse and a beautiful ten-foot ceremonial scarf (*khadagh*). In bidding me farewell, he wished me an enjoyable and successful study in Badghar Monastery, giving his blessings and words of gracious, valuable advice.

After all of these ceremonies, we departed the following day into the nomadic areas of Mongolia with a caravan comprised of over twenty camels and twenty of my followers and travelling attendants. We camped each night in five tents and two Mongol yurts. Our first stop was at the Khadan-khushuun Monastery in Chakhar. The official in this area was Jodbajab *amban*. Because this was my first visit to that area, I was given an official welcome in the main hall of the monastery and a ceremonial presentation of a *mandala*. At my tender age I felt that the most impressive thing about the monastery was its four great pillars encircled by golden dragons, all supporting the roof of the main hall.

Our next stop in Jodbajab's area was a place called, in those days, Ükerchin (literally meaning "cattle herders"), a term given to the area by the Manchu court. The people there felt, however, it was not very prestigious for their area to be referred to as the area of the cattle tenders, so in the 1930s they changed the name to Mingghan Banner (district), Mingghan meaning the "thousand"—a reference to the time of the Mongol Empire. Here we stopped briefly in the home of a Mr. Jimba. As a boy I was very attached to my little Pekinese dogs. I had left one of these at

Dolonor and the other I carried with me as we travelled, but I was so impressed with the hospitality of Mr. Jimba that I gave him the little dog as a present. Some ten years later when I returned to this same place I once again saw this dog, now quite old.

I have been asked why it is that many of the incarnations and high lamas have Pekinese dogs (khab) as pets. For one thing, these dogs are not so fierce and troublesome as large Mongolian dogs. They are gentle and friendly, and therefore make very fine pets for monks. These special little animals are almost human, are intelligent and emotional and, might even weep on a sad occasion. It was my custom when my dogs became sick to read a special scripture to the Buddha for them, and they were quickly healed. I must say that Mongols are very careful to give favorite pets auspicious names like Bayar (happiness) or Arslang (lion). It is our feeling that these small khab will be comfortable only in a friendly and proper home, and will soon die otherwise. Lamas also are pleased with the fact that these little dogs are easily trained. They lie very calmly as we read the sutras and do not cause any disturbance. As we go out to walk, they frisk ahead of us in a joyful, happy manner. These little animals lie on their back to express pleasure and enjoyment to their master. Some people even feel that these pets, after hearing so many sutras, will certainly be reincarnated as human beings in the next life. I, however, consider this only as hearsay.

After visiting with Mr. Jimba, we traveled on to our next stop. Many of my followers were concentrated in the western region of the Chakhar banners and others gathered from such distant points as the Keshigten, Ujumuchin, and Tümed Banners. They set up tents and organized a large committee for a welcoming reception and to assist me on my journey.

Among our people, before Chinese communist rule came in the 1950s an important relationship was that between the princes (noyan) and his subordinate people (khariyatu). As for the various incarnations (khubilghans), we generally spoke of our many followers as shabinar, people who recognized us as their teacher or master (baghshi) and whom we looked upon as our children and grandchildren. We did not think of them as our serfs or slaves in any way, nor did we feel we were exploiters of the common people, for we mutually served each other in many ways. Still in those days many of these people were regarded as hereditary disciples (*unaghan shabi*), and their obligation to an incarnation was passed on from generation to generation in a strict manner. Today we are somewhat conscious of this relationship because it has often been criticized by leftist radicals who came to power under Mao Tse-tung and turned the world upside down.

From Gul-chaghan Banner we continued our journey westward in Chakhar region to Aduuchin (horse herders), which name has now been changed to Shangdu Banner. Here we stopped at the Guushi Monastery and then continued on to Labai Fountains, a place of many natural springs. The weather was cold but I continued to travel in my yellow sedan chair with bearers and tried to find comfort in whatever way possible. Finally, after crossing the southern steppe lands of Ulanchab League, and as we drew near Badghar Monastery, we stopped at Serem *bulagh* (Serem fountain), a place particularly noted for its fine *oboo* shrine and as the place to which lamas from Badghar came during the summer as a retreat or hermitage. The lama officials from Badghar came here to meet me on my journey and erected a yurt for our quaters.

I don't remember the precise date of our arrival at Badghar monastic temple, but the weather was very cold and the occasion was most spectacular with some one thousand lamas lining the two sides of the path to the monastery. Part of the welcome consisted of the impressive playing of the monastery band. Ya *jasagh* had arrived previously and everything was put in good order; thus, my arrival was most enjoyable. Here again I was welcomed by a fine official ceremony in the main prayer hall of the monastery (*sogchin doghon*). Since this was my first arrival at this important place, where I was to spend much of my life, I was welcomed ceremonially just as when I visited the Peking and Dolonor Monasteries. The Duingkhor *gegen* presented me an official *mandala*, and I then returned to my own quarters (*labrang*). *Mandalas* are an important item in the religion and ceremony of Mongolian Lamaist Buddhism that I must mention from time to time, so it is fitting that an attempt be made here to explain this key symbol. There are many kinds of *mandalas* but their real purpose is to gather in spiritual powers and promote the operation of the Buddhist law (*dharma*). Popularly viewed as magic circles or squares, including Buddhist deities and decorations, *mandalas* are sacred symbols expressing various mystic doctrines, and as such are often used as offerings, in incantations, magical formulas,

[63]

teachings, yoga and so forth. *Mandalas* also express the mystic principles of cause, effect, intelligence and the fundamental realm of mind and being.

Life and Training at Badghar Monastery

The most important monastic center in all of western Inner Mongolia, Badghar is traditionally known for its strict discipline and for the profound Buddhological studies carried out by the lamas there. As most everyone knows, there is an hierarchy of monasteries among the believers of Lamaist Buddhism, and if a lama or some lay person has enough money, as first priority they make a pilgrimage to Lhasa or go there to study. If they are not rich enough to make this trip, they then go to either the Labrang or Kumbum monasteries. Those not fortunate enough to study in one of these centers will then come from anywhere throughout Mongolia to study at Badghar Monastery. This monastery became a particularly important center for the training of young lamas after the fall of Outer Mongolia to communism and with the death of the Jebtsundamba *khutughtu* during the Socialist Revolution. Since it was impossible for young men to go to Ulan Bator to study at the former great monastic centers, they came to Badghar to complete their preparation and vows.

A very special, large monastic center in Mongolia, Badghar is located on the border of the Tümed Mongols and the Ulanchab League, perhaps thirty miles from Pao-t'ou. But rather than being under the jurisdiction of either of these Mongol areas, Badghar Monastery traditionally had a high degree of autonomy and had attached to it a large section of populated territory. But with modern changes this autonomy was lost, as will be discussed. In modern times a large coal deposit was discovered on its lands and was developed as a source of income for the monastery. All the wealth of these lands, such as the coal mines, was taken care of by the administration of the *demchi*, a financial officer of the monastery and a very powerful figure in his own right, though he reported to the *da-lama*, or abbot.

Some people have the idea that monasteries are located on travel routes, but, as a matter of fact, many great monasteries were established in their present location long before the caravan routes passed near. It seems that in most cases those who were

[64]

establishing a monastery tried to find a quiet place conducive to the study and meditation of the lamas. Nevertheless, as monasteries became prominent and attracted many people, the trade routes were diverted and the monasteries became involved in trade. Thus, frequently people from Outer Mongolia in the north or from Peking and Dolonor in the east passed by Badghar on their way to Kumbum or Lhasa. The Dolonor group of monasteries is the best example of a place that also became involved as a trade center.

Our monasteries are generally of three architectural types: Tibetan, Chinese, or a mixture of these two. My home monastery of Badghar is Tibetan style with a flat roof, great stone walls, and with great wooden timbers used as supporting beams and pillars. The great walls are inclined inward toward the upper stories with small, slit-like windows toward the top. We were always pleased to see the beautiful whitewashed walls from a distance as we returned from a journey.

Dolonor Monastery, unlike Badghar, was a Chinese style structure made of wood with impressive sloping roofs, extended eaves, and upturned corners. Surrounding the temple was a fine porch or veranda. The whole, great central prayer hall was built on a stone platform and it was much more ornamented and gilded than Badghar. The gilded yellow or blue tiles of the roof appealed to many people. We had a beautiful plaque over the entrance with the monastery name written in Mongolian, Tibetan, and Chinese. Such Chinese style monasteries are much less common in Mongolia than the Tibetan style.

Usually through most of the year, except for the summer, I lived in the permanent buildings of Badghar, wearing my yellow ceremonial dress each day. My quarters in the monastery were known as the *baruun* (right or western) quarters, and the apartments of the Duingkhor incarnation were known as the *jüün* (left or eastern) quarters. Traditionally, the *baruun* quarters were considered superior, just opposite to the Chinese view. During summer months, while I travelled or vacationed, I lived in the Batchaghan, a unique large yurt handed down from my predecessors. The posts and wooden parts of this yurt were made of an elegant red lacquer, its outer coverings were three layers of felt, and its inner wall coverings were expensive silk. On the top exterior of this yurt was a partial red covering shaped in a special design. The bottom of the yurt was white. Because of this yurt's special

[65]

large size, it was necessary to have four large posts on the inside to support the roof.

Soon after my arrival, all the lamas of the monastery met for a great prayer meeting (khural), and I presented to them an obligatory mangja, ceremonial tea offering, with cakes and dried fruit. At the beginning of the tenth month, I officially joined the prayer mass (khural) of the monastery. I then began attending the "college of doctrine" (choyir datsang) or Buddhist philosophy and from that time forth resumed my study of the scriptures. I was then ten years old.

When I was studying and training as a child for my high and holy position at Badghar Monastery, the Chinese Republic was but a decade old and the problems of the civil war and the warlords continually spilled over into Mongolia to disrupt our study and daily life. Sometimes we lacked food, but could not slacken the ceremonies to be performed. Frequently I had to go hungry to the khural (prayer mass), even twice a day, to participate in the great assembly of prayers and ceremonies. Being hungry, cold, and miserable, in the winter time, if I did not pay close attention I would find myself subject to discipline and punishment after returning to my quarters.

In 1925, just the year after I came to Badghar, there was organized in Kalgan a group called the Inner Mongolian People's Revolutionary Party (Nei-Meng-ku jen-min ke-ming-tang also known as Nei-Meng-ku kuo-min-tang). It was a group of radical young militants among our people and I do not claim to be well informed about them since we had no direct contact. But they added to the other problems of our people—the bandits, Chinese warlords, and merchants. It seems that they were greatly influenced first by the "arad," leftist revolutionary types in Khalkha (Outer Mongolia: MPR) and by Sun Yat-sen's Nationalist Party.

They made common cause with the warlord Feng Yü-hsiang who had Russian support but were defeated in 1926 by the strong man Chang Tso-lin and fled west throughout areas of Chakhar and Tümed into the Yeke-juu League of Ordos where they preached revolution for a year or two before dispersing. They did not bother our monasteries directly but were active recruiting young men who may otherwise have become lamas. The worst complaints were heard from the Ordos Mongols, some of whom came into open conflict with the revolutionaries and suffered from their radicalness, some being killed or tortured. Some young, unstable lamas, like Wangdannima, even joined their infamous movement and were disruptive near us in western Inner Mongolia.

This group demonstrated that there was growing conflict and debate over our traditional religion and our hereditary political institutions in Mongolia. Decades later, from the 1950s through the 1970s, I met the leaders of this earlier radical party in Taiwan, namely Pai Yün-t'i and Li Yung-shin. They had long since become moderate, even conservative, and Pai Yün-t'i is still with us as a respected elderly leader, now (1978) in his eighties.

In each large monastic center there were at least four colleges, the one of first priority being the college of doctrine or Buddhology (*choyir datsang*), a more exoteric tradition within the tantric or esoteric learning. There are many specialized lines of study in the monastery and everyone must first complete, as a first degree, the introductory study of Buddhology in the *choyir datsang*. Some lamas then specialize in this college and devote themselves to a study of the Law of the Buddha; others, after the completion of their introductory courses, transfer to other colleges or lines of study. When I began to attend this college, I wore each day the yellow ceremonial monk's shawl.

My first teacher was a venerable lama, over sixty years of age, from Khalkha Mongolia to the north. This master had the great distinction of being an earlier disciple of the Dalai Lama and had many followers himself. He was most impressive in his ability to sit continuously in silent meditation for many hours. Unfortunately, soon after I began studying with him, he passed into *nirvana*, on the last day of the last lunar month of the year (23 January, 1925).

Another of my important tutors was Lobsangsambu lama from the Ejil-ghol (Volga River) region of the Torghud (Kalmuck) group of Mongols. He came to Badghar Monastery while I was still quite young and was soon considered a very learned lama. He held the ranks of both *gebshi* and *rabjimba*, and, because of his erudition, became the tutor for the important incarnations of Badghar and also for many *gegens* and *khubilghans* from minor monasteries in surrounding areas. To us he was a most remarkable lama because he never changed his clothes or bathed and yet always appeared very clean. It seemed that he rarely slept, that he meditated throughout the night, and that on those few occasions when he did sleep he did so sitting up in a meditative pose. I am greatly indebted to this man for teaching me many scriptures.

[67]

I felt even closer to him because he was somewhat accomplished in medicine, an area of great interest to me.

The day before my first teacher died, he said to all of us, who were assembled before him, that we must come to study the next day dressed in our best ceremonial attire, prepare all the offerings before the altar of the Buddha, and be prepared to read our scriptures. This we did, and after we had completed reading the scriptures, our teacher remained seated for a long time in a pose of meditation on the khanji (Ch. k'ang), a warm platform-like flue under which the smoke and fire was conducted and on which we used to sit to keep warm in severe weather. This seemed a little strange. That evening on checking closer we discovered that he had passed on.

It is the custom of Badghar Monastery that deceased lamas be cremated and their ashes deposited in various places determined by rank, age, and knowledge. The remains of this venerable teacher were deposited at the Altan oboo, an honorable, holy place. The following day, the first day of the new year, we all gathered for a great prayer mass and I, together with the Duing-khor gegen, lighted all the candles of the various altars. We then divided into two groups and made a ceremonial procession through the various halls and sanctuaries of the monastery burning incense and lighting candles in our official capacity. We passed the next two months with no special event except the task of my becoming further accustomed to the new environment and making friends with many of the lamas.

At this time we learned that the Panchen Lama was in Peking, having fled there from Tibet in an attempt to escape a power struggle in Lhasa. We decided to journey to the capital to meet His Holiness. The Duingkhor gegen was to accompany me with my attendants, and we requested the Suiyuan regional government to prepare a private car for us on a train to Peking. On this trip I was hosted at the shang of the great Yung-ho kung, monastic temple of Peking, by the Samsai gegen. Immediately, I paid my respects 'o the Panchen Lama, received his special blessings, and discussed with him the important matter of the appointment of a new teacher for my studies. The Panchen Lama then confirmed as my teacher a scholarly lama named Dimpiral, who had the honored, scholarly title of lharamba, and who was both a Mongolian and an incarnation. My former incarnation had been his teacher and now he was to be mine. Though a little ironic, this is not an uncommon situation in Tibetan Buddhism. This venerable teacher accompanied me and Duingkhor *gegen* on our return to Badghar Monastery to take up my new course of study.

The fifth month of each year was the occasion of a celebration at Marchin-lha, an important *oboo* to the north of Badghar Monastery. As we approached the *oboo*, it was necessary for us to ride up a rather mountainous area. Because Duingkhor *gegen* was only seven years old and unsteady on his horse, some of his followers had to assist him, so he would not fall and be injured.

When I was twelve years old (1926), the Duingkhor *pandita*, the second ranking incarnation in my monastery, was officially installed in Badghar. The situation in our area had been somewhat stabilized and to commemorate this occasion, a great *nair*, an occasion of feasting and tournaments, of wrestling and horseracing, was held and thousands of people gathered from hundreds of miles around. The feasting and festivities continued for many days.

At Badghar it was the custom in the seventh month to hold a *mani*, a large formal prayer meeting for the summer season. When a month had thirty days, we began the meeting on the twenty-fourth day; when a month had twenty-nine days, we began on the twenty-third. This prayer-festival had no particular characteristic, except that all the lamas assembled in one place to recite the sacred Buddhist prayer formula of the *mani*. On such occasions pilgrims and people from nearby areas would come to sit in the courtyard and recite in unison with the monks.

A key part of the *mani* prayer assembly was the chanting of the sacred formula *om mani badmi khon* (*om mani padme hum*), originally a Sanskrit-Tibetan term meaning "Hail to the Jewel in the lotus" (praise to the Buddha). Ordinarily this particular ceremony began very early, soon after midnight. Later, a second stage of the prayer festival began about dawn. The third session took place at two o'clock that afternoon, and the last session in the late afternoon about sunset. Of course, it was my duty to attend most of these prayer assemblies.

During these occasions the lamas and the lay people were forbidden to eat meat; we could partake only of *chaghan guntseg*, literally "white food," though this did not necessarily mean that everything was white—only that it was not meat or meat products. Usually this meant that we ate *boorsogh* (Mongolian cakes), milk, and millet. Buddhists in many countries are vegetarians and never eat meat, but Mongolian monks, though not vegetarians, on occasion are very strict about not partaking of meat. This strict discipline we observe because of the teaching of Ariyabul (Buddhist deity of a thousand hands and eyes = Ch. Kuan-yin, Skt. Avalokiteśvara).

The *mani* prayer ceremony would continue for seven days, during which time all the lamas would prepare *öröl*, a sort of pill. There are many types, but in this case *öröl* was a spiritual pill that was believed to cleanse a person who was ritualistically unclean because of something he had done, said, or thought, or to cure a disease contracted as a result of some evil action. About three large cupfuls of *öröl* were prepared from some type of herb and then placed in a large "bottle" or container (*bomba*) made of bronze or silver with golden decorations, covered with brilliantly worked silk, and sometimes adorned with peacock feathers. The *öröl* were then left in the *bomba*. One of the marvelous mysteries of our religion is that these pills would multiply spontaneously and when it was opened there would be a number much greater than that originally placed in the container. The Chinese have come to call them *tzu-sheng-wan*, "self-born" or "self-producing pills."

On the first day of the eighth lunar month it was the custom of all the lamas together to take the *bomba* and make a holy circumambulation, a Buddhist custom of making a pilgrimage around the monastery clockwise a certain number of times, after which the *bomba* was then opened. Always the lamas were mystified as they observed that the pills had increased spontaneously by several times to fill the container. Some of them had even flown out into various parts of the courtyard and trees surrounding the monastery, a mystic phenomenon we always attributed to the great power of Ariyabul. The celebration of the *mani* festival was not the same throughout Mongolia. Though the formula and ritual was fairly standard, there was some difference in the scriptures read. At Badghar we customarily read the Sumbum scripture, written by one of my previous incarnations.

The beginning of the new year was always a special occasion for us. In preparation for the lunar new year, on the day prior to the eve of the new year, we would assemble all the lamas of the monastery in a special prayer mass. Following this, it was customary for all of the *shabinar* or followers of the monastery, to enjoy *naadam*, a festival lasting for about eight days. In Outer

Mongolia today, *naadam* refers to a grand occasion of horse racing, wrestling, archery, and other festivities. When I was a boy at Badghar Monastery, however, *naadam* was only a rest from the usual routine of the monastery. On noon of the eighth day of the first lunar month the monastery was closed. In the afternoon of the eighth day a ceremonial tea assembly, *mangja khural*, was held, a large assembly at the first of the year which included the *miyandagh* or ceremonies for conferring and announcing degrees to those candidates who have earned promotions in the monastery. At this time each person who receives the degree of *rabjimba*, or "doctorate," presents the lamas assembled with a ceremonial cup of tea and is then introduced and congratulated upon his accomplishment. These ceremonies are part of the *miyandagh*. If those seeking the *rabjimba* degree were successful, this particular *khural* was called *molon rabjimba*.

On such occasions, because the Duingkhor *gegen* was so young, it was my responsibility to preside over these ceremonies. Certain set scriptures were read and, although I was very young, it was my duty to read them. This was a very awesome task for me, because I was required to recite before some of the venerable lamas of the monastery, but after I had successfully accomplished this task, they were very charitable and encouraging in their praise. A second stage in the ceremonies then took place, *khural*, a prayer assembly for blessings and good omens. These ceremonies continued until the fifteenth day of the first month.

On the sixteenth day of the first month, it was customary for us to perform a special ceremony in which we paraded the image of Buddha of the future, Maidar (Skt. Maitreya Bodhisattva), around the monastery in a sacred procession. This varied according to different monasteries, but ordinarily the image of Maidar was mounted on a beautiful, elaborate gold sedan and taken among the lamas and the people. The people would kneel and the image would be passed over them by the lamas as a blessing and dedication or prophetic omen. This indicated that they would be the disciples of Maidar in the future in preparation for the great final battle for Shambhala, the sacred city that would become at the end of the world, the battle site in the struggle between the forces of evil and those who support the Law of the Buddha.

As I grew in knowledge of the Buddhist scriptures, I found it a great challenge to remember all the scriptures and their deep meaning. In my studies my teacher, Yontson *baghshi*, constantly reminded me that I must study hard in order to obtain the special power (*jinung*) of the Bodhisattva Chaghan Manjushri. Thus, in the eleventh month of that year I retreated into a hermitage with my teacher in order to acquire the special power. This meditative retreat lasted for seven days, during which time we meditated from dawn until dark, eating only one morning meal. At dusk on the seventh day, Yontson took out three white peas, gave them to me, and told me to hold them in my mouth and to recite the sacred formula (*tarani*) of the Chaghan Manjushri. With great concentration and devotion, I recited the *tarani* all night. At dawn the following day, master Yontson asked me to show him the three peas. When I took them out, two had sprouted and the other was just about to sprout. This pleased my master very much and seemed to confirm in his mind that I had received the special power for the future to properly recite and understand the scripture.

During this long meditation we did not eat meat. At its completion we performed the *jinsereg* ceremony, for which we prepared a *baling*, a triangular shaped object made of butter and rye flour which had a fire design on it and which, after special prayers and recitations, was to be cast into the fire. Fire offerings will be discussed later. Following this it seemed to me that my intellectual ability for memorization was greatly increased, and from that time I was much more successful in my studies; I usually memorized six or seven pages of scripture each day.

At Badghar monastic temple there was a customary meditative seclusion beginning on the third day of the ninth month and continuing until the twenty-second of that month. All the lamas observed a solitary retreat in their quarters, during which time they did not communicate with each other or anyone else, devoting themselves solely to meditation and scripture reading. Only at noon did they open the door of their quarters briefly and prepare their own food. After this noon meal there was to be no smoke coming from any chimney of the lamas' quarters. All lamas of every rank were invovled, and there were no special favors or pardon due to rank. those of the highest degree, the *gebshi* (doctors), were treated as equals to the most lowly lama. At dusk everyone was required to put on his formal robe, stand in front of the door of his quarters, and recite what he had memorized during the day. During the daylight hours the *gesgüi* lama patrolled the quarters, it being his responsibility to investigate each area, determine if anyone was sleeping, and make a record of which scripture each lama was memorizing.

On this occasion, each lama recited for about three hours, and even though my status was highest of all lamas in the monastery, I was not excused. I still observed this period of study and bore this ordeal of recitation along with the ordinary young *shabi*. In addition, on the eighth and fifteenth of each month, each person was required to recite his studies for the entire night in the main hall of the monastery. We would then recite until four o'clock in the morning, at which time we were served tea by the monastery. Each lama was then allowed to open the door of his quarters and to prepare food according to his needs.

On the third day of the tenth month it was customary for all the lamas to meet in a special assembly for prayer and for Buddhist debates and dialogue (*choyir*). Actually, each of us looked upon this occasion as a time of examination to determine through our debating what we had learned the previous month. As we debated and discussed various topics, we were also required to recite certain scriptures verbatim. During our previous month's meditation, memorization, and preparation, we were constantly reminded of the coming of this special *choyir* debate during which we would be examined on our accomplishments.

The custom on these occasions was for a lama to state a certain thesis, whereupon he was challenged and required to defend it by citing proof for his ideas. Those who challenged him were also required to defend their position. All of this was done in a sort of free-for-all debate open to all the lamas and supervised by the older, more venerable monks. Close attention was given by all to the logic and the rhetoric of each lama's recitation. The topics of debate were set according to the text or subjects under study by the lamas at the time. All lamas dressed in formal robes and capes and there was much posturing as the lamas stood to courageously challenge each other without the customary reserve or modesty of the Chinese or Japanese.

This was often a very tense time and some of the lamas would become extremely excited, enthusiastic, earnest, and even emotional in their debating. After the completion of the debate, however, no one held any grudges and no fights ensued. It was our custom to debate in the Mongolian language but to also use many technical Sanskrit or Tibetan terms. All scriptures or evi-

[73]

dence submitted for proof or support had to be given in Tibetan, so the debates were not an easy exercise. The irreligious young intellectuals felt that this type of debate and recitation had limited value for the development of intellectual talents among the lamas. They felt that there was no real independent thought, that the analysis was of a very low order, and that the whole thing was a game of rote memorization. This is their uninformed, subjective judgment.

This debating and recitation occupied the entire tenth month. On the third day of the eleventh month, we rested from our studies, continuing until the sixteenth of that month. On the seventeenth another great *choyir* or debating recitation began. Then later, the first day of the twelfth month, a final examination (*damcha*) took place. The Tibetan term *damcha* can be translated into Mongolian more understandably as *nom kelelchikü*, meaning literally the "discussions or debate of the law," the law being the Law of Buddha or the sutras. This means that after completing a course of discipline, memorization and discussion on a particular text using this debating (*choyir*) technique, a person may have conferred upon him the particular rank for which he has prepared. This is somewhat similar to the procedures of modern graduate education, of the technique of oral examination of candidates for various degrees. The debate and graduation-like ceremony is held in the open courtyard or in the great prayer hall and all attending may participate and freely question the candidate. One difference, however, according to my understanding of the modern system, is that the examiners do not allow a lama student to come to an examination until his competence is recognized by his teachers and peers.

At this time only *rabjimba* degrees were conferred among all the lamas of the monastery. This *choyir* debating process included a testing, elimination, and challenges for the purpose of determining who would be the top three candidates for the final examination of the *rabjimba* degree. These top three candidates were then required to sit before the entire body of lamas to be challenged by any and all and to defend themselves in full debate. This session usually lasted from seven A.M. until seven or eight P.M.

After the three candidates for *rabjimba* were seated, they were not allowed to move for any reason, including food, drink, or toilet. Needless to say, this was an extreme trial of discipline.

This type of examination was then resumed each following day for a three-day period. The final examination debate was completed on the seventeenth day of the twelfth month. During all these various recitations and debates, a *tsanad lama* played a prominent role as superintendent of all the ceremonies and rituals of the temple. The role of *gesgui lama*, in policing the lamas of the temple and maintaining order, was also very important.

Following the final debate, on the seventeenth day of the twelfth month, a special prayer assembly called *duibsun khural* was held, which continued until the twenty-third of the month. This particular observance at Lamaist monasteries involved prayer for a good era in the time-cycle of Buddhism.

On the twenty-third of the twelfth month the special fire ceremony (*ghal-iin takil*) took place. Worship of fire is an ancient custom among the Mongolian people going back long before the introduction of Buddhism; it seems to have been influenced by the Chinese in the Mongolian areas near the Great Wall, as the date of the ceremony has been shifted from fall to winter. Fire is the symbol of light, intelligence, goodness, and the object of this ritual is the purification of everyone by casting evil, lust, ill-will into the fire with a prayer for good fortune. The time and nature of this ritual varies from place to place among the far-flung Mongolian people.

There were, in the seasonal rituals of the monastery, lesser ceremonial activities for the twenty-fifth, twenty-sixth and twenty-seventh days. On the twenty-eighth, a prayer assembly (*khural*) was held for observing *abral*, a prayer mass for blessings. At the completion of this *khural*, offerings were made to the *doghshid*, "the fearsome protectors of the Buddhist Law," those deities who exorcise the evil spirits. At this time it was very important that all of the more important offerings on the altars of the monastery be changed. Then, with this preparation completed, on the twenty-ninth a special ceremony was held and offerings made to Chorjil, the "Khan of Hell," who was the superior one among the various *doghshid*. Following all of these activities was a vacation period, during which everyone was free to relax and enjoy some recreation that was acceptable.

When activity resumed, *choyir* debating sessions extended from the first day to the seventeenth day of the second month. Then from the third day of the third month until the third day of the fourth month a spring *choyir* was held. During these activities,

[75]

it was easy to see who had been diligent in his studies, who had successfully mastered his lessons and the Buddhist scriptures. In between the special prayer assemblies, debating convocations and periodic seasonal cycle of rituals, the lamas carried on the regular activity of prayers, study and meditation. On the eighth day of the fourth month until the fifteenth of that same month was the ceremony of usun takil (usun meaning water, takil meaning offering), during which vessels of water were presented before the many images of the monastery. Then on the seventeenth day of the fourth month, the lamas once more resumed the activities of the Buddhist debates and dialogues (choyir), continuing these until the third day of the fifth month.

We always looked forward to our vacation beginning the third day of the fifth month and continuing until the third day of the sixth month. Then from the seventeenth of the fifth month until the seventeenth of the sixth month a summer choyir was held. One of the happiest days of the year was the forty-day vacation following the completion of the summer choyir.

Activities during our vacation period varied greatly depending on the individual interests of each lama. Younger lamas usually returned home to visit their parents while the older lamas relaxed around the monastery. Pilgrimages to some special place or distant monastery were also common for lamas who were more active, ambitious, or venturesome.

When I was in my twelfth year (1926), an elaborate ceremony was held in the seventh month for the installation of the Duing-khor gegen. During this great occasion many guests of all kinds from all the surrounding Mongolian Banners gathered to Badghar Monastery. The date for this particular occasion was always set for the time most favorable for the people and their animals. At this particular time, while we were all enjoying the many festivities and ceremonies at Badghar Monastery, our monasteries in Dolonor were attacked by a large group of Chinese bandits. The thirteen monastic temple compounds and the two great monasteries of the incarnations were plundered with the loss of many items of value.

In the winter season of that same year Ishighawa da-lama returned from visiting the Bargha area of northeastern Inner Mongolia, the area from which he had originally come, and extended to me a formal invitation from my patrons in Bargha to visit their region.

PART THREE

Life in a Monastery

The Organization of Monastic Temples

The monastery was the center of life for most lamas; indeed, for some it was their world. It follows, then, that something should be said about the organization of this important institution in Mongolia.

The single most important part of the monasteries was the *doghon*, the main hall, that contained the images of the Buddha, the abbot's seat, and other sacred objects. Next to this, possibly the most important part of the monastery was the *shang*, that housed the administration, with its own staff, and the treasury. The superior of the entire *shang* organization was, of course, the *gegen*, the incarnation. Below him, in all those monastic centers especially commissioned by the Manchu emperor, was a *jasagh lama*, and below him in rank, the *da-lama*. The *jasagh lama* ruled broadly over the entire holdings of an incarnation, whether in eastern Inner Mongolia or as far afield as Amdo (Kokonor).

If there was more than one person of da-lama rank, as sometimes happened, the monks were always divided into the categories of *tamagh-iin da-lama* and *khariin da-lama*. There was only one lama of the former rank, *tamagha*, meaning, literally, seal. The lama holding this rank held the official seals to do all business. Apart from him, those who had formerly held this post, who had for some reason been retired but still were looked upon in the temple as senior lamas and important men, would have the title *khariin da-lama* (*khariin* meaning leisure). Below the *tamagh-iin da-lama* rank was the *demchi* lama, who was usually responsible for the finances of the monastery and an administrative assistant to the *tamagh-iin da-lama* who was directly involved in many

[79]

affairs. In some cases there were several *demchi*, an important one being the *tamagh-iin demchi* who, as his name indicates, was directly responsible for the official seals of the monastery. The use of these seals was a serious matter, not to be taken lightly, and was used only with the occurrence of the *tamagh-iin demchi*, the *tamagh-iin da-lama*, and the *jasagh* lama.

My previous incarnations had achieved the rank of *gabji*, and later the lineage of my incarnation, as a whole and in perpetuity, was raised in rank to that of *Mergen nom-um khan*. With each higher rank my incarnation received a new seal or *tamagha*. These important old seals from previous incarnations were given to me, and I maintained them until they were finally lost in 1945 when I escaped from Dolonor as the Communists came in. One seal was of beautiful rare silver with a handle in the form of a cloud. The inscription on it was in three languages: Manchu, Mongol, and Tibetan; no Chinese name was present. The last great seal of my former incarnation was lost in the turmoil and devastation of the Chinese revolution and the invasions from Outer Mongolia into Inner Mongolia. Consequently, it became necessary for my staff to petition for a new seal in the early years of the Republic. It was inscribed in Chinese, Mongolian, and Tibetan; the Manchu Dynasty was gone so the Manchu inscription had been removed. Also, a new seal was necessary because the Kanjurwa lineage had been raised to the level of a *khutughtu*. The form was much the same as that of the previous seal, and on the side of the handle was an inscription stating that it had been cast by the Office of Seals of the Republic of China. As I have mentioned, all of the seals, both new and old, were lost during the war; but should they be recovered, they would no longer mean anything to me. They only represent worldly power and status.

The *shang* organization was responsible mainly for the finances, the temporal affairs of the monastery, the lay disciples, and the herds. Our monastery, like some others, however, had herds in distant places and their administration was taken care of by an *ar shang* (northern *shang*). In our case, the *ar shang* was located north of Dolonor and had many herds and animals. This branch office was administered by an official referred to as *shangtsad*. Under him was a *demchi* (deputy administrator) and below him two *nirab*. This latter man looked after all the day-to-day responsibilities and handled any problems that arose. The main concern of the *shangtsad*, and the *demchi* who assisted him, was the finances of the monastery. The *tamaghiin da-lama* was concerned only with things in his immediate jurisdiction.

The lamas who were selected to serve in this small and important staff were appointed only by the incarnation or the abbot of the monastery and served at his pleasure. In the ceremonial selection and appointment of this important staff, we would first bestow on the new candidate a new *khadagh*, a ceremonial scarf, upon which was laid a *janghaa*, a piece of red silk knotted in a special way and blown upon while being tied by an incarnation or another high lama. The lama kept this symbol of authority or office as long as he held the position conferred upon him. The *janghaa* is considered a protective amulet to the person who holds it. Upon his resignation, a lama returned the *khadagh* to the abbot, though he could keep the *janghaa*.

The fame, fortune and influence of an incarnation was strongly tied to the *shabinar* disciples under his jurisdiction who were organized into groups of ten households and presided over by a *daragh*. A *daragh* in turn was responsible to a *ghalai* who was responsible to the *shang* of the monastery. A retired *ghalai* was given the title of *jaisang* and was seated above the other *ghalai* on ceremonial occasions. *Jaisang*, who are ordinarily older, experienced laymen who have served as officials of the monastery, still had a voice in the affairs of the *shang* with which they were associated.

In areas of Mongolia where there were ruling princes, a prince quite commonly bestowed titles upon outstanding lay followers of an incarnation, though he could not or would not confer a special distinction or title upon lamas. Among the entourage of an incarnation, the *deberchi* (kettle bearers), usually two in number, were usually young men. An incarnation had much contact with people both inside and outside the monastery. Among his personal attendants the *soibon* dealt generally with common individuals who had some contact with the incarnation. More important individuals, such as princes or other incarnations, were dealt with by a *donir*; two men usually held this particular office.

An administrative staff of a *shang*, mentioned earlier, existed only for the highest or top level of incarnation. All lower *khubilghans* or incarnations did not have such an important staff. Neither did they have associated with them a *jasagh lama* or *da-lama*, but only *shangtsad* and lower officials. An exception to

[81]

this was the Jebtsundamba *khutughtu* in Urga who presented a special situation; the top lama official who administered his affairs was referred to as *erdeni shangtsad-pa*.

In all of Mongolia only a few exalted incarnations were designated as having imperial rank and recognition by the Manchu court. Over the centuries many other incarnations appeared who did not have independent, autonomous status but were instead part of the overall administrative system in Mongolia. Because of the great influence of the temples and the number of the lamas, society was divided into two parts: the ecclesiastical and the lay. This meant that there was what we commonly refer to as a division between the *shira* and *khara*, the *shira* (the "yellow") referring to the great multitude of lamas in the population and the *khara* (the "black") referring to the lay people. Thus, common incarnations were under the jurisdiction of a *jasagh*, the head of a Banner (district) in which their monastery was located. We incarnations who held special positions had special authority because we, like a *jasagh*, also had jurisdiction over both the *shira* and *khara* within our sphere, because there were lamas under us within the monastery and *shabinar* or lay disciples in the pastures or areas under our direct jursidiction.

Except in special circumstances, my food was prepared by one particular person called *jama*. No lay person was ever allowed in the kitchen. One other person assisted the *jama* in the kitchen and was referred to as the *deberchi* or *ghal-iin lama* (literally "fire lama"). In his work in the kitchen the *jama* always had to hold in his mouth a special kerchief to prevent him from contaminating the food. After he had prepared the food, it was served by yet another special lama, the *soibon*, and never by the *jama* or the *deberchi*. Part of the *soibon's* responsibility was to taste the food to determine whether it was edible or poison. There is only one large general kitchen for the entire monastery, though the *shang* with its smaller more restricted staff had a separate kitchen and cooking staff. After the meals were prepared and ready, a large gong was sounded to bring the staff to the meal.

As an incarnation I had my own personal scribe, *rungyig*, and the *shang* of my monastery had several additional scribes to handle the various records. Some of our great monasteries had lamas numbering into the hundreds. One of the most important functions of a monastery was the great *khural* or formal prayer assembly. Apart from the *da-lama* or abbot who was responsible for the affairs of the entire monastic community, a separate *da-lama*, with a somewhat lower status, but still a good deal of power, was over the *khural* itself. A *da-lama* served as his deputy or assistant. Always we had, in connection with the *khural*, a lama we called the *ongtsad*, whose function it was to lead out in the prayer chants and oral scripture recitations. Invariably this man had a magnificent bass voice and was well versed in the scriptures and sutras. He would first recite a particular passage or prayer, after which all the lamas would chant it in unison.

Another important lama in the life of the temple or monastery was the *gesgüi*, whose function it was to serve like a master of arms. He patrolled the prayer assemblies and the quarters of the lamas with his large stick to keep order, to maintain discipline among the young lamas, and to settle problems. Still another lama, who was quite important but whose status was rather low, was the *ghonir* who kept the prayer sanctuaries and various halls of the monastery clean and kept the various altars in order.

The large monastic temple centers in Mongolia had two important subdivisions, the *shang* and the *khural*, the main prayer assembly hall. Each had separate staffs, all of which were unified under the overall general authority of the *jasagh lama* and his deputy assistant, the *da-lama*. Apart from the great monasteries, the large majority did not have a *jasagh lama*, but only a *da-lama*. Each of the various monastic centers in Mongolia had its own unique situation. For example, Badghar Monastery had been honored by the imperial court, but it did not have a *jasagh lama*. Moreover, the *da-lama* of Badghar was not the most important official in its administration. He had only nominal power and actually had withdrawn to concern himself almost entirely with the spiritual, religious affairs of the institution. Thus, the most important figure in administrative or temporal affairs was the *demchi* lama.

Several important incarnations, such as the Panchen and the Jangjia, in addition to their primary monastic centers, also had an office (*pan-shih-ch'u*) in such important Chinese cities as Peking or Nanking beginning with the Republic of China. This office handled various matters of business which would arise, particularly in connection with the government or important individuals in the capital. My first incarnation established such an office, as also did the Jangjia *khutughtu* and later the Panchen Lama. This office had a small staff, supervised ordinarily by a *tsung-kuan*, a general manager, or a chu-chang, an office head with a few secretaries or assistants. The staff of these offices were not necessarily lamas. Sometimes Mongols or even Chinese were hired to assist in the various matters handled here. One thing quite distressing to some Mongolian leaders was that the very influential incarnation, the Jangjia khutughtu, invariably employed as staff for his office in Peking, and in Nanking, men pushed onto him by Yen Hsi-shan, the warlord of Shansi province. Though this may not always have been entirely according to the desires of the Jangjia khutughtu, he could have resisted the pressure of Yen without too much trouble. For a long time I had a branch office in Peking, but later, after the death of Ya jasagh, I felt it was not so important, not worth the expense, and could create problems as the staff became involved in politics. Therefore, we did not maintain the office after the death of Ya jasagh.

Most incarnations, had a sembon whose function, a minor one, was to act as a sort of assistant in taking care of minor chores and running errands. When we as incarnate lamas traveled in areas outside Mongolia, such as China or Tibet, we often had with us a lozawa (Tib. lo-tsra-ba) who assisted us as an interpreter in various problems of communication involving languages we did not know. Another important part of an incarnation's staff was the tseremba lama, an expert in mathematics and astronomy, and a mamba lama, the incarnation's physician.

Mamba lamas have, as part of their training, em-iin dörben sudar, the four important sutras or basic texts on medicine. They must study and master these in order to be adept at treating various diseases. The first sutra or text deals with the general understanding of health and illness, and the general presentation of diagnosis and medical treatment. The second important text has to do with diseases and the categorization of their symptoms and treatment. The third text deals with the problem of what medicine to use for which disease and which prayer to recite for the curing of a particular type of disease. The fourth text deals with the analysis and treatment of various diseases involving the urine and the pulse (sudal).

Our study of the complex interrelated categories of diseases required us to memorize a treelike diagram showing the association and relationship between various diseases. Another important part of our training involved a bronze or copper statue showing all the important critical points, complete with their

[84]

names, in which pins should be placed in the practice of acupuncture. It took much time to master the art of acupuncture, which seems to have come from China originally, speading to Tibet and then to Mongolia. Part of our training required us to cover up the image and the names and be able to thrust a needle into the right place, even though we could not clearly see the mark on the image where the needle should be inserted.

One who has mastered the various techniques in the medical academy (*mamba datsang*) receives the degree of *maramba*, a doctor of medicine. There were among our lamas a few great master physicians who were so adept and skilled that they could gaze upon a patient from a considerable distance and still determine whether his particular illness was curable or hopeless. We identified this miraculous ability on the part of some *maramba* as *shidi* (clairvoyance). There are various esoteric forms of this marvelous power. There are also special *maramba* who may have the son of a sick father come to them and who are then able, by sensing the pulse of the child, to determine what disease is afflicting the father and whether he can be cured. Since I have come in contact with modern doctors and skeptical intellectuals, I find that many of them have no respect for lama doctors. They feel they are all nothing but quacks or crackpots. This attitude is unjust. I am convinced, from my experience over many years, that lama doctors often have a high degree of capability and have made an important contribution to the health and well-being of the Mongolian people.

Another important occasion in the affairs and ceremonies of a monastery was a special prayer or ceremony carried on seasonally or at least once a year in honor of the *shabtang* or *choijung*, the protective deities of the institution. These deities are not strictly Buddhist and originally were adopted into Tibetan Buddhism from the Bon religion or the Shamanism of old Mongolia.

It is the impression or idea of most people now that all Mongolian monasteries are stationary and built in Tibetan or Chinese style architecture. When I was young, however, there were many moveable or seminomadic tents that were not stationary dwellings but could be moved from place to place. These were found particularly in Khalkha and Bargha. Many Buddhist scriptures were arranged in shelves around the walls on the interior of the yurt. Because these portable monasteries were moved from time to time, the lamas' belongings and their attendants were packed in carts to facilitate their movement from place to place. Their most valuable possessions were packed in specially prepared boxes and wrapped with felt and thus well protected. Some valuable possessions were kept in the boxes and left sitting on the carts outside the yurt. This was an indication of the security and honesty of the areas, a sign that the people did not have to worry about their property. Such areas were found particularly in Bargha and Shilin-ghol.

One of the important activities in connection with the monasteries was the annual sacred parade of *Maidar* (Maitreya). In this religious festival the image of Maidari was mounted on a sedan chair and carried on the shoulders of the lamas out of the monastery and around it in a clockwise circumambulation. This festival occurred at different times in different monasteries but always once a year and was symbolic of the belief that in the future Maidar will become the Buddha to turn the Wheel of the Law now turned by Burkhan *baghshi* (Gautama Buddha). The belief is that Maidar, the Buddha of the future, will come to preside over the world as it reaches a perfect state. All the lamas of the monastery and those disciples who came to attend the celebration either participated in the procession or else kneeled as the image passed over their heads. This they believe made it possible for them to attend Maidar and be present in the next era of his rule.

An incarnation ordinarily arose very early. Prior to this his attendants had already cleaned the room and put the altars in order. After arising, the incarnation first washed his face and took care of his personal needs and then, before morning tea, he prayed. After morning tea, almost daily, the officials of the *shang* or those of the monastery conferred on some particular matters of business with the *gegen*. Following this, a *gegen* ordinarily devoted some time to the reading of the scriptures. Sometime during this scripture study his cook inquires about what he would like to eat that day. Late in the morning the incarnation received some of his disciples. Whenever disciples come from a distance, they were given a special reception.

Although the lamas in general were restricted to one hot meal per day, those who attended the *gegen* were allowed two. I have concluded from personal experience and observation that the usual diet for an incarnation is strongly influenced by the Chinese diet including, for example, meat dumplings (*buuts* = Ch. *pao-*

tze), a type of meat pancake and hot stews. The Mongols of course eat many different types of milk products, and their most common dessert is *boorsogh*, a type of cookie. They also eat many types of *khurud* (cheese). A special type of cheese, which I doubt is found in other parts of the world, is *arja*, a soured cheese that is left after the water has been distilled from the milk.

I have previously mentioned the manner in which we study the Buddhist scriptures. Common lamas arise very early and together have *manja*, tea with milk, which is prepared in the kitchen in very large kettles. From a kettle the tea is put in a churn along with cream or butter. After it is churned it is put in a large kettle about two yards in diameter to be distributed to the lamas. The kitchen of the monastery is regarded as a very sacred place, and women are never allowed to enter. After completing their morning tea, all the lamas then attend the *khural* which may last over an hour. This prayer assembly is held in the morning, in the afternoon, and again in the evening, and in between times, the lamas study the scriptures individually or in groups. When there is a break or free time, those lamas who are particularly poor go into the hills or surrounding territory to find and bring back wood for the kitchen of the monastery. The monastery supplies only the morning tea, not that provided at later times during the day. It is a rule that there be only one cooked meal per day, and that it be at noon. The noon meal is cooked by the lamas individually, not in common by the monastery kitchen. For breakfast and in the evening there is only tea.

In our Mongolian monastic temples are a very few special lamas whom we refer to as *dayanchi*, meaning lamas who are dedicated to a discipline of meditation. Their approach to religious life is *dayan*, a Mongolian form of Zen. These lamas may meditate in the monastery itself, in the surrounding territory, in the mountains, or in caves. In *nunai*, a particular type of meditation, a person must concentrate very strictly on Ariyabul, a form of the thousand handed *bodhisattva* Avalokiteśvara (Ch. *Kuan-yin*), and must not talk, swallow, drink water, or eat. After a period of meditation, he may on the following morning drink a little something and then at noon partake of a vegetarian meal. Particular times are set for the *nunai* type of meditation; it may extend for one hundred days or for one thousand days. In this case the lamas count two days as one day, so the actual term is double.

[87]

The fasting I refer to has to do only with the actual term of meditation and does not extend throughout the full meditative activity.

For our study of scripture and texts, and for various rituals and ceremonies, we depend mainly on the *Kanjur*, the Tibetan collection of sacred texts. The *Kanjur* itself has been translated into Mongolian, but many other texts have not yet been translated and thus we must depend considerably on the original Tibetan texts. Because of our dependence on Tibetan texts, the Tibetan language has naturally become the liturgical language of Mongolia and has had a great influence upon the common language and the traditional literature of our people. Many of the learned *ghabji* (master or teacher) in Urga (present Ulan Bator) have even written a number of commentaries in Tibetan as well as in Mongolian.

Religious Ceremonies and Festivals

Lamas customarily participate in the worship at the *oboo*. Their duties include tending this shamanistic shrine, a pyramidlike structure of rocks with prayer flags attached to tree branches situated so that they jut out from the pile of rocks forming the shrine. Where possible an *oboo* will always be erected on a hill or raised area in the steppe. Great regional *oboo* are often flanked by six smaller oboos in a row on either side. The lamas tidy and arrange the shrine in preparation for special ceremonies each year.

My function in taking care of the *oboo* was not simple. On the appointed day of the worship ceremonies at the *oboo*, I first dispatched lamas to take care of any preliminary chores. They placed sacred writings on the stones and attached sacred prayer flags called *kei mori* (wind horses—for good fortune) to the tree branches. These *kei mori*, unique to Tibet and Mongolia, are customarily restricted to the colors white, yellow, blue, red, and green, black never being used. *Kei mori* flags are found not only on *oboo*, but each Mongolian family has them in the regions where Chinese and Mongols live together. Thus, one can often distinguish a Mongolian family by these flags. On the flags are scriptures and winged horses. As the wind furls the flags, the horses are continually moving and to our people this suggests that their good fortune is always moving ahead. The *oboo* itself is a shrine to the "Dragon King" (*loos*), our Mongolian people's local deities (*nibdagh* and *shibdagh*). Sacrificial offerings are assembled for presentation at the *oboo*. In some places the offerings consist of only milk products; in other places meat products also are presented. Along with the offerings of milk products, there may be offerings of tea. At very large *oboos* there will ordinarily be placed as offerings nine large cauldrons of an entire cooked sheep. A ritual known as the *seter* is traditionally held, usually at the same time as the *oboo* ceremony, to which people from many miles around gather, bringing their customary offerings of five categories of animals—horses, camels, cattle, sheep, and goats. At the time of the *seter* the lamas read sutras and offer prayers while the animals to be offered as live offerings to the *oboo* are marked in various ways and set aside, not to be used in any common way. This marking may take the form of cutting a notch in the ear, a brand made on the horn or flank, a brand placed on the foot of a goat, or a colored strand of silk or cloth tied to the mane or tail. Animals offered as *seter* to the *oboo* were never sold or used for food. If the *oboo* is near a monastery, the animals were cared for there; otherwise, they were taken back and cared for by the people making the live offerings.

When I, as a high-ranking *gegen*, went to the *oboo* to participate in the ceremonies, I was always accompanied by various high-ranking lamas and lay disciples. Inasmuch as this was not a Buddhist ceremony, I did not dress in a customary Buddhist gown, but rather in the costume of a lay leader, with a flint and knife in my belt. The dress is formal, with the knives on the right side and the flint and other ornaments on the left. The worshipful bowings at the *oboo* were not performed in the traditional Buddhist custom with the customary hand movements, but rather were a kowtow in the old tradition.

An important part of the ceremony was chanting in unison of a special *oboo* liturgy by the congregation of lamas attending. The prayers were invariably for the Buddhist monastery and the local surroundings. After chanting the scriptures, the special ceremony *dallagh* was performed on behalf of the monastery, banner and local people. This was an age-old Shamanistic ritual in which streamers of various colors are attached to an arrow. This arrow was then held by myself, or by the head of a family or some other group, by both hands high above the head and rotated in a circle clockwise in such a way as to gather in blessings. At the same time, those attending the ceremony chant "khurai, khurai, khurai," meaning "gathering, gathering, gathering," referring to the blessings that were to be gathered in. Then a khutugtu (myself or another) asked those present in a loud, formal request, "Have the blessings from the ten directions (arban jüg = the cardinal points of the compass plus up and down) been gathered?" Those attending then reply in unison, "Gathered, gathered, gathered." From this one may understand that the Mongolian people do many things for good luck.

Another important aspect of the oboo ceremony involves praises and prayers at the oboo in the form of vocal or instrumental music. This music, sometimes of different types and combinations, vocal and instrumental, usually involves one man who chants in solo, asking for blessings or giving thanks, perhaps asking for rain but no storm, or for breezes but no great winds. The solo chant on some occasions is accompanied in the background by a chorus that sings in unison and on other occasions by instrumental music and a man with a deep bass voice.

After the completion of the ceremony, the people descended from the raised part of the oboo to the level ground where many tents were pitched in a special semi-circular pattern by the people who had gathered for the special occasion. In the midst of the encircled tents was erected a large tatang, a very large pavillion-like tent in which dining and ceremonies are held. The smaller tents, arranged in a special U-shaped pattern, extended out from the sides of the pavillion.

The annual oboo festival was one of the happiest occasions of the year, a time when many people gathered to enjoy various games of amusement. The most enjoyable part of the celebration was a nair, a special festival including dining and such sports as horse racing and wrestling. The festivities of the nair at a small oboo festival concluded after a half-day of activity, while major gatherings at a great oboo extended for as long as three days, but not longer. The course of the horse races ordinarily was about twenty miles. The horses and the young boys who rode them were dispatched early in the morning after the ceremonial gathering, in which a large cedar smoke offering was made and prayers were chanted for the cleansing and blessing of the participants. The boys and horses were then sent off in the midst of loud singing. This particular type of bonfire was known as a sang or the "treasure of good fortune." The riders rode bareback during the races.

One contest we greatly enjoyed was the *tashuur chokikh* (*tashuur* is a whip and *chokikh* means to beat or throw), usually involving quite a number of men on horseback. The object of this game was the display of great skill and agility in riding as each contestant attempted to steal a whip used as a game piece and to ride away with it while everyone tried to snatch it from him. Frequently the whip dropped to the ground and a horseman had to show great skill in retrieving it while riding at top speed and bending down close to the ground. Because no score was kept and no clear-cut teams were involved, every man had to fend for himself in an attempt to steal the whip. If one man was able to gain a clear advantage over the others and to ride away with the whip, he then dropped the whip to the ground or stuck it in the sand, becoming the winner of that particular round. The game then continued again as the contenders struggled to retrieve the whip from the ground and to keep others from stealing it.

After the horse racing ended the wrestling competition began. The type of wrestling in this tournament-like *nair* was determined by the number of people in attendance. The limits were strict, beginning with thirty-two participants and extending up to 256, teamed in 128 pairs.

Another contest that was quite rough but very amusing to spectators was *dal-bulaakh* (steal the shoulder bone), that took place among wrestlers after the completion of the various wrestling matches and after the prizes were awarded. In this game the wrestling contestants struggle to get a game piece derived from a shoulder blade of an ox. Sometimes the bone is thrown to the group of wrestlers who then struggle over it, or it is placed in a particular spot and at a given signal the wrestlers run in and compete for it. In this very rough game virtually any means short of killing may be used to steal the bone. The foreleg of a beef is also sometimes used as a baton or game piece.

During the wrestling competition there also is special traditional folk singing. During the contest the spectators may sing some special heroic song in unison. Those seated in special positions for honored guests in the great *tatang* tent enjoy drinking *airagh* or *kumis*. After the wrestling is completed, and after the horse racers return, the great gathering is dispersed as many people depart with cheerful teasing, particularly as one person slyly

[91]

snatches away the whip of a friend and runs away to stick it in the earth. The friend must then follow and retrieve the whip on horseback, leaning down close to the ground to display agility and horsemanship.

In the Bargha district of northeastern Mongolia there was a traditional *nair* festival like those in other areas of Mongolia except that a particular type of archery takes the place of bareback horse racing. For this activity three poles are erected at set intervals; to each is attached a piece of leather to be shot at by the marksmen as they gallop past on their horses. I never observed this type of tournament in Chakhar where I usually lived.

At the Dolonor monastic center of Chakhar where large numbers of *shabinar*, lay disciples under the jurisdiction of the monastery, gather, the archers customarily stand in a particular posture and shoot at a leather plaque from a distance of about one hundred paces. In Bargha the arrows used for shooting are pointed, while those used in Chakhar are blunt. Ordinarily, lamas participate freely in wrestling but are restricted from archery, because it is too closely associated with the martial arts of war. I practiced both while a young man, however.

One of the functions of the lamas was to carry out divination for various important decisions. This art took many forms, but I will give just a few examples. The first was the tossing of three special dice we call *sho*. The dice are numbered one to six to correspond to the six syllables of the tantric formula *om-ma-ni-bad-mi-khon* (praise to the jewel in the lotus). By tossing the dice, one may decide a particular problem; for example, a marriage date or a decision on a journey. On occasion a person threw but one die. Another form of divination was to chant a brief tantric formula, quickly pass one's hands over the Buddhist prayer beads, and then count the beads between one's hands. A third common form of divination was to arrange black stones in different patterns to represent the date, time, and people involved to gain a solution to a question. Or one wrote down mathematical formulas derived from astrology and a consideration of various combinations of the stars. This form of divination was usually used in the *Duingkhor* College (*datsang*) of Badghar Monastery. We can see in these various forms of divination a combination of Tibetan and Chinese influences. The eight trigrams of the Chinese *I ching* (classic divination) combined with the twenty-eight asterisms of Tibetan astrology.

[92]

Divination for us is not a simple matter, for one must spend much time in meditation. Only after a special spiritual experience, a vision or something of a similar nature, is one prepared to perform the role of a diviner. Many people come with their problems to gain answers through divination, but the undertaking is sometimes hampered by evil spirits. If evil spirits interfere with the divination, any particular pronouncement or prediction given will most likely be a lie and misleading. The time and energy of a diviner thus is consumed in meditation, and as a result he cannot divine any oftener than once or twice a day. Not only must one chant sutras and recite formulas to exorcise evil influences; one must also meditate and pray faithfully and earnestly for the best possible divinations. As one begins to gain results, they must be careful to make correct interpretations regarding the association between the problem, the people involved, and the situation brought together for the divination. One definite problem is that while one is carrying out the divination process regarding a particular matter, alternative solutions may appear; and if one is not extremely careful, the prediction settled on may be no more accurate than the aim of a blind man trying to strike a dog with a stone.

The Mongolian form of divination is much more difficult than the Chinese form. While the Chinese merely shake the divination sticks on the floor and then read the answer desired from a handbook of divination, Mongols must meditate a great deal. The Buddha never lies, but the correct answer depends on the faith of one who seeks an oracle, and the art or faith of the person who carries out the divination. I frequently carried out divination in Mongolia until I was forced to flee to Taiwan. Here I have been asked many times by people to divine for them a particular problem, but I have rejected these requests because I have no scriptures to use in the important preparation of meditation.

Another most interesting rite is concerned with the special invocation of a spirit of a certain *choijung*, a Buddhist angel, the protector of the Law, which we call in Mongolian *sakighulsun*. Not all messengers or angels of the Buddha can be invoked, only a limited few, and no ordinary lama can achieve this manifestation of spirits, just certain special lamas. Such manifestations are not an element of true Buddhism, but something that has persisted from old Shamanistic traditions. Because this tradition is looked upon with disfavor by more orthodox Buddhists, a *gelüng* who

[93]

is a very holy person (a high level *bhikshu* or mendicant Lamaist monk) will not participate in such questionable activities. The type of lama who performs this kind of devination is known as a *ghurtam*.

My own belief is that the *sakighulsun* spirit was originally a sort of evil spirit. Only later, after it had heard the Law of the Buddha, surrendered itself and been converted, and had become submissive to Lobon-jugnai, the great Tibetan suppressor of evil spirits, did it become a good spirit and a servant of the Buddha. It is still not holy enough to manifest itself to a *gelüng*, however. There are several different kinds of Buddhist angels of the *sakighulsun* type. The *choijung*, for example, a protector of the Law of the Buddha, is commonly known by the Tibetan term *damsring*. Another, the *shajinai tedegegchi*, meaning literally "defender of the faith," is a protector of religious institutions. Images of this type are often found in the monasteries expressing fearsome wrath to frighten away evil influences.

In order to receive a spirit or manifestation, the lama oracle or medium must wear a special mirror on his chest. This mirror, actually an element from the old Shamanistic tradition of Mongolia, is very important in the practice of divination. During the manifestation the oracle, or special lama receiving it, customarily drinks a bowl of wine or *kumis*. At times a piece of gold is put in the bowl of wine. In the case of the great Dalai Lama of Tibet, the *ghurtam* lama performing some very special divination for him was given an ounce of gold, which he swallowed. To the ordinary person this would mean death, but this venerable lama was special. According to customary belief he received a mystical manifestation of the female protective diety Lhamo, and it was she, through possessing his body, who swallowed the gold. There is also an ancient custom that a special lama who seeks this oracle may have placed upon his head a special helmet type of head-dress. This piece is so heavy that ordinarily two people must lift it, but the strength of this lama is so great during the manifestation that even while wearing the helmet, he is able to dance and jump freely without feeling or exhibiting any restriction. Also, it is necessary for other strong lamas to hold down the special oracle by means of yellow silk ropes in order to prevent him from jumping too violently and injuring himself and others while in this turbulent trance.

[94]

During the rein of Emperor Ch'ien-lung (1736–1795) such manifestations were forbidden, apparently because the Ch'ing emperors feared what might happen if the people placed faith and confidence in them and the troublesome complications all this might lead to. Later in the dynasty, however, as the Ch'ing imperial power weakened, these manifestations rose again, and from time to time one would hear of the mysteries surrounding them.

It was common among Mongolians for a special lama inspired by a *choijung* deity to thrust a sword into his body or the body of others without harm as a demonstration of power and faith. Before the manifestation took place, however, the special spirit who was going to come gave a sign to the abbot of the monastery to clarify whether the spirit upon possession of the body would or would not use the sword or swallow the gold mentioned above. The manifestation that followed then proceeded according to a rule as set down in an oath. When a special sword was used, after it was thrust into the body of an oracle or someone else and then withdrawn, one saw no blood on it and no incision or blood on the person, only a red spot where the sword entered.

During this special manifestation, if some of the attending lamas who were assisting in some way made a mistake, the deity or special spirit which was manifesting itself cast the sword aside, thrusting it into the wall, as a sign of the deity's power and as an obvious reminder that someone had erred. There were other ways of confirming or demonstrating that a special spirit had been successfully invoked. For example, in Mongolian monasteries there were often found swords tied into a knot by the powerful influence of a visiting deity. This phenomena was not only common in my time but was handed down from ancient times. As indicated in the record of Saghang Sechen, for example, a venerable lama who came to preach the Buddhist law to Tümen Jasaghtu Khan (r. 1558–1592) had performed through him as a medium this marvelous manifestation of power.

Oaths or sacred formulas are extremely important to lamas and there are oaths pertaining to many different things. One is regarding special manifestations. In these manifestations only one real difference distinguishes the ancient practices of the shamans and the oracles of special lamas. Whereas the shamans had no oaths, the lamas do, and these must be closely adhered to in carrying out special manifestations. Through mediums in trance, various spirits or deities may come. For example, at my own Badghar Monastery the local deity known to us as *Uuliin ejen* (lord of the mountain) appeared. Each different spirit that was invoked had a different mode or manner of being called upon.

Uuliin ejen was a minor deity, and the ceremony for a special manifestation or visitation of this deity through a lama acting as an oracle in a trance was not very precise or elaborate, and was not restricted to a special lama oracle but was broadly practiced by others. We had special spirits or deities called *Jamsarang* and *Sereb* that had very high rank, almost the rank of a Buddha, and the ceremony for the invocation of these spirits was very elaborate. Each monastery or temple in Mongolia had a special protective deity or spirit (*sakighulsun*). Though one never hears the common people claim that a certain spirit is protecting their yurt, it is common for powerful families or the nobility to claim a certain protective deity. In the old records we are told that during the time of Khubilai Khan the protective deity of the royal clan and the nation was *Doghor* (Skt. *Usnisa-sitāta-pattra*), the Bodhisattva who bears a white umbrella. Thus, in the descriptions one reads of the court of Khubilai, the great white canopy over his throne was the symbol of Doghor and the umbrella he bears. Many believe that another common protective deity of the Mongolian people is *Lhamo*. Many festivals took place at different times of the year and at different places to celebrate a particular protective deity of that area.

I have already mentioned the various offerings made by the lamas. One of these, the water offering, had to be done very precisely. The cups for the offering had to be filled exactly; they must not overflow or be deficient. Should they overflow, this meant the wasting of blessings; should they not be full, this meant a deficiency of blessings. The cups of water were placed on the altar to symbolize purity and cleanliness, and those who made the offering were blessed by the Buddha with purity and cleanliness. Through these offerings the lamas gained a clearer mind and a keener intellect and better understood the teachings of the Buddha.

Another common offering was called *jula*, an offering made of high grade butter with a wick for a flame, and placed in a cup made of gold, silver, copper, or bronze. The oil was never of animal fat except for butter. *Jula* offerings were made as symbolic actions to dissipate darkness and evil, and show that the light of

[96]

the Lord Buddha is continually expanding and bringing understanding to the world. This offering designated that both the
monastery and the household of the one making the offering
would be enlightened by the Buddha. In all cases, whether a
water offering or a lamp offering, all the receptacles involved
were absolutely clean, or the symbolism would not be complete
and the offering would not be accepted. Later, as I came in contact
with the Chinese, it seemed strange to me to find Chinese monks
using candles, a thing Mongols never do, because they are made
of animal fat. It seems rather ironic that Chinese monks do not
eat meat but will use candles made from animal products whereas
Mongolian lamas eat meat but will not use candles.

Our Mongolian people have a traditional custom stemming from
ancient times which some describe as an "anointing" or "blessing"
called *milaakh*. The ceremony consists of taking a small amount
of butter or animal fat and rubbing it on one's finger, and then
rubbing the finger on the object to be anointed or blessed. For
example, a family, or more particularly a young, newly married
couple, who is establishing a new yurt, will rub a little butter
or animal fat on the inside of the roof near the opening in the
ceiling. In the anointing action they will pronounce some special
words of blessing such as a wish for many children, protection,
prosperity. Also, anointing the lintel of the door in the same way
is a common practice. At other times, when a family kills an
entire sheep to serve an extraordinarily good meal, they will,
before eating, perform the *milaakh* ritual by taking a small piece
of fat and putting it into the fire. The action here places a blessing
on the fire, a symbol of prosperity. On occasion it is also common
for grandparents or parents to *milaakh* their young children as a
simple symbolic blessing or anointing with the wish that they
may always have good food to eat and prosperity.

It has also been customary for Mongols to perform *milaakh* on
other special occasions, such as when a person obtained a new
bow. They take a little fat and rub it on the bow itself and on
the string so that the bow will be lucky and useful in obtaining
game. When a young boy begins to follow his father in the hunt,
it is also customary for the father to rub a little animal fat on
the thumb and index finger of a son's hand that draws the bow
so that it also will be strong and accurate. This custom has been
widespread among Mongols from ancient times. It is found, for
example, among Kalmuck Mongols living in the Don and Volga

[97]

regions of southern Russia. At the time of the fall *dallagh* festival (beckoning of wealth festival), it was common for each person attending to take a small piece of fat, to anoint their mouth with it while chanting, and then to swallow the piece of fat.

A variation of this *milaakh*, anointing ceremony, also traditionally takes place with newborn babies. A little liquor or fermented drink serves for a type of anointing and for washing the baby's mouth. It is possible that this practice also involved some traditional, pragmatic medicine with the function of disinfecting. The Mongolian feeling, however, is that this anointing is for blessing the baby and that a fermented drink rather than tea or milk, or some other liquid, is used because it is considered to be *de'ed amt*,(*de'ed* = superior or "topmost," *amt* = "taste.") Three days after the birth of a male child, a special festival is held by the family and the *milaakh* ceremony is performed. This anointing ceremony may also be performed by particularly devout or conscientious Mongols as an expression of gratitude when they obtain new furniture or some other desired object. Thus, religion has traditionally been inseparable from every aspect of life.

Images and paintings of the Buddha naturally played a very important role in our monastic life and ceremonies. Chinese paintings of the Buddha are rather different and not nearly so appealing as those done by Mongolian or Tibetan lamas. From my observation Chinese renderings were more relaxed or impressionistic and the body proportions were different from Mongolian or Tibetan paintings. Mongols and Tibetans, inspired by their faith, painted from the heart, whereas the Chinese painted merely to produce pictures to make money. Another difference was the colors used by the Chinese as compared to the Mongols or Tibetans. The former generally used only common painting compounds while the Tibetans and Mongols sought out very special ingredients and colors and even powdered precious stones for use in painting. Thus, our colors were much more permanent and brilliant. Also in Mongol and Tibetan paintings careful attention was given to the various instruments and objects held in the hands of the Buddha in different poses, revealing that these people believed in being very precise in basing their depictions upon the Buddhist scriptures. It is a Mongolian impression that Chinese artists by contrast have been somewhat careless in this matter. Because of the difference in art styles, Chinese temples to us are quite bare and foreboding while Mongolian monasteries have customarily been very beautiful, with their luxurious chimeg (hangings and drapes).

Pilgrimages, Visits and Common Customs

As a lama incarnation, I was invited at different times to visit the homes of the people and the various monasteries or temples. For such visits there were various customary observances; some would call it the ecclesiastical protocol of Mongolian Lamaism. In preparation for a visit, it was common for a monastery, a banner prince or some such important person to send a special messenger, perhaps several months ahead of time, to bear the invitation and make an appointment. When the time came for the visit, a special caravan was sent to bring me to the place. On occasion I would prepare this caravan myself. When we were within ten to fifteen miles of the destination, the host would send a party of twenty or thirty people to designate a place for the erection of a special tent to serve as a welcoming delegation. As we reached the place, a messenger from the host made a formal greeting of reception. In so doing, he approached my horse before I dismounted, knelt in respect and extended a formal welcome for the host. Later, upon conclusion of the visit, as I mounted my horse to return to my monastery, this same special messenger knelt on the left side of my horse to again extend the regards of the host.

Whenever I made an extended formal visit in Mongolia, it was common for me to have an entourage, perhaps a half dozen to a dozen people, including such special people as my *soibon*, a sort of chamberlain who arranged for my personal needs, meals, clothing, and sleeping accommodations. This lama was closest to me and most important to my official functions. Another lama accompanied me as a *donir*, to handle such official matters as protocol, visits with other people, acceptance of gifts and arranging of schedules. Still another lama accompanied me as a *deberchi* (literally "kettle holder"). It was this monk's task to serve tea and refreshments. He was close to me and took care of various other small chores and duties. His rank was not so high as the *soibon* and *donir*, however. Always accompanying me on extended travels was also a lama, known as *jama*, who cooked my meals. In addition to these people, two *kiya* (guards) accompanied me;

this according to a custom that arose in the early Ch'ing dynasty, originally by an order of the emperor. We know by their title that earlier each carried a sword, but in my day, they did not carry any weapons. An ordinary gegen would never be accompanied by such a bodyguard.

It was not often that I traveled with such a formal entourage accompanied by so many people. But in former days when I traveled to Ujumuchin Banner in Shilin-ghol League it was always a special occasion; and because of the continuity of the ancient traditions that are still strong in this area, I made a very formal visit only when accompanied by an impressive group of people. My arrival at a temple or monastery was a very special occasion which brought great joy and honor to me, because there were many people who came to receive me. The great musical instruments of the monastery, such as tubas, were played with loud and solemn music. Special lamas came with great bowls of incense hanging by chains to go before me on either side, to bring me into the main hall of the monastery, and to see that I was seated properly upon the highest ceremonial throne of the incarnation of that particular place. Then they presented to me a mandala. Depending upon the wealth of the monastery, I was given valuable gifts, perhaps a large sum of silver, beautiful horses or other such things, or perhaps only a symbolic mandala should the place not be so wealthy.

Another important part of the reception of my visits to the various monasteries was the ceremonial offering of tea and the series of audiences in which the various lamas came according to rank to bow in respect. Usually if there were not too many lamas, I gave each a blessing, as he passed before me, by placing my right hand upon his head. If there were many lamas, because of the inconvenience in reaching over the table where I was seated, I used a short instrument in the form of a scepter, perhaps one to two feet long, with a silk tassel hanging from it, which made it easier for me to touch the heads of the lamas as they passed before me.

After an official reception, I sometimes lodged at the monastic temple in the labrang, the residence of a high lama. There were several of these near some monasteries. At other times I lodged in the shang of the monastery, that was a little less private. After settling in these temporary quarters for the duration of the visit,

I would soon be served a formal meal usually consisting of a whole sheep boiled in a cauldron.

Still another important part of the visit was meeting with officials of the monastery after the reception and meal to discuss which *tsewang* I would perform during my stay. A *tsewang* is a scriptural recitation, a ceremonial presentation of scriptures as a form of ordination or the conferral of special blessings or authority. The lamas could then meditate on and discuss the particular scripture with special power and devotion. Depending on the time or the circumstances, I was at times requested by the officials and lamas to perform the *ramnai* ceremony, a special invocation of a deity or spirit to reside in a new image or painting or one that had been refurbished for use in the religious observances of the monastery. Until this special blessing was pronounced upon the image or painting, it was not regarded as a proper object of worship. Sometimes I was asked to perform the *dallagh* ceremony, to request a special blessing of wealth and prosperity upon the monastery and its vicinity.

Visiting various monasteries or temples throughout the land took a good deal of time. During some visits I was requested to assist in obtaining an oracle for the search of a new incarnation to replace one who had passed on. If several candidates had already been found for a new incarnation, I might be asked to assist in determining which candidate was correct and to provide some direction for his preparation and teaching. After the new incarnation had been identified, while he was yet a young acolyte, old friends of the earlier incarnation were invited to formally visit the monastery. There were also those occasions in the monasteries, after a *gegen* had died, in which honorable lamas or incarnations from various distant regions were called upon to visit and to recite sutras or to assist in the affairs and ceremonies of the monastery in the absence of its abbot or incarnation. The most enjoyable occasion for me was my visit to a friend who lived at a distance and while there to enjoy the *nair*, the wrestling tournament, the drinking of *kumis*, and other such activities.

Thus, there were many different types of visits or levels of protocol; those to a monastery, a prince, a lama friend, or the home of a common person, for example. Each had its distinct customary form. Official visits to monasteries took place during any season, but visits to friends and homes of the people or a prince ordinarily took place during the summer or autumn. The

[101]

common people were, of course, not so ceremonial and the gifts or observances were much more simple. For their welcoming ceremony, for example, I would upon arrival take the seat of honor in the yurt, facing the entrance, and the host would present to me in a formal manner a ceremonial scarf (khadagh) upon which was placed a bowl of kumis or milk. This I received and perhaps drank, but ordinarily I dipped my finger in it, sprinkled the liquid as a blessing to the deities, and placed it aside.

During these visits I was careful to bring only a few servants in my entourage so as not to burden the people with too many honorable guests. My personal feeling was that while they had faith in me personally or my role, they were not interested in those who accompanied me. On these common visits I ordinarily took with me only my soibon, personal chamberlain, or my deberchi, tea-kettle heater, and my kötöl, the man who attended my horses. When I did not take my jama, personal cook, it was necessary for me to partake of whatever was prepared by the family I was visiting. I found my soibon to be very helpful in assisting me in various chores and duties that arose, such as welcoming people who came from afar who had heard I was visiting in the vicinity. The size of the group that accompanied me of course depended on the distance I had to travel; hence, I found it necessary to take more people when I went on an extended journey.

Ordinarily, if it were possible, the host would roll out a welcoming mat of white felt for me to dismount on and then proceed on it into his yurt. Ordinary persons never mount or dismount a horse in front of a yurt. This is an honor reserved only for important people. Other people usually mount their horses at the left rear of the yurt. In some respects Chakhar was a little different in places because of long Chinese influence. Here, for example, the color of the felt carpets in the yurts was sometimes red rather than the traditional Mongolian white.

When I arrived at the home of a common person, I was also often welcomed by the blowing of a conch shell. In visits to a prince, however, the prince frequently invited a monastery orchestra or other musical group to play music upon my arrival. This was never part of the ceremony when I left, because to play music or sound an instrument on departure of an honored guest would have been a bad omen, meaning the person would never come to visit again.

On visiting wealthy people or a prince, I was usually presented a *mandala*, much like that presented at a monastery. The common people would present to me a few coins or some other gift wrapped in white paper and placed upon a ceremonial scarf. Though this was not actually a *mandala*, they would call it such. When they presented me *kumis* or some other drink, I often drank a little of it and then put it aside, and it was passed around among those present; if I drank it entirely, however, the people would wipe the bowl with the ceremonial kerchief. This kerchief would then be attached to the arrow used in the *dallagh* ceremony to invoke blessings upon the people. This first drinking was most important. Following it, I was usually given some common tea to drink and refreshments in the form of Mongolian cookies, *boorsogh*, made of flour boiled in butter or fat. These refreshments were always stacked in layers one upon another to form a square, hollow in the center and with small cookies placed around the top. In partaking of these cookies Mongolian *gegens* were always careful not to take one from the bottom of the pile and disturb the stack but always to take just a little from the top.

In my visits to border areas closest to the Great Wall, I was given food consisting of long white noodles thought to be symbolic of long life, a custom no doubt due to Chinese cultural influence. I always took care to refrain from giving any indication that I was hungry, even though at times I was famished after a long journey. I partook of only a small amount of the noodles, knowing that later there would be a large meal of finely cooked meat and other dishes.

The most important meal was delayed until evening, prior to which I was allowed to rest after the welcoming ceremonies. The most important part of this large meal was a whole sheep cooked in a cauldron. When the animal was brought to the dining area, it was customary for the host or for my *jama* (steward or cook) to cut off the head, tail, and hoofs, place them on a large platter, and present them as an offering before the altar of the Buddha. Those attending understood that these various parts were symbolic of an entire animal in the offering. On the head of the animal was incised a cross. It seems obvious to me that such an offering of meat to the Buddha was not in keeping with pure Buddhism, but that such an offering came from the traditional nomadic culture of our people as a persistance of the old offerings

[103]

to the protective deity of a place. An orthodox Buddhist offering would not require the taking of life.

While it was not a necessary thing, some people took a little of the fat of the animal and placed it in the fire as an offering to the fire god. It was natural that I could eat only a little of the animal presented in the meal, so what was left was given to those who accompanied me. They could never eat all of it, and what was left was then given to others present. The sheep would usually weigh from forty to fifty pounds and be almost too much for ten men to eat. If it were in season, the family always had *kumis* as a drink to refresh their guests.

After the evening meal, the guests enjoyed a program of music, whenever someone could play the string instrument we call the *morin-khuur*. This two-stringed instrument would remind one of a violin with an echo box, having a pleasant, low-pitched sound when played with a bow. The strings of the bow are made of horsehair. The instrument is also often called a "horse *khuur*" because the upper handle is shaped artistically like a horse's head. Always there was much singing and light conversation. When I was present, the people were careful to sing only proper songs. I know, however, that when I was not present they sang some which were not for the ears of a *gegen*. Ordinarily the singing was rather formal and the people did not get carried away. I recall during the Japanese occupation that some Japanese who desired to joyfully join the group were disruptive in their eagerness.

On the second day of the visit I was always requested to perform various ceremonies such as a *dallagh* blessing ritual or was consulted regarding some problem of a local family and asked which Buddhist scripture would be best to recite for such a problem. The family then sometimes later invited other lamas to recite the scripture, or they would request me upon my return to the monastery to represent them in the recitation. If I did not read the scripture for the family myself, they always had an itinerant lama do so in his regular visit on a set date as he moved from camp to camp throughout the region. If a high lama had not visited the region for a long period of time, I was commonly requested to perform the ceremony of *ramnai* in order to invoke the deities to come once again to reside in the images of the family shrine or to purge the yurts of evil influences and rededicate them for the good luck and fortune of the family. If the family requested that I perform the *dallagh*, they usually brought their animals and paraded them around the yurt in front of me. This was so that I could sprinkle them and bless them to be abundant in offspring and be protected from disease.

Upon departing from the family, I was invariably presented with a gift of larger animals—a horse, a camel, cattle, or a number of these animals, depending on the wealth and the wish of the host. One of the more important aspects of a visit, if there was illness in the family, was to confer a special blessing for assistance in curing the family member.

Thus, we see incarnations left the monastic temples at times to visit among the people or the princes; likewise, there were seasonal times when the princes (*jasagh*) came to the monastery to visit the lamas, such as new years or the *oboo* festival. Such visits were at times complex in that protocol etiquette depended very much on the rank of the person and the status of the monastery. For example, there were monasteries within the banners under the jurisdiction of a particular *jasagh*; there were also monasteries that were not within the territory of a banner, and not subject to any banner's rule, but coming only under the jurisdiction of Peking. One important rule was that whatever the high rank of a lay official who comes to visit the monastery, he was never placed on an equal level with a *khubilghan*; he was never invited to sit in the honored chair of the incarnation, but rather was hosted only in the *jisa* or *shang* sections of the monastery.

A visiting *jasagh* official was treated with hospitality at a monastery equal to that offered any honorable *gegen* who came to visit. He was visited by the officials of the monastery and the high lamas, but not all of the lamas paraded to pay their respects or to receive a blessing. A reception welcoming a *jasagh* depended on the nature of his visit. If he came merely as a believer to worship, he of course was honored and well received; but if he came officially in his capacity as the *jasagh* of the region, he was received officially by the *gegen* who was the head of the monastery. This last type of visit was very rare, for a *jasagh* usually came as a common believer. When a *jasagh* visited a monastery that was not within his jurisdiction, and with which he had no official relationship, he was hosted merely as a patron.

Official visits were seldom undertaken, because if a *jasagh* were to come in his official capacity he must come in honor, make an offering of significance, and provide *manja* or milk tea for the entire body of lamas of the monastery. This was, of course, expensive. In the old days it was the great wish of every *jasagh* to make a pilgrimage to Lhasa and there to offer *manja* to all the hundreds and thousands of lamas. Of course, everyone could freely come to visit a monastic temple, make offerings, and chat with the lamas, but in a large monastery such as Badghar, the regulations (*ghorlom*) were very strict. If visitors had women with them, the women were not allowed to stay within the compound (*kuree*) but had to leave by nightfall—even the ladies of the *jasagh*. Needless to say, this was rather awkward. Among the small monasteries in the banners, there were no such strict regulations. In most monasteries throughout Mongolia, the residence or dormitory of the lamas was surrounded by a wall that provided protection and privacy. Our Badghar Monastery was quite unique, however, in that the lama's dwellings were not surrounded by any heavy walls. We had the impression that walls around a monastery showed undue worldly concern. We also felt that within our monasteries everything must be kept holy and uncontaminated. For example, the lamas are not allowed to establish toilet facilities within their dwellings; they must walk far from the monastery compound to such a facility. An exception was extended only to old lamas, who were allowed to establish a yurt with toilet facilities behind their dwellings.

A very important activity of our religion was making visits or pilgrimages to sacred places and historic sites. The most important destination, as already noted, was a pilgrimage to Lhasa in Tibet and tens of thousands of our people have made this trip. The next important place was the famous Kumbum Monastery, but both of these are very distant and the great majority of our people could never travel so far; thus, a very popular place, that was more accessible, was the sacred site of Wu-t'ai-shan (five-peaked mountain) in Shansi province. The esteem in which this place was held would remind one of the veneration in which the Chinese hold P'u-t'ou shan.

For many generations Wu-t'ai-shan was an economic center as well as a religious center because many pilgrims came there; great sums of money circulated from the many donations made to the monastic temples and because of the service activities that catered to the pilgrims. These pilgrims, however, criticized the questionable activities which took place there among the visitors and the less desirable local people. We were all keenly aware that the famous warlord Yen Hsi-shan came from the Wu-t'ai district; he had long contact with the Mongolian people and was continually involved in Mongolian affairs. A popular story among our people is that Yen Hsi-shan originally came from a common family whose cottage industry made wooden bowls to sell to the Mongolian people.

For religious and economic reasons, then, the great monastic center at Wu-t'ai-shan had important links both to Peking and to Mongolia and later many of our people desired to be buried there. Our people believed that a burial there would assure one of a good rebirth in the realm of Manjushri, the protector of scholars and the venerable deity of this monastic center. Some of our people traveled for a year at great expense and difficulty to visit Wu-t'ai-shan. In addition, it was common for Wu-t'ai-shan lamas to travel widely throughout Mongolia gathering donations for their monasteries. It was such an important place, religiously, economically, and even politically, that during my own day the Japanese had agents and military intelligence men there.

Recreation and Special Occasions

People everywhere are concerned with recreation, and it is natural for them to ask about this aspect of life for the lamas in the monastery. Of course, there was a variation from the traditional play of the Mongolian people, but there were similarities. The national sports since ancient times have been horse racing, wrestling, and archery. The lamas, however, are prohibited from participating actively in archery because it is a martial art linked to combat and killing.

In many places in Mongolia for many centuries, our people have been greatly delighted in listening to storytellers as these men travel through Mongolia and came to visit the monastery. These storytellers were not entirely free within the monastery, however, for some people apparently felt that there was a possibility the young lamas would not be so interested in studying and reciting *sutras* if there were some competition or interference from storytellers. Though they could not come freely to the monasteries, or openly gather many people to their entertainment

[107]

there, these itinerant storytellers could tell their stories freely to a particular person who hosted them at the monastery. These men, whom we call khuurchi (khuur meaning a "stringed instrument" and the suffix chi signifying "a person"), are fascinating people who tell stories all in rhyme to the accompaniment of a khuur. While there was some limitation on the lamas gathering to listen to a storyteller, there was no limitation to their reading the text of the stories that were available in the monasteries, though they were not encouraged to do so.

Some of the most popular forms of entertainment among the lamas was shatar, a Mongolian chess; migming (a term from the Tibetan meaning "thousand eyes," which is really very much like the Chinese or Japanese games of "go," also similar to chess); sedbiin khorloo, a game played also on a board, which involved the religious Tantric or esoteric formula of the mani (sacred formula or chant common in Tibetan Buddhism). One game or sport that we enjoyed greatly when we were young and had free time was shagha. There are different forms of this game, all of which involved the ankle bone of an animal. One type of shagha, played with the ankle bone of an antelope as a game piece, took place indoors. The object was to flip the bone on the floor in such a way as to strike other game pieces of bone, and the person who won was the one able to flip the most accurately. Another form of shagha, also played indoors with the ankle bones of sheep, consisted of dropping four ankle bones on the table or ground and keeping score according to the position in which the ankle bones lighted. A third form of the shagha is played outdoors with the ankle bone of an ox which was kicked about like a hockey puck. Scores were kept also according to the position in which the puck or bone came to rest.

One of the games I found most interesting when I was young was tebeg, a form of "badminton." The cock for this game was made of a Chinese coin with a hole in the center from which there extended a number of feathers. This was kicked very agilely from person to person, and one must have great skill to prevent the cock from falling to the ground. Other people as well as lamas enjoy demonstrating their ability, almost acrobatic, in playing this game. We also enjoyed another game called shento (Ch. shein-to), a game played with a ball that is kicked in the air from player to player, mainly for fun and not for competition. We lamas did not play these games the year around, but usually on the New Year's holiday.

At Badghar Monastery there was the fine custom that in the sixth lunar month (July) of summer all of the lamas were allowed to vacation at a summer residence, a custom very important to the well-being of the lamas. Since the monastic centers were usually established permanently in a valley, the life-style there was very different from the traditional nomadic life of our people. The land on which the monasteries were established was regarded as *koros-ugei*, "dead land" (literally, "skinless," meaning it had no ground cover), and in the summer we wanted to be out in a yurt on the green grass of the *korostei* or "living land." If the old lamas stayed in the temple all year round, sometimes their legs would swell up, but if they went out to the countryside and stayed in a yurt and drank *kumis*, they soon recovered and were in much better health and spirits. People speculate that the swelling of the limbs was a problem of diet or exercise, but who knows? As for me, the Duingkhor *gegen*, and my teacher, we made our summer residence at Serem *bulagh* (Serem spring), mentioned earlier, as arranged by the *shang* of the Duingkhor *gegen*. Here we spent an entire month with great enjoyment, making offerings to the *oboo*, enjoying the wide open grazing areas, riding special horses and drinking *kumis*.

In the seventh lunar month (August) of the year we ended our vacation and returned to the monastery. We have very fond memories of those vacations, particularly of the springs that drew people to the area for health and recreation. One Mongolian poet, Tsongkor *noyan*, a patron of our monastery, has noted this in a poem: "the best waters are those of Serem *bulagh*, and the best people are those of my banner." I am not certain, but it seems that he was prince of the Urad Banner of Ulanchab League from the border near Badghar Monastery. Certainly it was a pleasant, beautiful place with many springs, streams, and trees. In the summers, if I was in the vicinity of Badghar Monastery, I usually spent my vacation there, where the Duingkhor *gegen* usually held a *nair* festival, with sports competitions and a fine banquet in the *Bat-chaghan*, a yurt for special occasions. This yurt was so high that it was not possible to reach up to the *tonno*, a hole in the ceiling, and it was necessary for a man to mount a camel to assemble this particular area in setting up the yurt. The interior was so large that it was not possible for a man sitting on one side of the yurt to hear another man speaking on the other side. I was but a boy the first time I saw such an immense yurt and the first time I drank kumis, that great drink. I was so interested in all the activities and watched the people milk the mares to make the kumis. I found this especially impressive since where I came from in Kokonor we had no such customs. Usually in the Badghar Monastery area when we were going to drink kumis, we would first eat some mutton broth and then drink the kumis so there would not be any distress arise from the fermented drink on an empty stomach.

The birthday of an incarnation or gegen was an important occasion, and the lamas made special preparations for it. These preparations include mainly the making of sereb, a pill symbolic of long life. Different kinds of sereb was prepared, some for the Ayushi Buddha (the Buddha of longevity) and others for the Chaghan Tara eke ("White Tara Mother"). There are many legends and much has been written about this latter deity, of her kindness and compassion. On the morning of his birthday, the incarnation came to the main prayer hall of the monastery where the lamas all assembled and presented him a mandala. Each of the lamas bowed individually, paid respect to the incarnation, and received from him a sereb pill to swallow with the hope of long life.

In Mongolia we had a special custom of celebrating the various anniversaries of a person's birth, a thing common in many countries. The Chinese celebrate every tenth anniversary of the birth of some important person, but we Mongols celebrate each twelfth anniversary according to the signs of the zodiac year cycle. I am not certain of the origin of this custom, but I think it must be Tibet. The common people and even common lamas did not observe this anniversary, though princes were certain to observe it and also high lamas. It was the general feeling in the monasteries that the observance of these anniversaries even for high lamas should be modest, not pretentious. When high lamas celebrated the anniversary of their birth, the twelfth, the twenty-fourth, forty-eighth, etc., a prayer ceremony was ordinarily held, to which all the lamas of the temple were invited. The person whose birthday was being observed made an offering to the Ayushi Buddha (the Buddha of long life), an offering of a special type of small pill, somewhat like candy, that was then passed to the monks of the monastery to be eaten.

A change in the nature of the birthday festival came when a person reached the age of forty-eight, which was a special anniversary based again on the dating of the Mongolian zodiac cycle. According to this custom, a special observance should have been held on my thirteenth birthday when I was living at Badghar Monastery. I was quite young, however, and no one paid any special attention to the occasion. But after the next twelve years of the cycle, my lama friends and my teacher did pay some little attention to my birthday. An occasion which caused great comment and festivities, and which we still remember, was the forty-eighth birthday of Prince Sodnamrabtan, ruling *jasagh* of West Üjümüchin Banner. Three days of feasting, horse races, wrestling, and other festivities were held, which attracted people with their gifts from far and wide over all of Inner Mongolia. This was in the late 1920s, when I was still quite young. Although I did not attend, I heard many comments about it because it was a rather unusual occasion.

Wherever we live or with whatever culture we come in contact, we find that a person's birthday is a special personal occasion and special observances are held in which we all are involved. This has been true from ancient times. We find, for example, in an old record, the *Altan Tobchi* (golden chronical), a comment Chinggis Khan made on an occasion when he was discussing birthdays with his sons. He asked them which day they regarded as particularly meaningful and important. One son replied that the most important occasion was the new year which brought many festivities and which was the new beginning of the future. Chinggis Khan disagreed, saying that even more important was a person's birthday, reasoning that if a person's parents had not given birth to him what then could he begin at any time? One's very existence, name, and fame—all stemmed from the birth provided by one's parents. Thus, it was important for them to commemorate this day with a special observance.

Accordingly, from early times, a birthday celebration has involved a certain filial element, a sentiment common among Mongols, who have a strong feeling of regard for their parents and ancestors. This is, of course, really the ideal, theoretical situation. As a matter of fact, the common people have not been so conscientious in the observance of birthdays, particularly of younger persons. Among richer, more aristocratic families, however, there is still a modest observance of the birthday of children. There

[111]

are no large parties or invitations to friends, only some special food perhaps, congratulations from the parents, and usually a bowing of the children to the parents in recognition and gratitude for their birth. One reason these things come to mind is that only when I came into close association with Chinese people did I become aware of the fact that some people pay such great attention to birthdays.

Lamaist Vocations: Medicine and Other Fields

Every large monastic center in Mongolia, such as Pandita Gegen Monastery (Pei-tse-miao) and Badghar Monastery, has within it a *mamba datsang*, a college of Buddhist medicine. While the culture and the society of our people are changing, medicine is always a necessity, a positive benefit. For this reason I was active in the practice of medicine in Mongolia. I did not formally study in a *mamba datsang*, but rather on my own. I read many books and practiced the healing arts.

Frequently a *gegen* was called by the people to assist in their problems, whether they were ill or just in need of counsel. In these situations it was common for us to decide by divination on a correct diagnosis of the problem and determine what proper measures should be taken to bring about a cure. Many *gegens* tried to impress others with their great learning and experience, but I did not pretend to high scholarship. Those who know me can confirm that in my contact with the people I tried to handle matters in a simple straight-forward manner. If someone had a minor illness, I did not exaggerate the problem for gain or to impress people. If it was necessary to recite scriptures as an approach to a problem, I did not drag out the ceremony unduly but tried to keep it brief. Actually, if I may modestly say so, I had a good reputation in Chakhar and in the Bargha banners of Hulun-buir as an effective doctor. And I can claim with some pride that I actually saved many lives. Through the course of time I had many experiences, both interesting and disappointing, in my practice of Buddhist medicine.

An important development for my personal career, for the Lamaist religion, and for all Mongolia was the Japanese occupation of Inner Mongolia. Before the Japanese army occupied our country, it was preceded by an important organization known as the Zenrin kyokai (Good Neighbor Association). Ostensibly, this society's concern was education, medical clinics, and other such civic enterprises, but some of us were quite curious, even suspicious, of these activities. I recall one early case in which a man whose face was swollen to an extremely abnormal size came to the Japanese for help. They tried various treatments unsuccessfully and finally decided to operate on his face. The man refused the operation and came to me. I gave him some special medicine—I don't recall what it was—but the results were excellent and the Japanese were surprised at the healing powers of what they thought were primitive Mongolian cures.

The Buddha taught that if a man desired to accomplish any good thing he must first have a good heart—the right intent. All good things originate first from a good heart. In some medical treatments there may at first be seemingly good results, but if the intent was evil, the results will eventually turn bad. Thus, the first concern of a lama is to develop a proper attitude, proper intent or purpose. From the beginning, I have been concerned with this. The Buddha made clear that the threat to religion is from the inside, that destruction or attack from the outside is not the main concern. Like worms eating away the wood, evil works from within to destroy something of beauty.

The Buddha also explained that it is not necessary for us to struggle against political power. Neither is it necessary for Buddhist monks to struggle against scientific or natural developments in the world. If Buddhism desires to develop and to spread, it certainly must work in accordance with the natural trend of the times, for any struggle against the wheel of time will bring only failure. In Mongolia we have a saying that everyone will walk according to his time and place: "In the land of the lame, the lame will walk. In the land of the blind, the blind will walk." Everyone is bound by their own tradition, by their own time and custom. Thus, the lamas feel that all they do and say is right and proper.

In Mongolia we always stressed that people should strive for *chaghan buyan*, white virtues or blessings, and to suppress or avoid the *khara nigül*, black sins. The origin of the "ten black sins" is the body, the tongue, and the heart. Three of these black sins are of the body: killing, stealing, and sexual impropriety. Three are of the heart: covetousness, malice, and incorrect views.

[113]

The other four are evils of the tongue: lies, saying things that may bring trouble, harsh words, and idle speech.

The ten white blessings come from doing those things opposite to the evils just listed. The role of the lamas has been to teach that people must do good deeds (buyan üildekü). When people inquired as to what was the best thing to do, we told them first to study and learn the teachings of the Buddha, second to make donations to maintain the monasteries and shrines, third to sustain the monks and feed them. These are buyan, or good deeds, for the religion. In addition there are buyan, or good deeds, for the world (yörtönch), such as helping the poor and giving all types of service to people. These different types of good deeds should really not be divided, but rather be regarded as one. Anyone who strives for good deeds without proper intent will do so in vain, however. To help the poor or to sustain the monks, both are meritorious services. Whether they are done by Buddhists or non-Buddhists does not matter; the results of both are good. A person may, of course, by constant good deeds and virtuous observances, build up merit. This accumulation of merit may benefit a person in a future life, or it may serve as a reward for other people, to heal their illnesses, or solve their problems.

In order to be recognized, we tried to properly train lama doctors and graduate them from the mamba datsang, a recognized medical college of a Lamaist monastery. There were doctors, however, who did not have these qualifications, who were either common lamas or ordinary persons, spoken of as emchi (doctor), but who really just assumed this role among our less educated people.

A lama doctor will not give medicine on the day of the ram of the zodiac time cycle, because many Mongols feel that sheep and goats are stupid and that diseases will tend to resist the good effects of the medicine. In my time, if an emergency arose when a lama had to give medicine on a wrong day, he was required by tradition to present with it the dried leg of a rabbit. The implication of this symbolic ritual was that the rabbit runs very rapidly and, thus, the medicine will be rapidly efficacious.

In this connection one may note a unique tradition in Chakhar different from the more nomadic areas of Mongolia. In north China a boy or a girl born in the year of the ram finds it very difficult to obtain a marriage partner, so few marriages took place in these ill-fated years, and this belief had some influence also in the frontier areas of Mongolia close to China, like Chakhar.

[114]

According to the teachings of the monastery medical colleges, we have traditionally had four basic categories of illness. One kind to be healed without any medicine by proper nourishment and care; a second type requiring medicine and the attention of a lama doctor for recovery; a third kind requiring the administration of medicine, plus prayer, and proper religious ceremonies; a fourth type recognized as terminal cases in which prayers and medical administrations are not efficacious. Here one could only hope to ease the final suffering and comfort the ill person. The medical college in my monastery spoke of four hundred and four types of disease. Sometimes a lama doctor in diagnosing a patient told him that his recovery would come only through *buyan üildekü* (good deeds). As a rule, a lama doctor was forbidden to request money of his patients, though it was customary for a patient in Mongolia to voluntarily give a ceremonial scarf, some animals, or other things as a token of his gratitude.

The lama doctors made or obtained their own medicine and do not freely sell it. Also, it was not freely administered without advice. Occasionally one heard the common people say: "Medicine accepted freely without a token of thanks will be of no effect." When Japanese doctors of the Zenrin kyokai (Japan's Good Neighbor Society) tried to freely serve the Mongols in an effort to impress them with their charity and good works, the Mongols still pressed gifts on them.

Among the various staff members of Japan's Good Neighbor Society, the Zenrin kyokai, operating in Mongolia, one of the finest men was Dr. Aoyama. He was a very personable man and was particularly successful in his clinical work in West Uju-muchin, near the banner administrative offices (yamun). He was working there in the late 1930s. Due to his success and the very favorable impressions that the Mongols had of his work, he was appointed an official government doctor early in 1940 and transferred from the Good Neighbor Association to a Mongolian government clinic located at the Shilin-ghol League administrative offices just east of the Pandita Gegen Monastery (Pei-tse-miao).

As his reputation grew and as more and more people were attracted to his clinic for treatment, he naturally came into competition with the Lamaist doctors resident at the monastery, but he seemed to be able to handle this situation without any great problem and no incident or serious conflict arose out of the situation. It seems that Dr. Aoyama was originally from the island

[115]

of Kyushu, where he reportedly was a specialist in the treatment of leprosy. Among our people in Shilin-ghol, he practiced general medicine, mainly treating eye problems, skin problems and the usual cuts and bruises, together with a little internal medicine.

One thing that was particularly commendable about this man's work was the fact that he took great pains to avoid involvement in political activities or spy work, an approach quite different from many of the other men who served as staff members of Japan's Good Neighbor Association. It is not surprising that, due to his great service, many of the people brought horses, sheep, brick tea, and many other things to him as presents to express their gratitude. He never really sought payment but, nevertheless, over the years of his work in Üjümüchin, he gathered a very respectable little herd of animals that were of considerable value.

Some people are curious about the prayers lamas offer up for the curing of diseases; they want to know about the significance and function or content of the prayers. Our feeling is that most importantly the prayers are for the benefit of all living beings, for their health, peace and happiness. During my many varied experiences, my purpose has always been to promote and build up the teachings of the Buddha and to care for the welfare of the people. While I lived in Mongolia, in addition to praying and preaching, I tried to be a good doctor to the people. Later in Taiwan, I continued my work for the good of mankind. I have never had an interest in money or politics. There is a long, venerable tradition separating our religion from such mundane things though, but of course there also have been many cases of exception to the tradition.

I practiced medicine in Mongolia because I felt it to be a great benefit to the people but also because it was very interesting to me. While I lived at Badghar Monastery, I had an upper room in which there were eight images of Otochi (deity of medicine) about full size. (The word *otochi* is an old Mongolian word, not a Sanskrit term; anciently it meant a medicine man, and a *chaghan otochi* was regarded as a very special, excellent doctor.)

The circumstances around my decision to study medicine may be of interest. One night I dreamed I had a very impressive interview with four of the Otochi in which we discussed many things regarding medicine. After awakening, I was impressed that this was possibly a revelation and that the Otochi were trying to transmit to me special information regarding the healing of illnesses. The following morning after the dream, my *soibon* (attendant), who was a *mamba* or doctor, happened to come into my quarters. His coming also seemed to me an omen confirming my dream, and I felt the occasion was a proper opportunity to request him to become my teacher in traditional Tibetan-Mongolian medicine since he had a very good reputation. This incident was the beginning of my medical career. From that time on, assisted by my teachers, I began to give medicine to patients who came to the monastery and had very good results, so my reputation as a doctor grew. My teacher was very encouraging, saying that it was fine for me to continue to develop in the learning and practice of medicine, and that there was no objection to it because it would at least be of benefit to my own personal health.

All of this took place before I was even seventeen years old, which seems now rather amazing. As I previously mentioned, after turning seventeen, I travelled to Üjümüchin and met the Panchen Lama. Because of my indecision regarding a career, I requested of him an *abral*, a special blessing to assist one in making a decision or to gain special spiritual advice. In response, His Holiness confirmed my earlier feelings and strongly encouraged me by saying that I should continue in my medical work, that my labors would greatly benefit the people.

I practiced medicine until I was thirty-two years old and generally had excellent success in healing people who came to me. Because of the turmoil of the wars, the Soviet invasion, and the chaos in Mongolia, however, I lost all of my books and manuals and dared not continue my practice of medicine. My medical practice was not for money, for in those days all my needs were most adequately satisfied.

Though it may seem that Mongolian lama doctors are completely superstitious, this is not the case. Lama doctors base their diagnosis on the examination of a patient's pulse and on a test of their urine. A common preparation lamas made for medicinal purposes involved the boiling of particular herbs. After the liquid or juice was poured from the herbs into containers, it was then given to the patients. For some medicines the liquid was put in hot water and used to bathe the body or the patient's affected part. For the treatment of arthritis and rheumatism we prepared a special medicine by gathering bones and boiling them for a long time. Then we used the solution to bathe the affected limb of the patient. For elderly patients we frequently prepared a tonic

[117]

called *mamar*. It was taken internally and reminds me of the vitamin preparations I hear of used in modern countries. For elderly patients we often prepared ginseng herb (*orkhodoi*). An important activity of a lama's medical practice was the gathering of herbs, and we were very fortunate to find many very useful and valuable herbs on the great grasslands of Mongolia.

We are indebted to a Chinese scholar of a late Ming period, Li Shih-chen, for his *Pen-tsao kang-mu*, an encyclopedia of herbology that is very useful in identifying, classifying, and preparing herbs. But its use has been limited since few lamas read Chinese. I made a comparative study of this Chinese reference work with that of the sutra on herbs in the Tibetan language and noted various differences in the preparation and use of herbs by Chinese doctors and by our Mongolian lamas. The Chinese have traditionally given patients a sizable amount of a particular herb that is boiled and drunk. Mongolian lama doctors have customarily given their patients only a small amount of the herb powdered and taken directly, without being boiled.

Apart from medicine, some lamas specialized more particularly in a study and practice of *jurkhai*, mathematics mixed with astronomy and astrology. These men were adept at predicting eclipses and determining which days were auspicious for special events and decisions. In our science of *jurkhai* we are able, for example, to determine the length of a man's life. This is done by calculating from the mathematical divination manuals. The general category of *jurkhai* may be further divided into the subcategoreis of *shira* (yellow), *chaghan* (white), and *khara* (black). The Mongol lamas have been devoted almost entirely to the practice of *shira* and *chaghan* mathematics and astronomy. Mongolian lamas identify the Chinese form or approach as simply *khara* (black). *Khara* has a negative connotation and here it arises from the view that Chinese *jurkhai*-type psuedo-science comes from the old Taoist, or some would say ancient animistic and shamanistic tradition of ancient China. It has similarities to the Mongolian tradition but is largely seen as alien to the Mongolian tradition so the lamas are skeptical of it. After the Yellow Sect of Buddhism became dominant in Mongolia, *khara jurkhai* practices, for example, those used to cast evil spells and curses were forbidden. But these practices still continued in Chinese *jurkhai*.

Intimately involved with this field of *jurkhai* was our Mongolian calendar that was given to us periodically from the seat of the

Dalai Lama in Lhasa, Tibet. From ancient times the calendar of a people had determined with whom they were associated or to whom they were subordinated. Many of our Mongolian princes followed the *cheng shuo*, the correct calendar of the Peking court, but the monasteries and the lamas followed the calendar of the Dalai Lama and the Tibetans. Both the Tibetan and the Chinese calendars are based on the lunar system so the length of the years and the various months are the same. In some cases there were a certain number of double calendar dates while other dates were missing. Also, there are differences in what Mongols or Chinese regard as auspicious dates; some numbered dates may be skipped or substituted for others.

Part of the important equipment of the *jurkhaichi* lama has customarily been a board on which is placed the ashes of a heated and ground shoulder blade of a sheep. These ashes are then smoothed out, and from these the lama writes, using a metal stylus to formulate his divination. Having once noted certain calculations, he can then erase these with his index finger and continue with other calculations. I have always been fascinated with the lama's use of these things and their association with religious education. Anciently, the shaman (Mongolian *böe*) used the shoulder blade of a sheep that was heated, cracked, and then read in the process of divination. Also in ancient Shang China, those who practiced divination frequently used the shoulder bone of an oxen or the shell of a turtle. In all of this I cannot help but wonder what changes are taking place in Mongolia, with so many changes due to communism, modernization, and the Chinese.

PART FOUR

Politics and Religion in Inner Mongolia

Visits to Peking and Mongolian Regions

Ordinarily lamas are quite sedentary and spend most of their time cloistered in the monasteries. But it seems that for much of my life I have been on the move, almost like a nomad and through the years I have met many interesting people and situations, a few of which I will note here.

In the spring of 1927, I journeyed to Bargha in eastern Mongolia. Enroute I stopped at Peking where I banqueted with Chang Tso-lin, then the generalissimo (*Ta-yüan-shuai*) in Peking and head of the Peking Government or, as most people said, the dominant warlord of North China. I heard reports that the Northern Expedition of the Kuomintang forces was marching to unify the country and there was much political excitement. Of my many activities in Peking, I recall we held a formal reception and banquet to which I invited various important Mongolian leaders and officials resident in Peking, including Prince Gungsangnorbu, Duke Ling-sheng, and Governor-General Hang Chin-shou who was then nominally the administrator (*amban* or *tu-t'ung*) of the Chakhar area. Also attending the banquet was Prince Sungjin-wangchugh. The background or experience of these leaders should be mentioned for they were all very important men.

Prince Gungsangnorbu, originally from Kharachin Banner, was at that time the head of the Mongolian Tibetan Ministry. Earlier in his career he had been a very progressive pioneer leader in that he introduced modern education, had even built a girls' school, and especially had been responsible for the establishment of the Mongolian Tibetan Academy in Peking. It was his unpleasant experience as a moderate, progressive prince to be caught in a tight political squeeze between the old conservative Mongolian leaders who wanted no change at all and the young radicals who wanted revolutionary change. Prince Gungsangnorbu was head of the Mongolian Tibetan Ministry for seventeen years, but because north China was dominated by warlords he was never able to enlarge his work or to realize the success he hoped for. In those days Prince Gungsangnorbu was commonly referred to as *tsung-tsai wang*, the "minister prince," since he was the only prince of all Mongolia who had been made a minister in the Peking government of Yüan Shih-K'ai. Following the Northern Expedition in 1926–1928, as the Kuomintang movement unified China, he resigned and retired to the foreign concession in Tientsin in 1928. He died two years later, greatly saddened by the political situation, the opposition of young radicals, and many other difficulties plaguing the Mongolian people.

Ling-sheng, another very important leader with whom I visited in Peking, was established in northeastern Mongolia in the Hulunbuir region, where his family was very rich and powerful. The son of an aristocratic, famous old Mongol leader, Kuei-fu, Ling-sheng was a very devout Buddhist, and a disciple of the Panchen Lama. He was also a firm supporter of the traditional Manchu imperial line and gave large sums of money to P'u-yi, who later became the puppet emperor of the Japanese state of Manchukuo. After the Japanese occupied northeastern Mongolia, Ling-sheng, because of his prestige, was made governor of Hsingan, autonomous Mongol Province. Later, during my travels to eastern Mongolia, this great political leader was executed by the Japanese Kwantung Army. Ling-sheng had been greatly disillusioned by some of their policies, had become strongly anti-Japanese, and, in collusion with certain Outer Mongolian leaders, plotted to free Mongolia from outside oppression from both Russia and Japan. His death was a tragedy for Mongolia.

Hang Chin-shou, an elderly Mongolian gentleman served, when a young man, in the office of the Manchu Governor-General (tu-t'ung) of the Chakhar region, learned to read and write Manchu very well, and later became the nominal head of Chakhar, which was a great distinction; indeed, the highest position in that area to which a Mongol could rise.

Prince Sungjinwangchugh, who also attended my banquet in Peking, had a very interesting career. He was born in a princely family in the Khuuchid Banner in Shilin-ghol League (region).

Because his elder brother inherited the position as prince of the banner, Prince Sung was placed in a monastery to be trained as a common lama. In this monastic role he had a very strict teacher who took him on a pilgrimage to the great monastic center of Kumbum in Kokonor; he had to walk almost the entire way, leading the camels in a caravan. Living in the monastery he directly experienced the difficult discipline of the common lamas. Fate apparently had a special mission for this young man who developed a most impressive personality and character. I was told by our Mongolian elders in Peking that because Prince Sung's elder brother joined the Mongolian Independence Movement (1911) and moved with half of the population of the Khuuchid Banner into Outer Mongolia the remaining half was weakened and without a head (jasagh). The young lama, Sungjinwangchugh, journeyed to Peking where some of the Mongol leaders there, knowing the situation, went through complex governmental and legal procedures to have this young lama established as head of the banner. Later, Sungjinwangchugh, a young lama his brother had left behind, grew to have considerable influence among our people in Inner Mongolia, eventually becoming the head of the entire Shilin-ghol League region and, during the 1940s, the head of the Mongolia Restoration Commission in the Kalgan Mongolian Government. I met him frequently in later days and, because of his devotion to Buddhism, we became very close friends.

From Peking I journeyed to Mukden, where I worshipped the protector of the Buddhist law, Makhaghala, who was enshrined in a temple of the same name. Because the deity Makhaghala was the protector of the Manchu imperial clan, a great national temple was dedicated to him in the outskirts of the Forbidden City in Peking. In Mukden I also visited the Eastern Tombs and the even greater Northern Tombs of the early ancestors of the Manchu-Ch'ing Dynasty. From Mukden I travelled north on the South Manchurian Railway, then dominated by the Japanese. At Harbin I transferred to the Chinese Eastern Railway, still dominated by the Russians, and journeyed to Manjur (Manchuli). In this place I was very pleased to meet a White Russian who had been an important patron in this area of my former incarnation. Now an important merchant in northern Manchuria, dealing with the Bargha Mongols, he invited me to his home where I enjoyed wonderful hospitality.

[125]

Dashimagh, the place I desired to visit in the Bargha region, was about twenty-five miles from Manjur. On arriving there, I was met by a contingent of Mongolian troops all drawn up in ceremonial array. They were under the command of Mongolian officials who were still wearing the traditional Manchu official, mandarin uniform, including the button of rank (jerig) and caps adorned with a peacock feather (otogh). In those days it was strangely anachronistic that the Mongols, who were under the Republic of China and later in the 1930s came under the Japanese, still had their princes and officials wearing the old traditional Manchu dress. This tradition actually continued until 1942 when the Mongolian Autonomous Government in Kalgan was organized and a few young nationalistic officials persuaded Prince De to abolish the costume.

Another thing that also surprised me very much was the fact that even at this late date the Manchu language was still the official language in the areas of Bargha and Butekha (Daghur). All of the official welcoming speeches on the occasion of my arrival were made in Manchu and I understood nothing.

As I arrived in that area, the people prostrated themselves before me in a formal kow-tow and later, after the ceremonies, I was taken to Shar-noghoi Monastery. The Bargha Banners in those days were quite small and there were only about three sumu ("arrow" = a civil-military administrative unit numbering about 100 households) in each banner. The amban official of Hulun-buir at that time was a Mongolian named Obgon. Even when the Mongol banner heads talked to each other among themselves in official capacity, they used the Manchu language. The terms they used in discussing the various administrative units of the Mongol areas were likewise designated by Manchu terms. All of this was because the area had long been under direct Manchu governmental jurisdiction. When I visited Barga, the military strongman over all Heilungchiang was the Chinese governor Wu Tsün-sheng.

Here in the Bargha area, at the Shar-noghoi Monastery I met the two major civil administrative heads (üker da). One was known by his personal name Shi and the other by Erkim. Their titles üker da is a mistranslation of the Manchu word niu lu; niu, meaning cow in Chinese, is translated into Mongolian as üker, and da is a Manchu word meaning "the head." The correct Mongolian term should have been ghar-iin-da. Though it was not commonly used, it means the head officer of a "flank," a military organization.

The term üker-da meant, according to the Manchu governmental system, that a person holding this title was the administrative head of a "flank," a large administrative unit. At that time one üker-da administered the affairs of four Mongol banners, and under him a subordinate official, ghaliin-da, administered two banners. Under these two sub-officials were other officials termed janggi, the head of an administrative unit called sumu, and a khafan, a governmental clerk.

All these various officials and the lamas gathered together in the main hall of the Shar-noghoi Monastery to welcome me, where I was seated on the official seat or throne of the monastery and ceremoniously presented the symbolic mandala. I was very fortunate, being only a boy of fourteen, to have the assistance of my teacher in all the protocol of the occasion. The people at the monastery prepared a special large yurt for my accommodation. The culture of the Bargha area was somewhat different from what I had been accustomed to in western Mongolia, in Ulanchab or Chakhar.

I was, by then, quite fluent in the Mongolian language and able to communicate with various people. There were some dialectical differences in the language that puzzled me a little at first. For example, in western Inner Mongolia in greeting a person we say sain bainu but people in the Bargha area say khain bainu. In the west we say süü for milk, whereas people in Bargha say ükü. The Mongolian dialect I had learned was like that spoken in Chakhar, but fortunately Ishighawa jasagh da-lama, who accompanied me, was able to interpret and help me when necessary. A custom that seemed very strange to me at the time was the method of greeting among the people. They would kiss a younger person on the forehead as they met them. Often they would kiss them first on the forehead, next on the cheek bone, and then lower on the cheek, this being symbolic of heaven, earth, and man. Because of the instructions of Ishighawa, I was able to understand these things rapidly and be effective and proper in my relationships with other people.

Later, after I went to the home of Shi üker-da, I was presented with a mandala and 1,000 taels of silver. In those days in the economy of that area 1,000 taels of silver was the equivalent of perhaps 500 to 1,000 head of sheep. I had many patrons in this

[127]

area and thus was very busy honoring the requests I received to perform for them individually a special *tsewang*, which meant that they would then be authorized to read a particular scripture themselves, both lamas and laymen. I went from home to home, visiting my more important patrons, and reading scripture to them.

Each time I arrived at a home, my patrons would have my horse stop directly in front of their yurt, which was a great honor, and they would also roll out a special carpet of white felt leading to the door of the yurt upon which I would walk. As I entered the yurt, I was seated on the place of honor facing the doorway and presented ceremoniously with a *mandala*. Along with this presentation there was ordinarily a gift of animals, money or wealth. I was then presented with *chagha*, white food presented to a high lama. Next came milk tea followed by cookies and other refreshments. Ordinarily on these visits I would also be served a light lunch and again in the evening a whole sheep specially boiled. The fare of this special evening meal would depend on the wealth of the family. In some cases I was presented a *jom*, an entire sheep, and at other times, the *uuchi*, the two hind quarters of the animal, or merely the shoulder or a large piece of meat. In addition I was always served rice soup. Upon the presentation of this feast, my personal cook (*jama*) would slice the meat and place the head, two ribs, and a hoof on the special platter before the altar of the Buddha. This meat offering seems contradictory to conventional Buddhism, but one must keep in mind that Mongolian society is traditionally nomadic and that meat, the most common food, also becomes a common, acceptable offering.

The yurts in which I stayed were always said by the people to be facing south, but actually it was the direction from which the sun rose so it must have been east. It seems that originally this was a practical arrangement to avoid the wind and dust from the north but then the eastern direction took on a religious meaning. Ordinarily a yurt in a stationary position faced the south east. I noticed as we traveled that the men erected our tents in a set, customary fashion, and raised them from the ground, beginning with the corner facing the direction in which we were traveling. This was symbolic of opening the path of our continuing journey to good fortune. And the tent was facing east when it was erected. The following day as it was collapsed for the continuation of our journey, the men carefully rolled up the canvas tent, beginning from the left or north side as one faced the east.

I became aware while traveling in Bargha and other regions of traditional customs and some taboos peculiar to that area. For example, it was taboo to lean one's hand against the pillar or door of a yurt upon entering, leaving, or standing by it. During the meal when the bones were cracked, the marrow was to be eaten only by the elders present. As we travelled in the caravan, it was always the *ghal-iin akha*, the captain or head of the caravan, who had the privilege of eating the marrow. In Mongolia the people often have great regard for some sacred mountain; in this region it was Mount Boghda, and thus I had my attendants carry special offerings to the mountain. In Mongolia as we traveled to such sacred places, the local people were very careful not to openly mention the name of a sacred mountain or river, for this was believed to be an offense that would cause some hindrance to the journey.

These various taboos in Bargha were similar to what I had observed on a different occasion in western Inner Mongolia as I travelled from Badghar through Gül-chaghan (all white) Banner in the Chakhar region. In Gül-chaghan Banner was a slope called Engiin Khairkhan, where, I was told, the bones of the *böe*, male shamans, and *üdgen*, female shamans, were buried in the old days. As we were travelling, I noticed that our traveling companions avoided saying the name of the place and I insisted on hearing what it was. Soon after they told me the name, a fierce wind arose which caused great problems with our tents and other traveling gear and put us in some danger. My teacher, Yontson *baghshi*, then prepared a special sacrificial cake made out of rye flour (*baling*) as an offering, and gave a special prayer. Thereupon the wind subsided and we were able to continue our journey.

Later, on another occasion when I was traveling to Ujümüchin in Shilin-ghol, as I stopped at the summer residence of the Prince of Abagha, called Küitün-shil (cold plateau), I innocently mentioned the name of the place. It seemed that the local deities were again offended at this and there arose in the night, on the occasion of the festivities which had been prepared by the prince, a fierce wind that carried away the tents and overturned the very heavy carts we were using in our travels. Thereupon Master Yontson read a special scripture we call *Shibdagh dorom*, *shibdagh* meaning local deity and *dorom* meaning prayer, and again the wind subsided. Thus, from rather sad experiences I learned to respect the shamanistic practice of the local people, the taboo forbidding the open mention of the name of local sacred places.

Another similar situation also comes to mind, a case at Dolonor regarding the Shandu River. The goddess of this river is considered to be a sister of the goddess of Kerulen River in the vicinity of Badghar Monastery and the people in the Shandu region are careful not to openly mention the name of the river. When they are a safe distance from the area and mention the name, they sometimes refer to it as the *ergü Shandu*, *ergü* meaning "stubborn" because of the river's many twists and turns.

On my return journey from Bargha country, we took the same route and made it safely to Harbin. Here the Chinese general Chang Tso-hsiang, commander of the Chinese troops in the Chilin (Kirin) region invited me to be his guest, to dine with him and accompany him on a boat trip on the Sungari river. This was the first time I had ridden a steamboat. By the time winter had set in, we had returned to Badghar Monastery where we spent the entire winter. I spent my fifteenth and sixteenth years (1928–1929) at the monastery here studying Buddhist scriptures.

The days of my teens, in the late 1920s and early 1930s, were very difficult. One particularly terrible experience was a great drought and a plague of locusts, which began in Shensi, covered some seventy districts (*hsien*), and moved into northwest China and the Mongol border, making it almost impossible for us to obtain grain. Circumstances became so difficult that even the Chinese farmers did not have food, and it became necessary for them to powder the bark of trees and eat it to maintain life. We even heard of cannibalism in distant places. Fortunately no one in Badghar starved to death because it was possible for us to obtain milk products and meat from the nomadic regions.

By my seventeenth year, 1930, Ishighawa *jasagh-lama* succeeded Ya *jasagh* as the administrator of my affairs. After completing the big prayer assembly of the third lunar month, I traveled to Chakhar by caravan as usual and passed through the region of Mingghan Banner, staying for a time at the summer residence of *amban* Jodbajab, the chief official in this place. A summer home for such an official was not so much a luxury, as it so often is for aristocratic people of other countries, but it was a regular necessity, for the *amban* changed his residence with each season, a continuing influence of the nomadic background of the people

[130]

and the climate of the area. This meant that in the summer the *amban* moved to a residence situated rather high in a mountainous area. In the winter he resided in a basin or some other place protected on the north by a mountain against the cold. In the spring and fall he sometimes had a temporary residence but not set in a particular place.

Progressive younger Mongols regarded Jodbajab as a conservative official, the senior of the various *amban* in Chakhar. He tended to be strongly pro-Manchu during the late Ch'ing period, and following the Republican Revolution in 1911 became equally pro-Chinese. Jodbajab was a courageous, single-minded man; and though he perhaps lacked good political judgment, he was famous for an incident at the time of the Republican Revolution when Outer Mongolia declared independence. The famous Manchu imperial grazing area of Darighanghai was under his jurisdiction when the Khalkha banners declared independence, occupied the strategic area of Darighanghai and moved into Inner Mongolia. In attempting to recover this area, Jodbajab made a military campaign or incursion into the area but was captured by the Khalkha forces and taken to Urga where he was imprisoned. Later he was repatriated to Inner Mongolia. Because of his loyalty and his courage in attempting to regain Darighanghai for the Peking Government, he was highly commended by the Peking government of Yüan Shih-k'ai and commissioned a lieutenant-general. This is one reason why he eventually became the senior *amban* among the eight banners and four pastures of Chakhar, each of which was governed by an *amban*.

After the Manchurian Incident (Mukden) in 1931 and Japan's expansion into Inner Mongolia, Jodbajab was very cooperative with the Japanese. Because of this, he was often criticized and strongly opposed by many Mongol nationalists. But some people forget that his faithful friend and close advisor, Nima-odsor, was assassinated by the Japanese and this was a very intimidating thing to Jodbajab. Finally, after the collapse of the Japanese in 1945, Jodbajab was captured by invading Mongol and Soviet forces and taken to Ulan Bator (Urga), where he died.

From Mingghan Banner we journeyed to Gül-köko (all blue) Banner, of Chakhar, where we also stayed for a time, being unable to continue on to Dolonor since it had been plundered by the Chinese bandits in the fifteenth year of the Republic (1926) and had not yet recovered. In Gül-köko I had a small personal resi-

[131]

dence, a *labrang*, where we were very comfortable. At that time the head man of Gül-kökö Banner region was Bawa *amban*. While there we received a report that the Panchen *boghda* had arrived to Üjümüchin Banner where His Holiness was going to perform a great ceremony, the *duingkhor-iin wang* described below. We felt it was very important that we attend this great occasion because everyone who attended had his name recorded on the special roster of troops who were to be the faithful ones to defend the Law of the Buddha in the last days of chaos in the great struggle for the sacred land of Shambhala. Representatives from the prince of Üjümüchin Banner were sent specially to invite me to this ceremony.

I, of course, was very eager to go, and immediately a caravan was prepared for our journey and we left for Pandita *gegen* Monastery (Pei-tse-*miao*) in Abakhanar Banner Shilin-ghol League. From this place we would then move on to Üjümüchin. At that time the incarnation of this monastery, the Pandita *gegen*, was still a young boy. Together we performed the special ceremony *samjin molom* and then I prepared to journey to Üjümüchin. While the men of the monastery were making special arrangements for our trip, I stayed in the private residence of the Pandita *gegen* who had seven special apartments in his suite. I especially enjoyed the *kumis* drink for which the Shilin-ghol region was famous. We first traveled to Khuuchid Banner and from there to Üjümüchin. Upon our arrival, we were treated with great hospitality and special quarters were prepared for us in a fine yurt. We were not hosted by the prince but rather were taken by his order to the Nunai *shang*, the *shang* here being a combination of an office and staff living quarters which looked after properties that belonged nominally to the Dalai Lama. In reality everything here was under the jurisdiction of Sodnamrabtan, the prince of Üjümüchin and head of the whole Shilin-ghol League. Nunai *shang* was not really a monastery although a small number of lamas lived there.

Üjümüchin Banner had for many reasons been one of the richest banner areas and the most nomadic area in all Inner Mongolia and thus had attracted many Chinese merchants hoping to make a fortune. After I became acquainted with the prince here, Sodnamrabtan (So *wang*), some of the people told me of an interesting incident that had occurred some years before in connection with the Prince's father. It seems that the old prince was very attracted to new hobbies, trinkets, toys, and other things that came from China. Realizing this, one particularly shrewd Chinese merchant brought him a special doll, a *pu-tao-weng*, which has a lead weight in the bottom and is rounded in such a way that it will always stand up and not stay knocked over when hit. The prince was quite pleased with this new trinket and in his enthusiasm gave the Chinese merchant the fantastic sum of one hundred taels of silver as a reward. Other merchants, seeing this generous bestowal of riches, were greatly impressed and felt they too must somehow take advantage of such a situation.

One particularly scheming type, knowing that the prince liked black donkeys because they were not native to that area of Mongolia and were quite rare, had a black donkey brought especially from north China into Üjümüchin for the Prince. In presenting his gift, the merchant subtly suggested that it would be fitting if he were given one thousand taels of silver as a reward for his thoughtfulness and trouble. The wise old Prince, seeing through this scheme, gained the best of the merchant by noting that since he, the merchant, had given him something valuable, he, the Prince, must give something valuable in return, and he gave the merchant the *pu-tao-weng* doll he had greatly prized as a gift from an earlier friend. This little doll was of course very common in the stores in north China, and the price of the donkey or the sum of silver expected by the Chinese merchant would have bought hundreds of them. This little story is somewhat representative of what was happening in Mongolia in those days as I travelled through the various banners, finding Chinese merchants taking advantage of our Mongolian people in many areas and in various ways.

To all who know Inner Mongolia, it is clear that Üjümüchin was a very special banner, because it had the largest grazing areas of all the banners of Inner Mongolia. Thus, with its many herds it was the richest according to the standards of a nomadic society, its prince was a most influential and important man. During this stay, I was visitd by him, Prince Sodnamrabtan. In all of the so-called "feudalistic" banners of Inner Mongolia this prince was the only one with the rank of *ch'in wang*, who was not a relative by marrige with the old Manchu imperial court. He was a well-known patron of the Panchen Lama, and when the Panchen came to north China, Prince So invited him to Üjümüchin.

[133]

At that time there was no temple or monastery in all of Inner Mongolia for the Panchen Lama, and it would be some time before one was built. The young Prince Demchügdüngrüb of the Sünid Banner, who was later to be the head of the Inner Mongolian Government, proposed to the other princes of the league that they establish a monastic temple for the Panchen in Inner Mongolia. Eventually one was built in about 1931 or 1932, sometime prior to the beginning of the Mongolia Autonomous movement in 1933.

This temple was not built in Üjümüchin as one might expect but rather in Sunid Banner, which helps explain the important relationship between Prince Demchügdüngrüb and the Panchen Lama. On looking back on the significance of this matter, it is obvious that Prince Sodnamrabtan of Üjümüchin was not an aggressive, competitive type man, while Prince Demchügdüngrüb of Sünid was an ambitious young prince with political objectives for a Mongolian separatist movement from China that were to arise but several years later in the Bat-khaalagh (Pai-ling-miao) Movement. Obviously he was already farsighted enough to see that connections with the famous Panchen Lama would be useful in the future. The pine trees for the wood to build this fine temple were transported from Kokonor (Chinghai) by caravan to the Yellow River and then floated down river and overland to Sünid. I think the plans were drawn by a Peking architect while the Chinese labor was contracted from Shansi.

Our quarters in Üjümüchin during our stay were several miles from the official residence of the prince (ordo), and each morning he sent a messenger to wish us well and to inquire about our health and necessities. I had already made the acquaintance of Prince So earlier during my first visit to Peking in 1924. He had come to Peking to pay his respects to the Panchen Lama during the earlier visit to Peking of this second most important incarnation of the world of Lamaist Buddhism. At that time a rather interesting occurrence took place. Prince So's mother was with him, and, being a very filial son, he always paid great respect to her. She was very distressed to see men pulling other men around the city in rickshaws like animals and instructed Prince So to forbid any of his people to ride in the rickshaws. Consequently, they were forced to hire horse carts, automobiles, or other such conveyances. For an elderly Mongolian lady coming from the nomadic areas into the big city, this was a rather enlightened view.

One reason Prince Sodnamrabtan of Üjümüchin and I had a close relationship was that my previous incarnation had gone to his residence to sustain him and to pray for his safe return when he made an important and difficult journey to Urga to pay his respects to the Jebtsundamba. I do not know the exact date of this visit; it took place before the Outer Mongolian Independence Movement (1911) but had no connection with it. Also, whenever Prince So came to Dolonor (Doloon-nor), he usually stayed at our monastery where we prepared a special yurt for his private quarters and held a reception for him. These and other similar occasions offered us the opportunity to develop a close relationship.

Because the visit of the Panchen Lama noted above was a very important occasion, many people came from all areas of Mongolia, both rich and poor, lay and ecclesiastical. Among them was the Molon-lama gegen, an important incarnation who was the abbot of the Lama-iin küree (monastic temple), the largest and most elaborate in all of Üjümüchin Banner, built strictly in Tibetan style. In 1945, at the end of World War II, as Soviet troops came in with Japan's withdrawal, there occurred here a curious incident that was witnessed by many people and reported far and wide. The Russians fired a large cannon at the monastery but the projectile became so wrapped up in the many khadagh and decorative fabric hangings of the altar of the monastery that it was stopped and left hanging before the image of Maidar (Maitreya). It hung there for a long time because everyone was afraid to remove it.

There were in this monastery at the time of my visit about eight hundred lamas. The Molon lama gegen and I from that time saw each other frequently and developed a close friendship. The great prayer ceremonies, the Duingkhor-iin wang, carried out on this occasion by the Panchen Boghda, lasted for seven days, and I and my teacher were given special seats in the front. The ceremonies consisted mainly of the Panchen Lama's personal reading of special scriptures accompanied by chants and monastic music of the lamas.

When the Panchen lama was performing the Duinghkor-iin wang liturgical ceremony in Üjümüchin, he was seated on a very high dais and surrounded by thousands of lamas and lay people gath-

[135]

ered from many parts of Mongolia, too many for me to estimate. They were gathered in the open air and, while many could not hear clearly, they felt that they would be blessed if they could only hear the bells of the ceremony. I was quite young at the time and, therefore, the impressions I have are of such obvious things as the great number of people and the fact that the Prince of Üjümüchin was a very large fat man. In Üjümüchin the common people traditionally believed that if the prince were fat the banner would be prosperous. Whether true or not, the prince was invariably a large man. While there was hardly any direct connection, Üjümüchin was in fact the richest banner of all the nomadic regions of western Inner Mongolia. In spite of the enormous number of people attending, the great prayer ceremony at Üjümüchin was much more orderly than a similar occasion at the Pandita Gegen Monastery that had been performed earlier by the Panchen. On this earlier occasion the people were very rowdy and ill-mannered in their competition to press forward to gain the blessing of or to pay respects to the famous incarnation.

During the ceremonies I was very pleased that the Panchen Lama looked at me kindly several times. Afterward, I paid my personal respects to him, and during our conversation he inquired about my studies and general situation. I explained to him what I was studying and that I was trying to become adept in Buddhist medicine, and he gave me much encouragement.

During his stay in Mongolia, there was considerable competition among the many princes and important people for honors from and for good relations with the Panchen Lama, and he had a close relationship with the princes of Üjümüchin and Sünid in the 1930s. I maintained a dignified distance, however, and did not at first become a close disciple.

Everyone knew that this Eighth Panchen Lama had fled Tibet and was traveling in Inner Mongolia under the sponsorship of the Peking government. Mongols are aware that when there is trouble in Tibet the Tibetans often prefer to take refuge in Mongolia. This happened earlier in 1904 when the Thirteenth Dalai Lama fled from the Younghusband Expedition of the British to Urga. Great Tibetan dignitaries like the Panchen Lama would come to the capital of Peking, and preferred to travel in Inner Mongolia since they regarded the people there as part of the same religion and found Tibetans in the various monasteries of Inner Mongolia. In the 1920s and 1930s there was a clash between the followers of the Dalai Lama and the followers of the Panchen Lama, and in the power struggle the Panchen Lama was forced to flee from Tibet. We welcomed this famous Tibetan incarnation with rejoicing and always felt that he was very warm and sympathetic to our Mongolian people.

During this stay in Üjümüchin, the Panchen Lama authorized me to perform the *Duingkhor-iin wang* ceremony and from that time I regarded him as my *guru* or master. Such an association with the Panchen Lama was very rare in those days and was a highly prized honor striven for by lamas and reincarnations.

There was one incident that came to my attention in this area of Üjümüchin. A very rowdy lama caused so much trouble that he was ordered to be beaten by Nasun-ochir *jakiraghchi*, an important man in West Üjümüchin Banner. In Mongolia one rarely hears of princes or banner authorities punishing a lama. It occurs, but it is quite rare. This case had a sad ending, however. It seems that Nasun-ochir *jakiraghchi* worried so much about the problem that he died. To understand his intense worry, one must realize that the aura of Pandita Gegen Monastery is notorious for its *khaaral*, black magic. The *jakiraghchi's* great fear was that he would be the victim of some evil tragedy that would come upon him because of the *khaaral* practiced by the lama he had beaten.

Religion and Politics in Change

1931 was a difficult year for us in many ways. There occurred a terrible epidemic, a fever illness that took the life of perhaps two hundred lamas at Badghar, many of them senior and venerable scholarly lamas. My close friend the Duinghkor *gegen* also contracted small pox, which made it necessary for me to take over all of his duties in presiding over the various ceremonies and prayer assemblies at the temple.

One of my respected teachers, *baghshi*, also fell seriously ill; when I visited him on the fifth day of the eleventh month (13 December), I found that he could not even open his eyes. In my distress over his illness, I made special prayers on his behalf and presented to him a *mandala*—a Buddhist graphic symbol of the universe, a circle enclosing a square with a deity on each side. One of his attendants whispered in his ear that the *gegen*, himself, had come to pay his respects and to present a *mandala*, which in this situation meant that we were beseeching him not to pass into nirvana but to remain with us and to teach us for yet a long time. I was greatly saddened when he slowly raised his hands in the pose of a prayer and beads of tears began to appear in his eyes. I knew from this that he would not receive my mandala, that his time had arrived, and I returned to my room with a heavy heart. The following morning messengers came to report that Master Yontson had already shown the düri of nirvana (manifestation of liberation from life and death). Later, a second messenger informed me that the venerable teacher had sat up, made the motion of prayer, opened his eyes, and then passed away. This was the sixth day of the eleventh month (14 December), the hour of the snake (9–11 A.M.). I then recalled that my teacher had earlier remarked that it would be better for him as an elderly lama to leave and take the plague with him. For seven days we performed the customary prayers and ceremonies in his memory and soon, to our great relief, the plague passed from the monastery. Even after the passing of my venerable teacher, we continued to pray that there would not be a recurrence of the plague. My teacher's body was placed at Altan oboo, the site of burial for all of the more important lamas of Badghar. Thus passed away this unhappy year.

It is interesting that all the lamas who aspire to be a great debater in the choyir competition of the monastery sometimes go to the site of Altan oboo and after clapping their hands in the special way we begin a debate, they actually carry out a debate. There were frequent reports that venerable teachers from ages past appear from the dead to debate with them. Other people who went there only to meditate report that they heard debates carried on by those who have long since passed away. The lamas of our monastery believed that after such an experience a lama is then superior in his wisdom and ability to debate.

It was in the following year that the Duinghkor gegen began to attend the formal prayer masses of the monastery. After I turned eighteen years of age, on the sixteenth day of the seventh lunar month (7 August), 1932, Arba-yampa, commonly known as Ya jasagh, died. This also was a great loss for me, because, as I have mentioned previously, it was this fine teacher who brought me as a young child from Kokonor and played an important role in my installation as the incarnation of Badghar Monastery. And it was he who struggled against the Jangjia *khutughtu* when he opposed and troubled the followers of my former incarnation.

That same year during the tenth and eleventh month (November and December) I completed the examinations and ceremonies necessary for obtaining the title of *gabji*, and in so doing fulfilled my obligation of furnishing *manja*, ceremonial tea, to all the monks of the monastery. Though these activities ordinarily required considerable money, they caused me no difficulty because of my status as an incarnation. Common lamas found it difficult to gather the necessary sum of money from various patrons in order to make a presentation to the monastery and to pay for the refreshments to be given to all of the lamas. The title of *gabji* may be an honorary degree and in this way is different from the degree of *gebshi* that is very roughly comparable to a high university degree for many people in the Western world, though prestige depended very much on the monastery from which the degree was obtained. In some of the less famous monasteries of Mongolia, obtaining the degree was not so arduous, but at Badghar it was highly prized and rather difficult to acquire. It was, of course, especially difficult to obtain such a degree from one of the three great monasteries in Tibet because of the very high standards and the difficulty in amassing enough money to host all of the lamas of such a great monastery in a ceremonial tea (manja).

On the seventh day of the eleventh lunar month (4 December) we customarily held the special ceremonies associated with the *doibsun*. I, of course, assumed responsibility for part of these ceremonies. Also the Duingkhor *gegen* now began to attend the formal prayer assemblies and prepared to share the ceremonial responsibilities. I directed the lighting of the incense, followed by the circumambulation of the temple with the incense, coming finally to the college (*datsang*) of the *choyir*, which specializes in Buddhology. I then performed the *damcha*, a ceremony in which I made a formal report to the Buddha of my success in passing the examinations for the *gabji*. This year passed without any notable occurrences.

The following year, 1933, when I was nineteen years old, we invited the Panchen Lama to come to Badghar Monastery. He was then staying at the Bat-khaalagh Monastery, well known as the second largest monastery in Ulanchab League and as a junction for the caravan routes from different parts of Mongolia. This year was particularly significant due to the fact that I officially came of age, assumed the Kanjurwa title and role and the management of affairs associated with it that previously were exercised on my behalf by the staff of the monastery.

From the spring of 1933 this place became very famous as the site of the important conferences that launched the Inner Mongolian Autonomous Movement, the most important internal political movement in Inner Mongolia during the next two decades. Bat-khaalagh was located in the Darkhan Banner governed by Prince Yundonwangchugh, who was concurrently head of the Ulanchab League and an important political figure of that time. It was later, as I came to understand a little more of the politics of Mongolia, that I understood that our Mongol leaders were forced to take action because the Japanese were occupying eastern Inner Mongolia and were preparing to move west into our areas. The Mongols had to be decisive and bring about a new Mongolian unity, a united front against such regional warlords as Fu Tso-yi and Sung Che-yüan, on the one hand and against the Japanese on the other.

In those days our strongest nationalistic leaders, Demchügdüngrüb and Yundonwangchugh, talked secretly among themselves about such strategy as *bölkomlin khamghalakh*, "collective security," and made the very daring move of holding special meetings far to the west, close to the area of Fu Tso-yi at the Bat-khaalagh Monastery. The Panchen Lama indirectly encouraged the movement, though he had to be very careful, very subtle in such political matters or he would certainly be in trouble with the Chinese.

It seems evident in these ecclesiastical politics that the Jangjia gegen was greatly influenced by the Chinese, especially warlord Yen Hsi-shan who always involved himself in Mongolian affairs. The Jangjia was going to come to Bat-khaalagh to neutralize or counter the autonomous movement. But it seems that the Mongolian students and intellectuals in Peking demonstrated against him and even threatened bodily harm if he moved against Mongolian political aspirations. I felt that he was wrong to get involved in politics, but at the same time I disapproved of the radicalness and militancy of the students. Actually the incident was misdirected, for as long as the Panchen was there it was not possible for the Jangjia to do anything. The Panchen stayed at Bat-khaalagh during the entire time these important meetings were being held;

but finally, when it appeared that everything was quite successfully settled, he traveled to Badghar Monastery, on to other parts
of Mongolia, and then to Peking.

When the Panchen Lama visited the Badghar Monastery, he
brought with him an entourage of some forty or fifty people. Our
temple was not rich and could not give him large sums of gold
or silver as could the prince of Üjümüchin. Consequently, our
gifts to him were rather modest. We were able, however, to
establish a very close relationship with him on the basis of our
Buddhist faith. As his disciples we were able to receive from
him certain *wang* and *lung*, the right through ordination to preach,
read, or promulgate certain sutras or perform other special ceremonies.

I requested that he bestow upon me the *sanwar*, the oath of
the rank of *gelüng*, the second-stage oath of a lama. Before His
Holiness, the Panchen Lama, performed the ceremony (*dorumb*),
it was my role to gather all of the lamas and to perform the
damcha ceremonies, which are important to the acquisition of
the *doromba* degree of academic excellence in the monastery.
The Panchen Lama himself sat by to observe. I had been studying
very intensely to prepare for this monastic degree, but I had
mastered completely only one and a half of the five texts required.
I was pressed by my teacher to achieve this degree from the
Panchen Lama while he was there and I tried, but my preparations
were not complete. Still the Panchen said that he would confer
the degree upon me with the agreement that I continue my studies
of the necessary texts under the very capable teacher Sambu
rabjimba, a Torghud Mongol. After this was decided, the degree
was conferred as I stood behind Sambu *rabjimba*, who vicariously
received the ceremonies in my stead. After the Panchen conferred
upon us much merit of the Law, he left Badghar for a short time
on the seventh day of the fourth month and went once more to
Bat-khaalagh Monastery. Before he left, all the lamas in our temple
beseeched him to confer upon them the *lung* of *Shambhala*.

Several days later I left Badghar Monastery to travel to Gül-
kökö Banner in Chakhar. Here at the Yeke Burkhan Monastery,
I presided over a large prayer meeting, and also officiated at some
of the surrounding monasteries and even at some of the local
oboo shrines. The following year I made a similar circuit to visit
some of the temples in Chakhar for the same purpose. I spent

[141]

most of 1934, my twentieth year, residing in Gül-kökö, in the Chakhar area where I had many followers.

In 1935 I received another formal invitation to journey to the Bargha region of northeastern Mongolia and made preparations to travel there by caravan. After traveling through the Chakhar Banners, my entourage and I stopped for a time at various places in Shilin-ghol League, visiting my followers there, including those in the Abagha Banner, the Pandita Gegen Monastery, and the Khuuchid Banner. We also stopped in Üjümüchin East Banner and visited with Duke Dobdan who was serving as a regent in handling the affairs of this banner because the prince here was but a boy. Duke Dobdan prepared a caravan for us including ten men as an escort guard and we traveled to Bargha via Soyoliji mountain and Tabunsalaa, on the border area of Khalkha. Here the three conflicting spheres or forces of Russian oriented Khalkha Mongolia, Japanese-dominated Manchukuo and western Inner Mongolia came together.

A year or two before undertaking this journey a rather strange rumor came to us that there was a communist incursion from Outer Mongolia into Chakhar. In spite of this rumor, I traveled from Badghar to our monastic center in Dolonor and during this trip learned how the rumor, actually baseless, was started. It was due to a misunderstanding on the part of Mongol people who had little awareness of the outside world. The rumor was that the "Oros" (Russians) were invading. To us the term Oros means the Russians, but some people use it in reference to all foreigners, as shira oros (yellow foreigners = Caucasians). As a matter of fact it often also referred to the "Eriben oros," literally Japanese foreigners also called khara oros (black foreigners). The rumor was caused by some activity of the Japanese. By that time, all of Khalkha had, of course, been taken over by the communists and was then known as the Mongolian People's Republic (Mongghol arad ulus). It was somewhat risky to travel in this border area, because many places were a no-man's land where one might be shot at or arrested by border guards patrolling the area.

Our stop at the hot and cold springs at Khaluun-arshan was particularly enjoyable. These springs have for centuries been a special place to which many people gather to be healed by the special waters. According to the Sanskrit name of this place these are not common waters, but rather specially blessed of the Buddha for the healing of people. Here there are some seventy different springs of varying temperatures and mineral content, each known for its power to treat a different disease.

Khaluun-arshan is very close to the border of Outer Mongolia, or the Mongolian People's Republic (MPR), so close in fact that the springs where we were staying were just east of the border and on the other side of a nearby hill or mountain was the territory of Outer Mongolia. At the time of our visit we felt we were under a cloud of pressure; there was great tension between the Japanese on this side and the Russians on the other; both sides involved the Mongolian people in a confrontation. The place had become a recreation area for the Japanese and also a base for operations against the MPR. It really was not possible for us to relax and be at ease.

The fine, famous retreat of Khaluun-arshan was also widely noted as a religious retreat. The lamas often remarked that the overall outline of the many springs, as viewed from a distance, formed the appearance of an Otochi, the god of healing and medicine (Skt. Bhaisajya-guru-raidurya-prabhasa). Amazingly the hot springs are never so bubbling hot as to be uncomfortable in the summer and the cold springs never so cold as to freeze in the winter. The total area of this retreat covers several acres. In each place where the springs come to the surface there were small huts in which one could live and rest.

From the retreat of Khaluun-arshan we traveled to Ch'angch'un, then the capital of Japanese Manchukuo. Here the Mongols were better treated than they had been earlier under the Chinese warlords and regional Chinese governments, for example in the matter of land problems. We then continued on north to Bargha where we visited many places throughout the various banners of that region. This was a most enjoyable occasion.

On our return journey to western Inner Mongolia we visited a number of the eastern Inner Mongolia areas, stopping at some of the larger Chinese cities including Mukden, Chin-chou, and Jehol, and finally arriving at Dolonor. In Jehol we visited many large monasteries and temples, particularly those built under the patronage of the Manchu court.

I spent that winter in Dolonor, which was now occupied by the Japanese, although they had not yet moved too far west into Inner Mongolia. We were nonpolitical, but were in a difficult position between the warring forces of the Japanese and the Chinese. Though I had traveled widely in Japanese occupied areas of eastern Mongolia, it still seemed advisable at this time that I not remain at Dolonor, because it was fast becoming an area of intrigue, pressure from Japan's Kwantung army, and activity of their military intelligence groups. Therefore, I moved a bit farther west to the Gül-chaghan (all white) Banner of Chakhar. Our important temple center, Badghar, was still to the west under the political influence of the Chinese warlord Fu Tso-yi, who was felt to be the greatest immediate threat to the Mongols.

My twenty-second year, 1936, I spent almost entirely in the Chakhar region, traveling among the various Mongolian areas serving as a diviner, a medical doctor, and offering special prayers on various occasions. My major purpose was to raise the spiritual level and the general well-being of the people.

As one of the most important incarnations of all Mongolia, it was frequently my responsibility to receive many lamas from various temples and to perform the ceremony we call *mörgöl tabikh*. In this ceremony the lamas and the lay people, young and old, male and female, would come one by one and kneel before me to pay respect and I would then place my hand on the head of each person in a symbolic gesture of blessing or cleansing. For lamas I would always use my hand, but for lay disciples I would only on occasion use my hand, touching them at other times with a *darkhad*, a sacred sceptre. When someone came to me of high rank, an incarnation such as the Duingkhor *gegen*, for example, it was our custom to bow together in such a way that our foreheads touched. When I met incarnations who were superior to me in rank, I customarily bowed to them in deep respect. The *mörgöl tabikh* ceremony ended with a *mani*, the six-syllable sacred *tarani* formula repeatedly chanted to invoke the name of the Buddha.

There were, of course, different levels of formality in our ceremonial greetings and exchanges of courtesy or ecclesiastical protocol. When the *mörgöl tabikh* was formal, the lamas or lay disciples would present to me a *khadagh* (ceremonial scarf) and perhaps also place some silver coins upon the *khadagh*, which would then be taken by one of my assistants who stood by me on such occasions. Whenever I received or went to visit someone of equal rank, we customarily exchanged *khadaghs*.

I was just twenty-three years old when there occurred the great tragedy of war between China and Japan beginning on 7 July, 1937, with the Marco Polo Bridge (Lu-kou-ch'iao) Incident. While this great conflict broke out, I was spending the summer in Gül-kökö Banner of Chakhar. At first the war did not directly affect Inner Mongolia, but it did affect us indirectly, and we spent long hours praying for the end of the killing and for the restoration of peace. The winter of 1938 I spent at Dolonor and in the spring traveled to Kalgan by car.

This important center is known to Western people by the name *Kalgan*, to the Mongols by the name *Khaalghan*, and to the Chinese only as *Chang-chia-k'ou*. Both the Mongol name and the Chinese term *k'ou* mean "gate," referring to the importance of this place as a passage through the Great Wall. This city has been a strategic place and an important administrative center from ancient times when it was built around two large fortresses known as Shang-pu and Hsia-pu, the upper and the lower fortresses, about one mile apart. If one searches hard, one may find in the Hsia-pu area a small hole in the great wall which is the entrance referred to in the famous name Chang-chia-k'ou. Certainly this is a reference to the gateway of some old Chang family who lived in the vicinity. Though these fortresses were no longer of any importance, this site became, through the Ming dynasty, an important place for the stationing of Chinese armies on the Wall and also an important border market where Mongols and Chinese met. It was to this area that most of the great caravan trains from the Khalkha Mongol region came into China and where exchanges were conducted just outside the Great Wall, in the vicinity of a large gate known as Ta-ching-men. By 1937, large numbers of Japanese troops had come into many of the areas of Inner Mongolia; it was virtually all occupied.

After staying in Kalgan for a time, I traveled west by train back to Badgher. That following winter the Duingkhor Pandita *gegen* received the high degree of *gebshi*. There were many festivities and ceremonies and people came from far and wide to enjoy this grand occasion. I attended the very special occasion of the *mi-yandagh*, a special ceremony for conferring degrees of rank in Tibetan Buddhism. I was happy in the presence of all the assembled lamas and dignitaries of the monastery to make a formal presentation of the ceremonial scarf to Duingkhor *gegen*.

During my twenty-fourth and twenty-fifth years, the learned lama Yontson, upon the request of Duingkhor *gegen* and myself, journeyed from the Naiman Banner of eastern Inner Mongolia to visit us and teach us certain important scriptures. This lama was

[145]

noted for his learning, but did not have any particular prestige in political, economic or other matters. Sometimes during these years, Dimpiral Iharamba, generally known as Naiman Toyin Gegen, became one of my more important tutors. Besides being a venerable teacher he was also an incarnation from Bor-keüken Monastery and a brother of the prince of Naiman Banner.

In 1940 I once again left Badghar Monastery and traveled to Dolonor via Gül-kökö Banner in Chakhar. By this time we had reestablished our monastery in Dolonor which had earlier been plundered and destroyed during the turmoil of China's early Republican period. The new buildings were erected with the help of Chinese contract labor. We were then able to refurbish the benches, paint the walls, guild the images, and other such things. I continued to live in Dolonor during 1941 and performed many important ceremonies and rituals.

During this period we heard news of a new development in Japan's war in Asia; that is, the attack on Pearl Harbor and the outbreak of a war with the Americans and the British. This did not have any immediate impact on us, secluded as we were in the monasteries. We were not to realize the real significance of the conflict until the defeat of Japan and the occupation of Mongolia by Communist forces. Even now the complexity of political developments during these years is a puzzle to me. But one thing impressed upon my memory is that in these years the political leaders of our Mongolian Government in Kalgan, such men as Prince Demchügdüngrüb, and Prince Sungjinwangchugh of Shilin-ghol, were more fearful of danger from the north, from the Soviet forces, and radical Mongolian communists than from any other quarter. This danger seemed real but did not come until the collapse of Japan in 1945.

With the Pacific War there was no disturbance in Inner Mongolia and life went on much as before. However, as the months passed the greatest distress came from the demands of the Japanese for heavy economic requisitions from our herds and resources due to the pressures of the war crisis. Also, it became difficult for us to obtain such things as cloth, tea and sugar. Most of our leaders who were aware of the situation felt that Japan's launching of the new offensive against the Americans was most unwise; some said it was suicidal, the beginning of the end, and brought the necessity for the Mongols to plan for the future without Japan's protective domination.

In 1942 I again received a formal invitation to visit the Bargha region where the lamas desired that I once more perform the great duingkhor prayer assembly. This custom in the Bargha region was first established by my previous incarnation and two men from Bargha, Ghombudorji and Jungnai. After deciding to develop the elaborate ceremonies of the duingkhor loilung, they contracted with Ta-ch'eng-yü, a rather famous company in Dolonor that was very expert in manufacturing various containers and objects necessary to Buddhist religious ceremonies, such as bronze images and silver and golden objects. They had many beautiful items made, mostly out of copper and gilded with gold, a number large enough to fill a large prayer assembly hall in the great monastic temple in Bargha.

The word loilung is a Tibetan word for city, but in our ceremonies it meant that there was created in the main prayer hall of the monastery a large and impressive replica of the sacred city of Loilong which then became the focal point around which the religious ceremonies took place. This was the second largest holy replica of loilung in the world, the largest in all of Mongolia and second only to that in Tibet. While these ceremonies were begun and a plan for their insitutionalization were inaugurated by my former incarnation, it took some thirty-six years to complete the work because of the fall of the Manchu dynasty, the Chinese Republican Revolution, and other events such as the "disturbance of the Year of the Cow (1913)," the Khalkha expansion into Inner Mongolia during which my previous incarnation was killed. The ceremony was finally completed in 1942 when I was twenty-eight years old.

Meanwhile all of Manchuria and much of Mongolia was occupied by the Japanese, and it was a large task for us to transport the numerous manufactured sacred images and implements by caravan to Bargha. The people in Bargha determined that the Duingkhor loilung or replica be established to the north of the Namghor monastic temple on a large hill. First it was necessary to erect a large hall into which all of the sacred objects were installed. Because this was such an immense project to plan, and because the erection itself was a great task, all of the various Bargha goldsmiths, coppersmiths, and others gathered at the site near Namghor Monastery to assist in the completion. In Inner Mongolia it was very common to contract Chinese labor for the

[147]

construction of monasteries and temples, whereas in Bargha this was done almost entirely by Mongolian hands.

It is of interest that most of the money for this great undertaking was furnished by the Buriad Mongols according to our reports. As the Buriad people came under the domination of the Russian Soviet forces after the Russian Revolution, a sizable group of them escaped to eastern Mongolia under the leadership of such men as Namdagh *noyan* and Ayushi. After much trouble they finally settled in the region of Hulun-buir in a place called Shinke. Later, a sub-group of these Buriads, who had escaped from the revolution in Siberia, migrated from Bargha to Shilin-ghol League and settled on the Modon plateau under the leadership of Er-inchin-dorji. Soon after, they became disciples of the Panchen Lama.

It seems that these Shilin-ghol Buriad people broke off from the parent group in Bargha because of some internal problems, but as they migrated into the Shilin-ghol region, because they were outsiders, the local Mongols were reluctant to have them settled in their area. The Buriad Mongols asked various banners to allow them to settle in their lands, but problems arose over pastures and administrative jurisdiction and they remained isolated. The group, numbering about one thousand, finally found an area in the southern part of West Khuuchid Banner which was not occupied because half of the banner had migrated to Outer Mongolia when the great Jebtsundamba Boghda declared independence from China (1911). Here the Buriads finally settled.

Soon after, when the Panchen Lama visited the Üjümüchin region of Shilin-ghol, they paid their respects and beseeched him to intercede for them with the *jasagh* of Khuuchid and the prince of Üjümüchin, who was then head of the entire Shilin-ghol League. The Buriad Mongols wanted the Panchen Lama to arrange for them to become his *shabinar* (disciples) and to gain permission for them to live in the rich grass pastures on the Modon plateau. This the Panchen Lama did, and as a result they enjoyed a special status in the league, not being subject to any particular banner nor to its taxes or recruitment of troops and other customary controls. They paid only a token rent for the entire, extensive pasture area. As time passed, with Japanese involvement they became even more isolated and, because of various problems, a hostility grew between them and other Mongolian peoples.

With the Japanese occupation, the Buriad group in eastern Bargha was organized into a special banner unit with its own administration. The group in Shilin-ghol remained separate and soon came under domination of the Japanese military intelligence organization (tokumu kikan). The organization was suspicious of Mongols who had migrated from Soviet areas but also saw special uses for them in possible future operations in Soviet Mongolian areas, so they guarded them closely, at the same time giving them special privileges. This special treatment, of course, caused further trouble with the other banner peoples in Shilin-ghol. At the end of World War II the Russians invaded this area, and the majority of the Buriad people were forced to return to Siberia. Several hundred were fortunate enough to escape Soviet hands and migrate to Kokonor and Sinkiang in the far western areas of China. Some of them passed by Badghar on the way.

One reason I became involved with the Buriad people is that after they settled in Bargha a certain friction developed between them and the other local people. When the Buriad later decided to build a large monastery to the Buddha, the neighboring Bargha Mongols were worried because the monastery was to be built on Bargha land. Finally, after some problems and discussion, the Buriad and the Bargha decided to compromise—they invited me to the monastery, dedicated it to me and thus it belonged to neither.

The Duingkhor loilung, a sacred, symbolic replica of the holy city mentioned above, was to be installed in this monastery and dedicated by the performance of special ceremonies called the Duingkhor wang. Since I lacked experience, being only twenty-eight years of age, and because I felt that these ceremonies were too extensive, too complex and important for me to handle alone, I requested assistance and had some twenty lamas and scholars from Badghar accompany me, particularly my teacher from Naiman Banner, Yontson lama.

All of the lamas from Badghar came from the Duingkhor college and even before leaving Badghar Monastery made extensive preparations for the ceremonies in Bargha. For one thing, they prepared a special replica of the holy city made by a special dolsum ceremonial process that uses various colors of powder and which is complex, difficult, and very artistic. We Mongols associate this dolsum ceremony or function with special prayers for rain, for avoidance of natural disasters, diseases, and prayers for peace.

[149]

There was a large rain in Bargha just prior to the beginning of the Duingkhor ceremonies. Now I cannot help but be melancholy, wondering whether these sacred objects still exist or whether they have been destroyed by the communists.

A very large number of people, perhaps thirty thousand, gathered to observe the ceremonies and the dedication. It was a most impressive sight—this extremely large number of people camping round about with their yurts and animals. While the Buriad were a minority, they were very prominent and some of their important leaders attended the ceremonies, including General Urjin, who later became an important commander of most of the Mongol troops in Hsingan Mongolia under the Japanese, and Erinchindorji, leader of the Buriad group that had migrated to Shilin-ghol.

The prayers and ceremonies continued for seven days, after which I remained for another month, visiting with the people. After leaving Bargha, I returned by train via Harbin, Ch'angch'un, and Mukden, continuing through Peking to Kalgan. By this time the Mongolian Autonomous Government had already been established in Kalgan for several years.

The Japanese and Mongolian Buddhism

In 1943 I was invited by the Japanese to travel to Japan in company with some dozen other high-ranking lamas to inspect various Buddhist centers in Japan and to observe conditions generally. The trip was approved by Prince De, head of the Mongolian Government in Kalgan. Over the years many lamas and others went to Japan for visits of different types. On my journey I was accompanied by a group of Mongolian Buddhist leaders, including the shabrang (lowest ranking incarnation) of the Yongjigiin Monastery of West Üjümüchin, the shabrang of Ghaikhal Monastery of East Üjümüchin, and also the Toyin lama of Yangdu Monastery of Abagha Banner. This Toyin lama was from a very influential family and his older brother Budabala was at that time the deputy head of the entire Shilin-ghol League. His father, Yangsang, a venerable old prince over eighty years old, earlier had been one of the most influential princes in all Inner Mongolia. He was a very conservative old prince who hated the Japanese and also opposed all progressive reforms promoted by liberal, young Mongolian nationalists. He said, "no good ever comes from reforms." Jangchub Lama of the Tümed Banner of Bayan-tala League (Suiyüan) was also in the group, along with the Mergen gegen, incarnation of the Urad Front Banner of the Ulanchab League and Tobdanjams Lama from Badghar Monastery. I was appointed the chief representative of the group by Prince De, head of the government. Previously lamas had gone as individuals or as small groups to Japan, but this was the first time such a large influential group made up entirely of lamas had gone.

Our entire expenses were paid by the Mongolian Government in Kalgan and ostensively the objective of the journey was to visit various Japanese Buddhist centers and to observe conditions generally in Japan. Indeed, we did visit many places such as Tokyo and Kyoto and were welcomed and treated very warmly and hospitably in Japan. It was our feeling that the Japanese objective in this undertaking was to impress the Mongols that they also are devoted Buddhists, to have us observe the ceremonies in their temples, and thus to influence us and, in turn, Mongolian Buddhism. This was not a direct and forceful influence, but rather a tactful and subtle one. In addition to such visits as the one made by our group, a number of young lamas were taken to Japan to live in Buddhist centers, mainly at Koyasan and in Chionin in Kyoto, to be trained in Japanese Buddhist ways.

In addition, a number of so-called Japanese lamas came to Mongolia and stayed in various monastic temple centers. They were very conscientious in attending the khural prayer masses and various ceremonies in the monasteries during the day. At night they often seemed to be very busy writing things and this seemed curious to us; it seemed to involve some connection with Japanese officials or intelligence people. It is our feeling that the spiritual development of all lamas who come to the monastery is an individual matter, it was for each to determine his own relationship between Burkhan (Buddha) and himself. But the monasteries were, of course, very strict concerning a person's status within the monastic community; this was a long-standing tradition. Consequently, the so-called lamas from Japan were not enrolled on the official roster of the monastery; they were entered on a separate list maintained for guests or visiting lamas.

Before my groups of lamas visited Japan, others went as individuals or in small groups. One rather important group that preceded ours in about 1938 included the Chaghan gegen, the incarnation of the Chaghan-oboo Monastery of East Sünid Banner just near the border of Outer Mongolia. In this group were the Mergen gegen, an incarnation from Mergen-juu Monastery situated in Urad Front Banner of Ulanchab League, and also the Gabji Lama of the Gabji Monastery of East Üjümüchin in Shilinghol League. At this time two groups of lamas were sent to Japan at different times for the purpose of seeing some of its historic places, especially the great temple centers of Kyoto and Koyasan.

The objective of the Japanese for requesting such visits was, as noted earlier, to impress the Mongol lamas that Japan was indeed a Buddhist nation and had great, ancient Buddhist centers. Such visits were significant partly because many lamas had serious reservations about whether the Japanese were truly Buddhist. While they saw the Japanese armies and their impressive military equipment and political, cultural or economic activities, they did not see much that convinced them that the Japanese really were Buddhist. Another reason for the Japanese sponsoring excursions for Mongolian Buddhist leaders was to promote their Buddhist reform activities in Mongolia. They were hoping to make changes in the monasteries, and in Mongolian Buddhist doctrine, so they brought a number of young lamas to centers in Japan for education and special training. It was their objective to convince the older leading lamas that these activities were good and that they should not be opposed. It was also the intent of the Japanese militarists to promote the idea among the lamas that their war was a "holy war" in the cause of Buddhism.

My memory of this visit to Japan is still very keen. Not only were we extended gracious hospitality but were given the opportunity to visit some of the ancient historical temples in the region of Kyoto and Nara. We were hosted by the great Honganji Temple, headquarters of the important Shinshu sect of Buddhism that is the predominant sect in Japan. Our party was deeply impressed with the temple center at Koyasan, near Osaka, in a beautiful secluded area in the forested mountains. This center serves as the headquarters of the Shingon sect of Buddhism, the sect in Japan that is closest to Tibetan Buddhism, both religions being of the esoteric tradition of Mahayana Buddhism. Prior to my visit, a training school had been established for lamas brought from Mongolia, and we were interested in visiting with these young monks. It seemed to us that the Japanese were having difficulty changing their ideas and attitudes. Although quite young, in their twenties, these young men were already somewhat set in their ways. Japanese Buddhism seemed to us much closer to Chinese Buddhism and to have a spirit rather different from that to which we were accustomed.

We were greatly impressed with the fine gardens, with the numerous plants and shrubs set in a very natural landscape, something lacking in our own monastic settings. Japanese temples seemed to us to be too close to the cities, though we realized that such beautiful gardens would attract worshippers to the temple and allow them to feel close to nature. Our Mongolian monastic temples are mostly established in the rather boundless expanse of the steppes and dominate the landscape, and our people are attracted to their solitary magnificence. It is my impression that the Mongols who come to our monastic temples tend to identify more with the institution itself, whereas Japanese, as they make a pilgrimage, feel closer to nature.

A point often stressed to us was that the Japanese have magnificent temples but few monks and that it would be well if we Mongols also could have more elaborate monastic temples and fewer lamas. Another important difference that impressed us was that most Japanese priests and even the highest abbot of the great temples marry and thus there is a hereditary lineage in the perpetuation of temple administration. Though the Japanese tried to encourage Mongol lamas to marry, we never accepted this custom. Anciently, lamas in Tibet were free to marry, and when Buddhism first came to Mongolia, this marriage custom came also and has been perpetuated at two important centers in Inner Mongolia, one in eastern Mongolia at the Lama Küree Monastery in Josotu League and the other in western Mongolia at the Shireetü-juu Monastery of the Tümed Banner in Hohhot.

These two institutions were, of course, exceptions in Mongolia and were greatly criticized by lamas from other temples who felt that such a practice was a compromise of spirituality with carnal or temporal life. The followers of Tsongkhopa adopted a custom of having the most important leaders of our religion and the great heads of the monasteries reincarnated from generation to generation, thus preventing a hereditary monopoly of the institution by the powerful families. This policy kept the monastic institutions more open to all the people and to new blood coming into the religion's top leadership.

[153]

Mongolian Buddhism settled this problem of marriage versus nonmarriage among the lamas long ago, and our policy was supported by the Mongolian Government in Kalgan, although for quite different reasons. They believed they could more effectively limit the growth and influence of the church by restricting the lamas from marriage. This meant that young lamas inclined to marry had to leave the temple and return to the secular world with all its responsibilities and problems. We were very impressed with our visit to Japan and welcomed closer relations with the Japanese Buddhist leaders, but we did not welcome changes in our traditional culture, least of all our religious institutions.

After returning to Badghar monastery, in the fifth lunar month (June) of 1943, I participated in the prayers and ceremonies at the *oboo* shrine. It was at this time that the Duingkhor Pandita *gegen*, my life-long friend, passed into *nirvana* and I presided over the various necessary ceremonies in connection with his death and burial. Then I returned once again to Dolonor.

In 1944 I was invited to Bat-khaalagh Monastery (Ch. Pai-ling-miao) where a new *oboo* shrine had been established, and I participated in the dedication ceremonies. All of this took place because of the destruction that occurred when Fu Tso-yi, warlord governor of Suiyüan province, invaded Mongolia. In a battle that took place there on the tenth day of the tenth lunar month (23 November) 1936, Bat-khaalagh Monastery was damaged and the *oboo* shrine was entirely destroyed.

I digress to note that this battle was one peak in the growing confrontation between the Japanese and the Chinese, especially Fu Tso-yi, who was the strongman in our area. Japanese influence was growing and some of their military agents had settled in Bat-khaalagh. With Japanese backing, Prince De's Mongolian forces were becoming more active, and in this new situation General Fu attacked to intimidate the Mongols and to strengthen his claim that Prince De had turned against China. Fu Tso-yi's attack was very successful and came to be known by the Chinese as "the great victory of Pai-ling-miao." From Bat-khaalagh I had the exciting experience of flying in an airplane for the first time to the capital at Kalgan enroute to Dolonor. There was nothing important about the trip but I can never forget the airplane ride.

Lamas, Princes and Politics

The relationship between khubilghans (incarnations) and noy-ans (princes) in Mongolia, or in other words between religious leaders and lay leaders, was rather unique or sensitive. On one hand an incarnate lama is one who has left his home to enter the Buddhist priesthood and thus has neither family nor wealth, neither children nor personal worldly possessions. Though living under a prince's territorial jurisdiction, an incarnation was not responsible in doctrine or religious life to the prince. The prince, however, traditionally had full authority over all affairs of the banner region and over matters that affected the arad (people). Accordingly, temples or monasteries within the boundaries of a banner, including its khubilghan and lamas, came under the jurisdiction of the prince in certain matters. But since the prince himself was ordinarily a devout Buddhist, and moreover, since the religion had great influence among the people, the relationship between a khubilghan and a noyan was at times somewhat com-plex and delicate. All affairs associating the two were normally handled with care to avoid problems.

Generally speaking, a monastery was exempt from the taxes and corée exactions of the yamun (official office), but there were situations in which it was necessary for a monastery to give financial support to the yamun. And a prince often felt some responsibility for the welfare of the monasteries within his banner, hoping they would flourish, become famous and raise the prestige of his domain. This is not an easy matter, however, in view of the fact that a monastery and the lamas were not ordinarily involved in secular work and had no visible means to support themselves as did the lay people. Although, strictly speaking, a monastery was what is now called a nonprofit institution, it was often quite wealthy because of the many donations from the people.

It seems paradoxical that while an incarnation and a monastery were under the political jurisdiction of a noyan, an incarnate lama was above the prince in spiritual affairs. This means that there were many times when a prince came to an incarnation to receive advice and blessings. Even though an incarnation was not directly involved in political affairs, it was common knowledge that he did influence political decisions. Theoretically, it was possible that the jasagh-noyan or chief of a banner might ban

[155]

donations to a monastery and thus eliminate it. But this never happened. The princes or *jasaghs* were themselves often chief patrons. Traditionally anyone who set himself against the lamas and the religion found himself isolated. Just as there is no sum that does not show forth light, there is no Buddha who does not have a monastery and no monastery that does not have *shabinar*, disciples. In short, there is no monastery without some influence in the society around it. Though the princes had difficulty limiting the influence of the religion, the religion in many ways influenced both society and politics. Though involvement in politics was not proper for the lamas, the princes had to be cautious in matters that affected the religion in order not to alienate the lamas.

Occasionally difficulties arose with some lamas or *khubilghans* due to problems of personality or personal tendencies. Sometimes a *gegen* became very worldly. This, of course, caused difficulty, because once an incarnation had been recognized and installed, his disciples and those within the monastery gave their oath to support and maintain him as an incarnation. There was really nothing they could do to retract their oath or to remove the incarnation, so they had to suffer in silence. There were rare exceptions, however, where a lay official not bound by any oath, a brave man with no overwhelming fear of punishment, inter-vened and removed the incarnation.

There was, for example, the case of the dissolute young in-carnation in the famous monastery of Pandita Gegen Monastery (pei-tse-miao) in eastern Shilin-ghol League. Because of his dis-graceful, scandalous activities, and because the monastery au-thorities feared to handle his case, a banner official came one night in 1941 and told the Pandita *gegen* to leave immediately; he was not even given time to pack his personal belongings. This incarnation was dispatched without delay on a pilgrimage to Lhasa, and was instructed not to return to the monastery without official permission. He became a sort of exile. I heard later that he went first to Kalgan and then to Peking where his case was reviewed by a high lama, the Toghon *khutughtu*, whose advice was requested concerning another embarrassing problem, the Pan-dita *gegen*'s scandalous activities in the houses of ill fame in Peking. The Toghon *khutughtu* said that the incarnation should be beaten by his master-teacher. This was done very reluctantly, but energetically. This punishment we call *khal barikh* (offering of suffering). This was distressing for a humble teacher to beat a superior but it was an important service for future development and success of the young gegen. It seems that this was the first beating the young incarnation had ever suffered and it was a turning point in his life. It seems that he repented and became a respectable gegen. There are reports of his good study and behavior in the great monastery of Berabon (Drepung) in Tibet. There he died before he could return to Mongolia.

To understand the situation, one must remember that the relationship between a baghshi (teacher) and his shabi (disciple) was very strict. When an oath was taken by the shabi to obey and to follow, he did so until death. Though he frequently suffered, he did so in silence, not taking any action, as in the case just mentioned, without outside pressure.

In the changing world of that day our young Mongolian intellectuals were often very critical of religion. They said that all of the earlier problems of Mongolia were due to the corruption of the khara and shira piudal leaders (khara means the layman and shira means the lamas; piudal is a loan-word meaning "feudal" that came into the Mongolian language after 1921 with Marxist influence in Outer Mongolia). This criticism causes us distress. Many of our people throughout Mongolia did indeed have difficulties because of taxes. The princes' demands were frequently extreme because no restrictions were placed on the taxes they could exact from the people. In the old days a prince who went to Lhasa and made donations, or to Peking to establish a fine residence, was not supported by his personal wealth. His expenses were paid from exactions upon the people.

We heard the distressing rationalizations of the old princes who said that if they made an expensive pilgrimage to Lhasa or established a monastery from the blood of the people, that it was really for the people's blessing and they should be thankful. Even the people themselves often accepted this view and felt that from their sufferings would come blessings. In cases where the people resisted the exactions of the jasagh, they were brutally whipped, a policy that I feel was extremely foolish. Our situation in Chakhar was not bad, however, because the old system of princes was abolished quite early by the Manchu, and the amban (officials) dared not make extreme demands on the people as happened in other places.

There was a very difficult situation in our religion in the old days. High incarnations were believed to be supermen and they

[157]

possessed power both for good or for bad. A good *gegen* never misused his power to press the people for donations or wasted the finances of the monastery. But if a bad *gegen* was inclined to misuse his power, the money of the monastery, or its disciples, it was difficult to counter his weakness. Ordinarily the incarnation of a monastery had no direct administrative power, for this was in the hands of a *jasagh-lama* or *da-lama*. But problems arose in the relationship between the *gegen* and his *shabinar* or lay disciples. I think the real problem in these cases was not always the fault of the *gegen*, since he was brought to the monastery and installed at a very young age. The fault was often with those who surrounded and instructed him. If they did not train the incarnation properly, he all too often tended to do evil things. Oppressing the people and behaving in a scandalous manner is not in accordance with the teaching of the Buddha.

A basic principle of our religion is *üil ür* (*karma*), the Buddhist law of cause and effect. The word *üil* means "behavior" and *ur* means "seed." As interpreted by Mongolians, this means that one reaps the fruit of the seed he plants; in other words, evil deeds bring their own reward. Thus, many lamas whose actions have been evil, later receive their just reward. According to Buddha, *üil ür* (*karma*) is the same for all men. There is no distinction between the prince, the lama, or the common people. Now we hear of "equality before the law." Retribution is certain; and even if a person does not receive his punishment in this life, he will be punished in his next incarnation. Although I am myself a *gegen*, I cannot deny that some lay nobles and high lamas have caused trouble for the Mongolian people. At the same time, however, one cannot say that the lay nobles' exactions from the people and the people's donations to the monasteries constitute the same thing as the communists' evil practice of taking everything from the people.

During the dark ages of Mongolia, from the collapse of the Mongol-Yüan empire (1368) to the readoption of Buddhism by Altan Khan (1571), the schools, monasteries, art, and medicine as known in my day were virtually non-existent. These contributions can be attributed to the lamas and the monasteries. Some people say that the decline of the population and the economy of Mongolia is due to the Buddhist religion. I believe, however, that the real problem was the lack of development in medicine and hygiene and due to the great wars among our people. There were and are many other things contributing to the poverty of the people that we cannot merely attribute to religion. It is unfair for people to place all the evils and problems of Mongolia at the door of the religion. Anciently Chinggis Khan created the great Mongolian Empire. Can one say that the religion also caused the fall of the empire? I know personally whether I, as an incarnation, have done anything good or bad, but still the people have the right to criticize. If people say that I am good, I am pleased; but if they say I am bad, this does not change the facts. None of us is perfect; each of us has some shortcoming for which he will be personally responsible to his own *karma* (*üil ür*). All of us want to be praised, not criticized. If we become overly worried about criticism, we exhibit a type of worldly, vain concern.

From time to time people are curious about my connections with the Jebtsundamba *khutughtu*, and wonder whether it was proper for this great incarnation of Outer Mongolia to be involved in politics as he certainly was from time to time. I am somewhat reluctant to comment on some of these things, however. While I may give personal comments, it must be kept in mind that I was born in 1914 and was only ten years old when the Jebtsundamba *khutughtu* left this sphere in 1924. Therefore, such knowledge really pertains to my previous incarnation and is something about which I personally do not have a clear understanding. I have had numerous conversations with people who were close to the great Jebtsundamba *khutughtu*, however, and they explain that his controversial political activities were not really of his own volition but must be attributed to those around him.

Our people commonly never refer to the Jebtsundamba *khutughtu* by this title. Instead we use the term Ar Boghda, *ar* meaning "back," the Mongolian equivalent of "outer," and implying "Outer Mongolia," and *boghda* meaning the Holy One. Everyone knows of the two great incarnations in Tibet, the Dalai Lama and the Panchen *boghda*. We see the Ar Boghda as the supreme incarnation in all of Mongolia, and indeed he was the spiritual leader of all Mongolia, more particularly Outer Mongolia. The Mongolian princes throughout the land were his followers and they unquestioningly followed whatever instructions he gave. All Mongols know that the Eighth Jebtsundamba *khutughtu* came as a small child from Tibet. According to Manchu policy he could not be a native Mongolian incarnation. But, the last great Ar Boghda was indeed Mongolian in his feelings, just as myself, for he had

[159]

been raised there and was entirely surrounded and greatly influenced by many important Mongolian lamas in Urga such as the various *shangtsad-pas* and the *soibon-khambu*. The *soibon-khambu*, as his title indicates, was an important personal steward or chamberlain to the Ar Boghda. The *shangtsad-pas*, Badmadorji for one, were administrative officials of the *lama-jasagh*, the controlling office of the monastery, which means their real concern was not with spriritual matters directly but rather with the property and wealth of the monastery, with its many disciples and patrons and other temporal affairs. The high lamas holding this post were essentially the most important administrative assistant to his holiness and his authority or position was confirmed by the Manchu-Ch'ing Government. I am told that these men were shrewd and capable politicians, very ambitious men who had contacts with all the princes and leaders throughout Inner and Outer Mongolia and other places.

These men, probably more than any one else, influenced the Jebtsundamba *khutughtu* and were particularly important prime movers in promoting the independence movement of Outer Mongolia in 1911. They urged the Khalkha princes to rally around the Jebtsundamba and raise him as a new emperor in an independent Mongolia. Thus, they played an important role in the very critical transitional period between the decline of the Manchu Empire and the rise of the Chinese Republic. Because of the great influence of the Jebtsundamba, and in spite of the complex situation in the China-Mongol frontier, the independence movement extended throughout Mongolia. But there were varied responses to the cry to rally to the flag of the Jebtsundamba, particularly in Hulun-buir, and Ulanchab, but also in such strategic areas as Josotu and Juu-uda from 1911 to 1913.

During this crucial time, the situation in our area of Inner Mongolia around Badghar was most complex and there were a great many debates among the princes and other lay leaders and to some degree among the lamas about what should be done. There was really no unity among the people as to their view of the situation. For example, according to one widely spread report, the prince of the Naiman or Bintu Banner very frankly told Gungsangnorbu, prince of Kharachin, that it was fine to have an independent Mongolia but "If we have an emperor, he certainly should be a descendent of Chinggis Khan or someone of his blood, and not a Tibetan lama. It should be either you or I." After much debate and controversy, the high monks and princes of Khalkha finally drew together in a new movement, declared their independence, sought assistance from Russia, and received armaments from that country. What these monks and princes sought was a united Mongolia, not the fragmented Mongolia of my day. They even sent troops into various parts of Inner Mongolia in an unsuccessful attempt to unify a Greater Mongolia.

It is common knowledge that during the Ch'ing Dynasty (1644–1911) the political administration of Inner Mongolia by Peking was much tighter, more consolidated or integrated than that of Outer Mongolia or Khalkha. After the consolidation of the new Chinese Republic in 1912, its military and political strength was once again extended into Inner Mongolia after an extended period of disruption and chaos, so the Chinese were once again able to take control of Inner Mongolia. The lamas in those days had no objection to developing a Greater Mongolia and supporting the Holy One, the Jebtsundamba, as the emperor. They welcomed this on the basis of their ethnic and cultural feelings. I have heard many stories of how the lamas felt that the new Mongolian nation could be a great Buddhist nation, but they greatly feared the Chinese *geming* (a loan word from the Chinese *ke-ming*, having very bad connotations to the Mongols), the revolutionaries, who they heard were determined to tear down the Buddhist religion and destroy the faith. As Mongols we certainly could not condemn any movement to preserve the religion and maintain the Mongolian nation. All of this is only what I have been told. It all happened before I was born; moreover, I have never inquired much about political movements.

The year 1913, just one year prior to my birth, was the worst year in Chakhar, where my disciples were mainly located. The events of this year were known by the people there as *Üker jil-iin uimeen*, the disturbance of the year of the cow. In those days many people wondered why Khalkha troops were coming into Inner Mongolia, and the answer, according to the slogans of that time, was for "the unification of the Mongol people and the protection of the faith." Some of the great leaders of the army were powerful lamas such as Jakhantzun *gegen*, who was a high ranking and intimate friend of the famous Dilowa *khutughtu* in west Khalkha, who was discussed earlier. We heard of the great miracles performed by these powerful lama generals during the movements in those days. During the great incursions of the

[161]

Khalkha troops into Inner Mongolia, the lama general Jakhantzun gegen met my previous incarnation. One great tragedy that occurred during this *Üker jil-iin uimeen,* the disturbances of the year of the cow, involved my earlier incarnation. He was inclined to be involved in politics and was very sympathetic to the independence movement of the Khalkha; consequently, as waves of Khalkha were coming into Inner Mongolia and as Chinese troops were coming to force them out, there were many problems. My former incarnation was an extremely influential and powerful gegen, but his political role was complicated by the fact that there was also residing in Dolonor another famous incarnation, the Jangjia *khutughtu,* who was superior to my Kanjurwa incarnation. Between the many followers of these two incarnations was much competition, struggle, and ill will. The Jangjia *khutughtu* was only a boy, but his disciples, great supporters of Peking, made secret accusations that my former incarnation was rebellious and disloyal to Peking. The final result was that my former incarnation was killed by Chinese troops.

The patrons and disciples of my previous incarnation were scattered in many places of Mongolia but were concentrated mainly in the areas of Chakhar, Bargha, Buriad, and Khalkha. In the latter place they were located mainly in Sechen Khan *aimagh* and concentrated in the San Beise Banner of this *aimagh,* an area particularly well known for the fine horses it had produced. I have heard that the animal herds of my former incarnation in Khalkha and Buriad areas numbered as many as thirty thousand. But in my day the Khalkha herds were lost to Communist confiscation during their takeover in the MPR. However, when I escaped from Dolonor in 1945, I had there herds of over one thousand horses, one thousand cattle, and three thousand sheep. Most of these animals were donations from my various followers and together they constituted a very large herd (süreg). Apart from these herds I had a fine income and therefore it was not necessary to sell my animals to meet my needs. Their natural increase was very great, and I distributed these herds among my *shabinar* (followers) to arrange for their care.

Mongolian princes could perpetuate their properites and status hereditarily from one generation to the next, a tradition quite different from the Mongolian monastic system in which there was no arrangement or provision for incarnations to hereditarily

[162]

perpetuate their properties to personal decendants, since the lamas did not marry nor have offspring.

I have often been asked what the view of the lamas is regarding private property and the possession of things. We know that the Buddha said people should not become attached to possessions and should not acquire property, but lamas are human and naturally acquire some possessions. There are, of course, poor lamas and rich lamas. Those lamas who had some possessions, such things as personal effects or animals, ordinarily brought these with them as they came to the monastery. Also, some lamas acquired a few possessions from the donations of the people after coming to the monastery; these they kept but such possessions were not great. As for the transmission or inheritance of property, when a lama died, his property was passed to his disciples. If a monk had no disciples, his property was placed in the *jisa* or *shang*, the treasury of the monastery. But the property of an incarnation was reserved separately and transmitted to his successor when a new incarnation was installed.

It is commonly felt among our people that the richer a person is, the more he can do for the Buddha; therefore, there was a tendency for Mongols to overlook, or rather not to condemn, the acquisition of property. Whenever lamas acquired considerable wealth through donations or natural increase, they almost always voluntarily donated a large proportion of it to the monastery treasury. Since much of the wealth of a monastery and its donations came in the form of animals from the people, a problem resulted because the animals could be sold only to the markets of north China. Although we knew they were going to be slaughtered, we tried not to think of this, because there was nothing we could do about it.

Another matter that people are curious about is the status and function of *shabinar* or lay disciples of a monastery or an incarnation. My comments on this matter refer only to the *shabinar* of a recognized incarnation who had the status of a *jasagh* and possessed a *tamagha* (seal). A *tamagha* was a seal and symbol of authority and administrative power, and a *jasagh* was one who performed an administrative role. An incarnation or *khutughtu* was concerned with spiritual affairs and, therefore, usually delegated his authority as a *jasagh* to a disciple assigned to look after the monastery's affairs. The relationship between an incarnation and his appointed *jasagh* was a delicate one, for if the *khutughtu* was a capable man, he controlled the *jasagh*; if, however, he was not capable, he was often controlled by the *jasagh lama*.

As for *shabinar*, there were various categories which should be mentioned. There was a general, common type of *shabinar* who were mere believers, disciples without any particular obligation or assigned function. They come voluntarily to pay devotion to the incarnation and to receive his blessing. Though they call themselves his disciples they are really only nominal *shabinar* and their obligation is purely religious. They come under no jurisdiction or administration of the incarnation and are not subject to his taxes. A second type was *unaghan shabinar* who were directly controlled by a *jasagh lama* or by the office of the *tamagha*. These people derive their status from an old custom according to which a Mongol prince who gives men or even families as gifts to a monastery or an incarnation prompted by a desire to show religious devotion and to gain divine favor. These people are commonly referred to as the "property" of the institution. They really were not "property" in the usual sense, however, because they could not be freely disposed of. It was not possible, for example, to take their personal belongings from them. At the same time these people were not free to come and go as they pleased and leave the jurisdiction or service of the incarnation or monastery. Moreover, the descendents of such *unaghan shabinar* were perpetually, from generation to generation, in the service of or under the jurisdiction of the institution to whom they had been donated.

In our areas of Inner Mongolia, it was possible for a prince to give *arad*, the common people, as a gift, as *shabinar* in this way. However, there was a special group of people we called *khariyatu* who were personally attached to a prince of a banner. Their status was similar to that of the *shabinar* of monasteries or high lamas in that they also were attached to him hereditarily for service. But they also were not considered slaves or property and could not be sold or disposed of freely. In some places these persons were not entered on any roles for military recruitment or taxation. In other places they could not be used for service in the banner administration, but they could be given to the daughter of a prince to follow her in marriage to a new household.

The main purpose or role of *shabinar* was to serve the *khutughtu* and to sustain the religious system in which they were involved.

[164]

When their khutughtu passed on, it was important for them to obtain a new incarnation in order to maintain their role and perpetuate the world as they understood it. Their devotion to the khutughtu was not merely a spiritual dedication, but rather a total dedication. They made whatever sacrifice was necessary to support and serve him, and administer to his needs.

Incarnations had two different approaches in arranging their shabinar. According to one approach, rather than drawing them together, the shabinar were distributed among the people and had no definite pasturing or administrative area (notogh). Then there were those cases where an incarnation had a definite section of grazing land on which their shabinar were drawn together and could be taxed to support the incarnation and expand his influence.

The Kalgan Mongolian Government and the Lamas

Buddhist monks generally view themselves as being apolitical. Though their influence on politics is seldom direct, one cannot escape the fact that political changes in Mongolia have often been linked to religion and the lamas; the influence went both ways. Certainly the long period of China's Republican Revolution, then the period of the warlords and the unification of China by the Kuomintang (Nationalist) forces, followed by a period of rule by the Central Government all had a great influence on the functions of the religion as well as the lives of the lamas.

Another major political development influencing all Mongols, both in and out of the monasteries, was the rise of Mongolian national consciousness and a desire to achieve self-determination. Young Mongols of that time were strongly influenced by the currents of nationalism when they went to such places as Peking and Japan for education. The young people's sense of nationalism became stronger particularly during the 1920s and the early 1930s.

I was very young then, living at Badghar Monastery isolated from political involvement, and, of course, I am no expert on political movements that took place in Mongolia at that time. The political developments were very important, however; the Mongols were fighting for their very existence during those years and none of us could entirely escape. Naturally all lamas did not respond in the same manner to the various political movements.

[165]

They reacted in different ways depending on their age, background, family, personal associations, the location of their monastery and past experience.

From the beginning of the 1920s, with the weak central government in China, our area of western Inner Mongolia fell under the domination of the northwestern warlords. Among them was the Moslem leader, Ma Fu-hsiang, later minister of the Mongolian-Tibetan Affairs Commission in Nanking in 1930. Though he was a Moslem he did not interfere with our religion nor trouble our monasteries. Still later in the warlord period, our area came under to so-called "Christian General," Feng Yü-hsiang, around 1925. We all knew that he was not favorable to Buddhism. However, he was so occupied with military affairs that he had no time to interfere with our religion. After the Northern Expedition (1928) civil order in Inner Mongolia was improved, but, unfortunately for us, Suiyüan Province was established by the Nanking Government and the dominant overlords here were the Shansi clique headed by Yen Hsi-shan. Finally Fu Tso-yi was appointed governor (*chu-hsi*). At first he was Yen's man from Shansi but later became quite independent. He was shrewd and capable and tried to put all our Mongolian league and banner administrative areas under his own provincial and *hsien* governments and to assimilate the Mongols. Even so he showed some respect for Buddhism and our monasteries as part of the policy of Yen and the Shansi clique to buy off the Mongols. On the other hand because of the valuable production of the Ta-ch'ing *shan* coal mines which were our property within the territories of Badghar, our monastery drew greater attention from him for, either good or bad, than in earlier periods. In the mid-1930s the Japanese came on the scene in southern Mongolia and the whole situation changed, never to be the same again for the communists' takeover followed the Japanese occupation.

Most everyone knows of the tragedy that resulted from the lack of Mongolian unification and of the great persistence of regionalism, class differences, and other factors that fragmented our people. The Mongolian autonomous movement of the 1930s introduced great change for the good, however.

All Mongols, from the conservative princes to the radical students and youth, cooperated to overcome their differences and to work toward self-determination for the Mongolian people. I believe the facts confirm that even most of the conservative

[166]

princes, supported by the high lamas, tried to protect the people's best interests, even through a nationalistic movement, to maintain their rights and the traditional structure and teachings of the religion. Some young Mongolian nationalists exerted great effort to achieve not only Mongolian autonomy, but also to abolish the special privileges of the princes, to promote atheism, science and democracy, and to limit the influence of the lamas and the monasteries in the social, economic, and political affairs of the Mongolian nation. A few of the more radical elements even tried to totally abolish the religion.

One major result of the rise of the Mongolian autonomous movement, as it concerned the religion, was the serious dilemma it presented Buddhist leaders and senior lamas. On the one hand, they desired political autonomy and unity with greater security from the threat of Chinese warlords in the border areas, and from Chinese bandits, landgrabbers and other bad elements, feeling that all of this would greatly benefit our people. On the other hand, the lamas were threatened by the younger radical nationalists who wanted to restrict and even abolish the influence of religion.

Now, after looking back many years, I believe the more far-sighted lamas tended to support the autonomous movement with a hope for the benefits mentioned above and a better life for the people. I would include here the Mergen gegen of the Urad Banner, Ulanchab League, the Dilowa khutughtu of Khalkha who had escaped from communist oppression in Outer Mongolia, and the Chaghan gegen, of the Sünid Banner of Shilin-ghol League, who, although not very active, still was sympathetic toward and supported the autonomous movement.

The single most important event launching the autonomous movement was a general conference held in August 1933 at Bat-khaalagh Monastery (Pai-ling-miao), attended by almost all the important leaders of Inner Mongolia. The first meetings of this movement were held, significantly, in the main office (yeke shang) of the monastery and were greatly welcomed by the senior lamas, but as the weeks passed and as young nationalists gathered from eastern Mongolia, from Peking, from Nanking and other places, the religious mood of the meetings began to change as the young intellectuals refused to venerate the images or to show any respect for the religion and the lamas.

[167]

The conference made a declaration for autonomy and gained recognition from the central government, then the political situation began to change rapidly. The nationalists led by De *wang*, Prince Demchügdüngrüb, with the approval of the central government in Nanking, established the Mongolian Autonomous Political Council—what the Mongols at the time called the *Batkhaalaghiin khural*, also widely known in Chinese as the *Mengcheng-hui* (abbreviation for *Meng-ku ti-fang tzu-chih cheng-wu wei-yuan-hui* = Mongolian Council for Regional Political Autonomy).

With the official establishment of this council, that in time was to become a new Mongolian government, Prince De soon sensed a contradiction, a potential antagonism, between the lamas and the young, radical nationalists. It came about in this way.

The monastery was a convenient site for assembling representatives from far and wide, but a group of militant nationalists who soon congregated preferred to eliminate from the proceedings all so-called "decadent, unprogressive, religious influences." They were very critical, even violently opposed to any involvement by the lamas in the affairs of state, whether economic, social or political. They were offended by the mixing of sutra chanting and monastic ritual with discussions for autonomy or independence from China and the building of a new Mongolia.

The lamas were pleased at first to have the recognition and distinction that came from having important conferences held in their monastery, but as the series of meetings dragged on from the spring of 1933 into 1934, with many people coming and going, the lamas became distressed with the disruption of their customary, quiet monastic life and began to complain to Prince De and other leaders. They urged that the political activities be removed from the monastery while the young liberals still wanted to use or even take over the buildings. Thus, there was an undercurrent of conflict between the conservative religious interests of the lamaist monks and the secular, nationalistic views of the young Mongol nationalists.

Meanwhile Wu Ho-ling, a practical and persuasive leader with considerable experience and influence, was continually pushing for a separation of religion and politics. Finally Prince De decided to follow this latter course of action and in the spring of 1934, the headquarters of the autonomous movement with its organization was removed from the monastery and established in a group of yurts one or two miles eastward across a river. This compromise protected the religion from the radical nationalists and at the same time restricted the influence of the religion in politics.

During the events that began the autonomous movement many people frequently spoke critically of the *geming*, a corruption of the Chinese word for revolutionaries, *ke-ming*, that to our Mongolian people meant militant, destructive radicals who tried to tear down the church and destroy all other good traditional institutions of our people. The Mongols were very antagonistic to anyone they considered *geming*. Any movement they considered revolutionary in a neutral sense of the word, they referred to as *khubisghal*. The lamas did not make such a distinction, however, and generally had a negative feeling toward all such movements. The majority of our lay people felt this same way as well. At the meetings at Bat-khaalagh Monastery, as more of the radical element manifested itself, the senior lamas began to feel that many of these young Mongols were really *geming*. Consequently, the lamas began to have some anxieties about the possible result of all the political activities.

Certain conservative princes, according to the rumors I heard at that time, were disturbed by the attitudes and the words of the young radicals they suspected as being *geming*. One of these princes, Pan *wang*, Prince Pandegunchab of Dörbed Banner of Ulanchab League, opposed the autonomous movement, and associated with him was A *wang* (prince Altanochir), the deputy head of the Yeke-juu League. Some of these princes were influenced or intimidated by Fu Tso-yi, the most important Chinese warlord in the western Mongolian border region, a man greatly opposed to the autonomous movement. But Dewagenden, a capable *tosalaghchi*, administrative head, who held the real power within the Dörbed Banner, supported the autonomous movement, and thus the nationalists were able, in part, to diminish the influence of conservative princes like Pan *wang* in Ulanchab to the west.

During the debates our lamas at Badghar Monastery, far removed from the site of the meetings and the movement, were unaffected; we neither supported nor opposed the movement. Our position, partly due to the distance, was largely because of our traditional tendency to avoid political matters. Although I was unaware of the fact until later, the most important political development during my life was without doubt this movement in the 1930s to develop a new Mongolian government.

This autonomous movement, that greatly affected my career, first began with the development of nationalism and the famous meeting held by Prince De at Bat-khaalagh (Pai-ling-miao), as related above. This complex development, that I cannot adequately explain, was a reaction to a threat from both the migration of the Chinese into our region and to the western expansion of the Japanese from Manchuria. In an attempt to protect our people, and as a result of the important conferences mentioned, our Mongolian leaders gained from the Chinese Central Government in Nanking in 1934 an agreement that no more Chinese districts, or hsien, would be established in Mongolian territory. About this same time, however, ignoring the policies set down by the central government, the governor of Chahar, General Sung Che-yüan, on his own authority and in spite of great opposition by the Mongols, established a Chinese hsien (district) at Jabsar and named it Hua-te, a term implying that Prince De (Teh wang) was in the state of being pacified. Moreover, it had the political implication that General Sung was "melting away," "assimilating," or prevailing over Prince De, the main leader of the Mongolian movement for political resurgence.

In 1936 the situation changed radically. General Sung withdrew to Peking as the Japanese came in, and Prince De established a Mongolian Military Government at Jabsar (Ch. Hua-te) in an attempt to protect our people and territory from the threat of General Fu Tso-yi. It was a tense time of confrontation between the Chinese and Mongols, complicated by the rise of Japanese political and military pressure. The Chinese name of the place, Hua-te, was changed to Te-hua—referring, in political symbolism, to the idea that the people were being acculturated by "virtue," that the area would come under or be properly ruled by Prince Demchügdüngrüb, whose Chinese name, Te, was the same character as that used in both names, Te-hua and Hua-te. The formal Mongolian name of the place, hardly used by anyone, was written in the documents as Erdem-soyoltu, literally "virtuous culture," a translation of the Chinese term. This was not the end of name changing, however. When the area was retaken by the Chinese Central Government at the end of the War of Resistance against Japan (1945), the name was once more changed back to Hua-te. While the politicians and young nationalists make much of this name changing, the lamas viewed it merely as political games. But, I suppose one must realize that both the Chinese and the Mongols have always been very concerned with the symbolic meaning of place names.

The new Mongolian government was set up in Jabsar largely because of Japanese pressure. Their strategy was to use the Mongols against their common enemy Fu Tso-yi. But many Mongols were surprised, even a little distressed, that the new Mongolian administration was located at Jabsar, perhaps feeling just a bit superstitious, that it was not an auspicious place for the government because of its name and history.

In Mongolian the name *Jabsar* means literally a break, or gap, between two points. The town grew up at this place located between two hillocks because it was on the main trade route from Urga (now Ulan Bator) to Kalgan. It was located in the Aduuchin Imperial Pasture, later known as the Shangdu Banner of Chakhar.

The rapidly changing political situation soon confirmed that the regime here was an interim, temporary setup with no promise of security or stability, for with the rapid movement of events the Mongolian Military Government was soon moved from Jabsar to Hohhot (Koke-khota, Ch. Kuei-sui) was reorganized as the Mongolian Allied Leagues Government (Mong. *Mongghol-un chighulghan-ig khoboju öbesüben jasakhu jasagh-un ordun*; Ch. *Meng-ku lien-meng tzu-chih cheng-fu*). This move and reorganization took place shortly after the outbreak of the Sino-Japanese War (1937).

Important political and economic changes took place around Badghar Monastery with the new Mongolian Government at Hohhot. The Tümed Banner, the four Right Flank Chakhar Banners, and some of the Chinese districts (*hsien*) were reorganized into a new regional government, Bayan-tala League, in 1937. The governor of this new league was Buyandalai, an intimate friend of Prince De. He tried hard to put Badghar Monastery, with its wealth in coal mines, herds and people, under the jurisdication of his new league government, but the senior lamas of Badghar resisted. I was the monastery abbot at the time but avoided involvement in these political affairs. Such problems were handed by the *demchi-lama* of the monastery.

At issue in this political matter was: first, the monastery was traditionally like an independent local government, just as the

[171]

Tümed Banner or the banners of the Ulanchab region. But this newly established league government wanted to take the wealthy, influential Badghar Monastery into its jurisdiction. Secondly, the Tümed Banner people of Bayan-tala League by this time were greatly influenced by Chinese settlers and Chinese culture but the neighboring Ulanchab area was much less troubled by them. Consequently, the lamas preferred to be associated with the more pure Mongolian area of Ulanchab League to the north. Thirdly, the Mongolian Government's position was to not recognize the secular administrative power of the monasteries. Its policy was to put them under government jurisdiction. So, for a time, Badghar Monastery was caught in a political struggle regarding jurisdiction between the two regional governments. Actually, Ulanchab felt less strongly about the whole matter.

Another great monastery, Shireetü *juu*, was caught in a similar difficulty. Its main center was in Hohhot but it had branches, land and *shabinar* (disciples) located along the border of both Tümed and Ulanchab areas. The abbot of Shireetü Monastery, Samtan *da-lama*, was very ambitious and he reasoned that his monastery and disciples had a larger population than some Ulanchab banners so he pressed for the status of a banner that would confirm more local control plus more influence in the regional government. In the controversy, Shireetü Monastery allied with Badghar and petitioned to be recognized as a special administrative district under Ulanchab League. After an extended period of debate, the two monasteries were finally put under Ulanchab League and given a status similar to that of a banner or district. The final decision, of course, was confirmed by the head of the new Inner Mongolian Government, Prince De.

Two years later another governmental reorganization took place, and the Mongolian Allied Leagues Government at Hohhot was merged at Kalgan (Ch. Chang-chia-k'ou) with two small Chinese puppet regimes of the Japanese that had just been established in the region of Ch'a-nan (southern Chakar) and Chin-pei (northern Shansi). This merger pushed by the Japanese military was against the interests of and distressing to the Mongols. The new government was called Mengchiang (Mongolian territory or dominion).

Many Mongolian people had misgivings about this the Mengchiang government in Kalgan, and the Chinese derisively called it the "false Meng-chiang" regime, a Japanese puppet government. The Mongolian people did not like the name Mengchiang because it implied that our territories, the Mongolian *kijaghar* (Mongolian border) was really a Chinese border and belonged to them. We usually refer to this government simply as the Mongolian Government or the Kalgan Government, but its official title was the Mongolian United Autonomous Government (Mong. *Mongghol-un kholbon neileldüjü öbesüben jasakhu jasagh-un ordun*; Ch. *Meng-ku lien-ho tzu-chih cheng-fu*).

It was no secret that within this new government there were struggles between the Mongols and the Japanese, because our leaders were greatly troubled by Japanese policies that forced them to join with puppet Chinese regimes to begin with, but also this unification greatly affected Mongolian welfare in every facet of life.

With the development of the Kalgan Mongolian Government, and even before, there was a growing tendency for the separation of religion and politics, and at the same time a tendency toward a revival of Mongolian administrative organizations. Consequently, in 1939, because of the large population and the complexities of the Dolonor area, where one of my main monasteries was located, a banner administration was organized that was concerned only with secular affairs. Among the Mongols it handled matters related to education, taxes, conscription of troops, public health, and new cooperatives for the buying and selling of commodities (*khorishia*).

The lamas felt that such administrative innovations were especially pushed by young Mongolian leaders, but for us there was no great break with the past. Our *shabinar* continued to look to us rather than to the new banner government which was supposed to have jurisdiction over them. There were some changes, but these lasted for only a few years, until the end of the war when everything was radically changed with the return of the Chinese and the communists. Though we lamas were not happy with these innovations in our region, we generally maintained our silence, never openly criticizing the government or resisting the new leadership. The wartime situation and the weight of Japan's occupation added to our continuing, though sometimes vague, sense of crisis.

During the period of the Kalgan Government (1939–1945), one of the most important issues, what the lamas spoke of as *chagh* (fate or destiny), concerned policies for our religion and was discussed at all levels by Mongol leaders. There were many

[173]

different opinions, but one thing upon which almost everyone agreed was that the number of lamas must be reduced and limited. Different men had different ideas about how changes should take place. Naturally the senior lamas were very distressed with such discussions. While the objective of many was to reduce the number of lamas and to limit the religion in other ways, such fine sounding terms were used as the "consolidation" or "revival" of Buddhism in Mongolia. Within the government in Kalgan a reform of Lamaist Buddhism had been under discussion for some time, but no one had done anything because the religious situation in Mongolia at the time was quite complicated.

It is important to see the background to the controversy. Changes in many aspects of life were taking place rapidly among our people, and with the growth of education and opportunities for travel, many young Mongols began to have less interest in the religion and, in fact, became quite critical of it. There was a strong tendency for them to blame all the problems and difficulties of modern Mongolia on the lamas and the religion. The atheistic inclination among the educated people was very strong, and it seemed that the majority of the intellectuals, particularly those who were more nationalistic, desired to completely abolish the religion.

There was a significant group in the leadership of the Mongolian government, however, who thought more in terms of religious reform. Closer to them than to the radicals was another strong group of princes, lamas, and lay people who wanted to maintain the Buddhist religion just as it was and to make no changes whatsoever, but they tended to reserve their discontent and did not try to exert their influence.

Some important leaders, particularly Prince De, were strongly devoted to Buddhism and tended to resist the pressure of the young, somewhat radical, nationalists. Prince De would not entirely ignore their influence, however, and he began to allow changes to take place. Nevertheless, these changes, he felt, should not be carried out in the spirit of radical iconoclasm, but rather in the spirit of Buddhism, to bring the religion closer to its ideals. He felt that some religion was better than no religion. The conservatives felt that changes in the religion should allow it to maintain or regain vitality and not choke or kill it.

An important element in the discussions at the time was the Japanese. Among them also there were different views, but many

[174]

of them felt that changes must be made in the orientation of the religion, that Mongolian Buddhism should be brought closer to Japanese Buddhism and reorganized in such a way as to facilitate Japanese influence or control. Actually, I became aware of the religious reform issue in the government in the early 1940s, around the time of my trip to Japan.

One thing on which both conservative and radical Mongols agreed was that changes in the religion should not be dictated or manipulated by the Japanese. Still, they could not ignore the fact that the Japanese were paying considerable attention to this issue, were very anxious that something substantial be done, and were taking action themselves, often without consulting the Mongols. Some wise leaders felt that if changes in the area of religion took place too quickly serious problems would certainly result and this would only weaken the Mongolian society's ability to resist the inroads of the Japanese. Even some active nationalists with rather liberal tendencies chose to maintain a somewhat conservative policy in order to maintain the integrity of Mongolian society and to strengthen it while making certain limited changes.

Between 1941 and 1943 the pressures on the government for reform had become quite strong, and it began to take certain measures for instituting change. It began to limit the number of lamas in the various monasteries, to encourage or require the use of Mongolian texts in the ceremonies and studies of the lamas, to hold examinations for literacy and other qualifications among the lamas in order to determine which ones were to remain in the monasteries and which were to become secularized, taken into the army, sent to school, or involved in some productive activity. Later, in 1943 and after long discussion, a decision was made to organize a *Lama tamagha*, an Office of Lamaist Affairs to coordinate policies and programs related to the religion (this will be discussed later).

Early in the spring of 1941 an important meeting regarding Lamaism presided over by Prince De was held in Shilin-ghol League at Pandita Gegen Monastery (Ch. Pei-tse-miao). The meeting changed life for many young lamas, though not so radically as when the communists came. The circumstances regarding the meeting should be explained. It was just in that period of the early 1940s when Prince De and the Mongolian leadership were weakened because of the overshadowing power of Japan's occupation.

Blocked by the Japanese from handling major problems of government in the area of politics and military affairs, Prince De and other leaders turned their attention to such matters as were within their scope of management such as education and religion. The meeting at Pandita Gegen Monastery was mainly concerned with religion but all top governmental heads from the eight administrative sub-regions (banners) of Shilin-ghol gathered here and it worried the Japanese. Their own situation in China was shaky and tension with the Americans was getting critical. They must have wondered if the Inner Mongolian leaders were plotting some major move to resist Japan, to contact Outer Mongolia or some other such thing. At the meeting it was decided to limit the number of young boys who could be taken into the monasteries to study and become lamas. It was also determined that education in the monasteries must be in the Mongolian language. Other decisions stressed the necessity of lamas learning to do productive work, and the policy that lamas with a bad record of discipline or advancement in their studies should leave the monastery and be secularized. Also it was decided to examine the records of the monasteries throughout Inner Mongolia, and on the basis of this examination, all lamas who were the only son of a family would be immediately returned to their homes. An additional program decided upon was to hold an examination of all lamas as to their literacy and the level of their understanding of five basic sutras. On the basis of this examination all lamas who scored below the level of sixty percent were to leave the temple. All of this was certainly distressing to most senior lamas; but because our Mongolian leaders insisted that the measures were for the welfare of the nation and for the building of a greater Mongolia, there was nothing that could be done to change the new policy.

Later in the winter of 1942 another conference was held in Kalgan and attended by most important religious leaders throughout Inner Mongolia. The overall matter of the future of the religion was discussed and also ways in which a rectification of Buddhism could be accomplished to restore true standards. While it was not openly debated, it was obvious that some compromise must be made between the demands of nationalism and the traditional role of Lamaism or the vested interests of the monasteries. Actually little more was accomplished than a discussion of very broad principles. The meetings were conducted under the auspices of the Mongolia Restoration Commission (*Mongghol-ig mandugh-ulkhu tüshimed-ün khural*). Apparently this particular conference was not of great importance, but there was more yet to come.

In May 1943, a very important conference was held, again planned and conducted by the Mongolia Restoration Commission, particularly under the presiding authority of Prince Sungjing-wangchug, head of the Commission. This larger meeting was attended by most Buddhist leaders and heads of monasteries and was significant in that the policies determined earlier, at the conference held in Shilin-ghol, were, after some resistance, officially set forth and approved by the Lamaist leaders of Inner Mongolia. I attended but cannot clearly remember everything that took place. One incident was a rather dramatic challenge of the measures proposed by Prince Sungjingwangchug by a strong-minded lama from the Shira-mören Monastery in the Dorbed Banner of Ulanchab League. The challenge was dramatic and impressive because, although it was an official government meeting, this particular lama jumped up, clapped his hands and debated with many gestures, just as though he were involved in a traditional doctrinal debate in a monastic assembly. Some of the younger nationalistic officials present were rather distressed with this performance, but Sungjingwangchug, a conservative gentleman who had himself once been a lama, took the whole thing in good grace and smoothly handled the situation in an admirable way. This challenge was a delicate situation in another respect as well. Prince Sung was himself well-known as a very devout Buddhist, while at the same time he was the spokesman for the government and had to implement government policies for change to the religious leaders present at the conference. It was not a comfortable situation for Prince Sung, particularly to confront the rather stubborn, conservative lama who debated everything strictly from the traditional viewpoint of Lamaist Buddhism. As for myself, I was inclined to keep my ears and eyes open and my mouth shut.

In my long experience and study in various monasteries I have seen many formal debates, *choyir*, of Buddhist principles and philosophy, but I must say that this was a rather strange *choyir*. We were accustomed to jumping up and challenging each point in a debate, but this meeting was ordered in such a way that anyone who desired to speak must first raise his hand and get the attention of the chairman, and then speak his mind. This

[177]

was generally done, except that the hard-headed lama from Ulan-chab had his own approach to the situation, as mentioned. The meeting, attended by over one hundred lamas and other officials, was held in the government assembly chambers and lasted for three days. The food was acceptable enough, but there was no entertainment and the general mood of the lamas present was quite subdued, as they lacked any enthusiasm for the whole affair. The main result of the meeting was the official establishment of the *Lama tamagha* (Office of Lamaist Affairs) already mentioned. It seems that this decision was prompted behind the scenes by Wu Ho-ling who served as prime minister for the Kalgan government. A few months later in the autumn of 1943, this office was actually opened in one of the former fine residences of Kalgan.

The *Lama tamagha*, or coordinating office for Lamaist Buddhism under the direction of the government, was not really a new innovation, but was actually an adaptation of an earlier, similar institution organized in Peking during Manchu rule under the direction of the Li-fan yüan, the top-most agency in Peking that set policy and supervised governmental administration in Mongolia and Tibet. This governmental institution, concerned with the control of our religion in Mongolia, continued after the Chinese revolution into the Republican period as the *La-ma yin-wu ch'u*, Office of Lama Affairs. There were other *La-ma yin-wu ch'u* offices or *Lama tamaghas* in Dolonor associated with this old center of imperial monasteries, and also at Wu-t'ai shan. These were each independent and in the old days reported to the Li-fan yüan. In my day they reported to the Mongolian Tibetan Affairs Commission (*Meng Tsang wei-yüan-hui*). Each of these offices was presided over by a *jasagh da-lama* with the title of khutughtu— he was, in other words, an incarnation. He was assisted by a *ded-lama*, an administrative assistant. Thus, the new *Lama tamagha* organized by the Mongolian Government in 1943 derives from this earlier institution.

One can perceive in all this that the Kalgan Government was very cautious and followed a strict policy that temporal or secular affairs be handled by each banner or league government, while religious affairs were supposed to be coordinated under the jurisdiction of the *Lama tamagha*. De *wang* and Sung *wang* took the lead in appointing the staff of the new organization. The person appointed as *jasagh da-lama*, or head of the *Lama tamagha*, was the Chaghan gegen of the Chaghan-oboo Monastery in the East Sünid Banner of Shilin-ghol League. Under him were two deputies, known as ded-lamas, one of which was the Mergen gegen of Mergen Monastery in the Urad Banner of Ulanchab League. I was also designated as a ded-lama; my role was to represent the Chakhar area and the important Badghar Monastery. The demchi, who was actually the most active in this new office, was the Ghabji Lama of East Üjümüchin, Shilin-ghol League, who will be discussed shortly. In those days, Japanese advisors were involved in all branches of government, and there was one, Lieutenant Colonel Yukei Kogan, who was attached to the office of religious affairs. This man had been raised in the family of a Buddhist priest and was supposed to inherit the family temple, but with the outbreak of war he was taken into the army and given special training in a military intelligence school. Thus, he had some background for a special assignment connected with Lamaist Buddhism when he was stationed in Mongolia.

The Chaghan gegen, head of the office, was a very popular incarnation in Shilin-ghol League and a senior figure among the religious leaders in Inner Mongolia. He was the head lama of the Chagan-oboo Monastery, located very strategically on the border of Outer Mongolia in East Sünid. This monastery was shown special attention and goodwill by the Japanese military in the hope of influencing people north of the border in Outer Mongolia. The head of this Monastery, the Chaghan gegen, was very careful in political matters, but nevertheless had a very close relationship with Prince De, head of the Mongolian Government (Kalgan). For these various reasons he was appointed head of the Office of Lamaist Affairs (Lama tamagha) in the government. In 1945 with the Soviet-MPR invasion, for reasons we do not understand, there was no killing and looting at this temple as there was in other places in Mongolia. It is noteworthy that after the Chinese People's Republic was established this Chagan gegen was made head of the Buddhist Association of all China. We assume that he died before the Cultural Revolution, but we have no news.

The Mergen gegen, known by many to have been very sympathetic with the Mongolian Autonomous Movement from the early days of the 1930s, was a good deal more nationalistic and active in politics than most lamas in those days. Of the three top leaders, I was the youngest and the only one to have the distinction of the rank of khutughtu. The Ghabji Lama mentioned was a very intelligent and progressive man with a tendency to be active in politics. It is my impression that the Kalgan government officials created a religious organization, the *Lama tamagha*, at least in part, to give the Ghabji something to do, at the same time preventing him from becoming involved in other political affairs of the Mongolian Government.

The career of this Ghabji Lama is interesting and worthy of discussion here. Originally he was head of the Ghabji Monastery in the East Üjümüchin Banner of Shilin-ghol League. He was a handsome, intelligent person, a relative of Duke Dobdan, one of the most influential men in the region. This monstery was located about fifty miles south of the administrative center (*wang-fu*) of the banner, and included a dozen larger buildings and adjacent living quarters for some two hundred lamas.

The Ghabji incarnation was rather unique among the lamas of Inner Mongolia. He was young, progressive, interested in the outside world and undertook some ambitious projects to introduce modern innovations among his disciples in education, small scale handicraft industry, and a cooperative venture. Inthe early 1940s there were very curious reports from those who visited the monastery. The Ghabji had in his room many pictures of world-famous people—a strange mixture, including such figures as Bismarck, Einstein, Karl Marx, Engels and others, although, it appears, he did not really understand who they all were.

A school was organized by the Ghabji Lama including perhaps twenty or thirty students, both boys and girls on the elementary level, and the classes were held within the monastery. The financing for the school was derived from rather heavy taxes levied upon the Ghabji's hundreds of disciples (*shabinar*) in East Üjümüchin.

Another of his efforts was to establish a rather collective, communal system in his area. In this connection he brought the people together and encouraged them to adopt a more sedentary, pastoral life and move away from their traditional nomadic ways. He even organized a small manufacturing enterprise to make textiles, clothing, and felt cloth for yurts, using lamas to do the work and even participating himself.

The Ghabji Lama began his ambitious program in about 1940 after his return from an earlier visit to Japan in the fall of 1938. The origin of his ideas is unclear; he did not have any real contact with Mongolian intellectuals and it is unlikely that the ideas came from Outer Mongolia. It is more likely that the inspiration was from the Japanese. Certainly the Japanese military intelligence people (*tokumu kikan*) supported and encouraged him. The Japanese group was located for a time at Nunai monastery, perhaps fifty miles to the southeast of the Ghabji Monastery near the Manchurian border.

More important, the Ghabji Lama's modernization movement brought him into conflict with the governing *jasagh* of the banner, one Dorji, who was also young and ambitious but somewhat erratic and, unfortunately, surrounded by unenlightened advisors who were inclined to exploit the people through taxes and various ill-advised levies. The Ghabji Lama's activities came as a challenge to *jasagh* Dorji and gained support because many common layfolk and lamas felt that his efforts were for the benefit of the people.

To the distress of many people, the confrontation between the Ghabji Lama and *jasagh* Dorji was causing a split in the banner with bad feelings, bitter debate, tensions and trouble. The real conflict between the two leaders was probably due to the Dorji's fear that the Ghabji Lama was gaining too much power. The Ghabji Lama protected his disciples and this made it impossible for Dorji to obtain revenue from this important part of his banner or administrative district. The more active the Ghabji Lama became in developing his enterprises and in taxing his people, the more he infringed on the authority and sphere of interest of Dorji. The latter was then unable to gain revenue in taxes from the area for his own needs, which often meant self-serving personal power and pleasure.

It seems, as one looks back on the situation, that the attitudes and views of the Ghabji Lama and of Dorji were contradictory for the time and situation of the two men. The Ghabji, with his rather progressive socialistic tendencies, was inclined towards a basically conservative Japan, but Dorji, a rather conservative *noyan* (prince), looked towards the Mongolian People's Republic with its radical communist tendencies, not really knowing what it was all about, but no doubt being motivated by emotional considerations of his consciousness as a Mongol while still being unaware if not irrational about how he, as a hereditary noble, would fit into a communist sytem.

Prince Demchügdüngrüb (De *wang*), head of the government in Kalgan, also Prince Sungjingwangchugh and other leading officials, were alarmed over the reports of Japanese influence on the Ghabji, not to mention the political schism growing out of the situation. Even though the Ghabji's enterprises were progressive and basically very good, if they were tied to the Japanese in any way, they came under a shadow. There was suspicion of and resistance to anything that might increase Japanese influence on the grass roots level among the people, and there was broad concern about the lamas' open involvement in political and temporal affairs. Finally, De *wang* dispatched the elder statesman Sung *wang* to the East Üjümüchin Banner in the summer of 1941 to resolve the problem.

As Prince Sung was dispatched to settle the problem in Üjümüchin, he was accompanied by his young secretary or administrative assistant, Sechin Jagchid. Both factions, the Ghabji Lama and *jasagh* Dorji, had been advised of his coming and both were worried as to what lay in store for them. Before making a decision, Prince Sung visited both parties, heard their opinions, and considered the situation. He first visited the administrative center of the banner (*wang-fu*) where Dorji was located. Prince Sung already foresaw that it would be necessary to remove Dorji from power but he wanted to see what alternative existed. Particularly, he wanted to see Dorji's young son of four or five, who would be Dorji's successor according to the traditional rule of succession. Also, he wanted to meet Dorji's mother, who could influence the situation. Dorji wanted to present his side of the case and try to gain the ear of Prince Sung, but he was largely ignored during the visit. Instead, Prince Sung consulted with Duke Dobdan, a deputy administrator (*tusalaghchi*), who was a popular person with broad support among the people of the banner, the "silent majority." Prince Sung then traveled to the Ghabji Monastery to observe the situation there.

Having made his inspection and after much discussion, Prince Sung then settled at Ghakhail Monastery to make a final judgment. This monastery was somewhat neutral ground located in between the base of the two competing factions. Here representatives of both sides were brought together and informed that Dorji was to resign in a reorganization of the banner administration. He was to be succeeded in his position as governing *jasagh* by his son, with administrative authority exercised for him by Dobdan as regent. The common people were much relieved with this settlement for there was had much goodwill for Dobdan and many were happy with Dorji's removal.

On the other hand, Prince Sung reaffirmed the policy that lamas were to keep out of politics. The monastery school of the Ghabji was dissolved, and a strict traditional injunction was reiterated that girl students were not to stay in the monastery. The students were transferred fifty miles to a boarding school at the site of the banner administration. The common herdsmen and families who had been brought together in a community at the monastery were released and told to go back to their usual grazing lands. They were quite happy about this because it was against their nature to be crowded together in a close community around the monastery. The cottage industry, only a small productive unit, was allowed to remain in the monastery since Mongolian leaders favored developing some productive work for the lamas.

Still Prince Demchügdüngrüb admired the enterprising spirit of the Ghabji Lama and soon appointed him as a leader in a new organization being set up to coordinate the policy and activities of Mongolian Buddhism, the Office of Lamaist Affairs (*Lama tamagha*) in the central government at Kalgan. The Ghabji actually proved to be most active and enthusiastic in this organization and spent a lot of time in Kalgan.

But there was more. At the end of the war in 1945, the conflict between the Ghabji Lama and Dorji was most likely one reason for a final split in the East Üjümüchin Banner as the former *jasagh* Dorji broke away and led hundreds of people north into Outer Mongolia (MPR). Dorji and the group were welcomed with much hospitality and finally settled in eastern Outer Mongolia some distance south of the important town of Choibalsan. Finally, Dorji was purged in Outer Mongolia and meanwhile, with the Chinese Communist occupation of Inner Mongolia, we lost track of the Ghabji Lama and heard no more of him after he was taken by the Soviet-MPR forces at the end of the war. Duke Dobdan's fate, it seems, was the same as the Ghabji's.

It should be clear that the purpose of the lamas and most incarnations in the various activities of those years, was to find some means of restoring the vitality of the religion and to correct certain bad practices, while strengthening the organization and drawing our people together in a unity, which had never been accomplished prior to this time. This was, of course, a tremendous challenge. I am sorry to say that we were never able to accomplish our objectives. The time was too short; before we could really begin the Japanese withdrew and Mongolia was invaded by Communist forces. We lost our freedom and were forced to flee for our lives.

One of the most illustrious and venerable incarnations in Inner Mongolia during the years of the Japanese occupation in the 1930s and during the Mongolian Government (Kalgan) was the Dilowa *khutughtu* who escaped from the Mongolian People's Republic (Outer Mongolia) and fled into Inner Mongolia with several hundred Khalkha followers. He was a wise and energetic person and very opposed to the radical changes made by the Communists in Khalkha (MPR) with a terrible suppression of our religion there in the 1920s and 1930s. It seems, from our reports, that he had plans to establish a movement, with a base in Inner Mongolia, to recover Outer Mongolia from the anti-religious Communists and to restore Buddhism. The Japanese naturally supported these ideas and tried to exploit the Khalkha refugees from the north for their own expansionist plans. They gave special treatment to the Dilowa's group through these years.

We have learned later that part of these plans was the restoration of the great Jebtsundamba *khutughtu*, who had left this life in Ulan Bator in 1924 and whose succeeding incarnation had been prohibited by the new revolutionary government there. In pursuing this plan, the Dilowa, with Japanese assistance, left on an expedition to Tibet to obtain the approval and assistance of the Tibetan authorities in Lhasa to accomplish the restoration of our most eminent incarnation of all Mongolia. Prince De had reservations about this plan but did not actively oppose it. Also, the Dilowa *khutughtu* was diverted on his trip to Tibet at Hong Kong by the Chinese and spent the latter part of the war near Chungking. With changing conditions in Mongolia after the war the plan was abandoned.

I turn now to a different but related aspect of our discussion on the period of Japan's occupation. We have seen that the late 1930s were very crucial years in the political development of our people, largely because of increased Japanese pressure to consolidate their domination of North China and Inner Mongolia. One result, as related before, was the new Mongolian government established in Hohhot in 1937 and its forced unification with two Chinese puppet regimes of the Japanese in southern Chahar (Ch'a-nan) and northern Shansi (Chin-pei) in 1939. It seems that the Japanese were rather anxious about the Mongols who were very proud of the fact that they had established an autonomous government even before the Japanese came in. The Mongols were inclined to an independent approach but the Japanese wanted to curb their autonomy and constrain them in a direction suitable to Japanese strategy. A key to the political situation was the fact that the Mongols occupied a very strategic area on the northern frontier between the spheres of Russia and China.

As the years went by, and as I became more familiar with the situation through conversation with Mongolian leaders, I realized that one big problem for the Mongols was largely due to the scheming activity of a group centered around an influential Japanese "advisor" we called Altan Khudagh. His real name was Shoji Kanai—his Mongolian name, Altan Khudagh, "golden well," comes from the Chinese characters for his name, Chin-ching. A very capable man, Altan Khudagh was earlier involved in the administrative development of Manchukou. As Japan's Kwantung Army moved into the Mongol-China border area, he was given the main responsibility of consolidating the complex administrative organization for this area. From our Mongolian point of view he was too inclined to continual interference in Mongolian affairs, and such actions served only to create a bad image in the minds of the Mongols. but I recall that he was very friendly to me, no doubt because he thought I could influence many lamas. My actions during those years confirm that I did not myself have any personal ambitions. At the same time I sensed that Kanai's contact with me made Prince De and other high officials in the government uneasy because they were fully aware of the Japanese ambitions to control Mongolian politics. Altan Khudagh (Kanai) was a man who thought purely in terms of power, administration, and efficiency. He had no sympathy with the Mongolian people's aspirations for self-determination. In those days communications were often a mixture of Mongolian, Chinese and Japanese languages, and funny combinations resulted. Speaking of Japanese advisors I note that there is a good Mongolian term for advisor, asuughchi (asaghughchi), but in those days the Mongols often used the term guowen, a misadaption in Mongolian mispronunciation from the Chinese ku-wen (advisor). This was an unintentional but ironic pun because this Mongolian guowen may come back into Chinese as kuo-wen, meaning "interference." In fact, Japanese ku-wen were more interference than advisement.

It seems that this advisor was distressed by the attitudes and behavior of those Mongols who resisted outside pressure and

[185]

interference from anyone, whether Chinese warlords, Japanese politicians, or others. Apparently Altan Khudagh wanted to neutralize Mongolian feelings of independence and to gain the people's total compliance to Japanese directives so the Japanese could better set up their defenses, and gain requisitions in Mongolia. In the summer and autumn of 1939 the spirits of the Mongolian leaders were very low. Whenever we met them, they shook their heads and groaned about the new difficulties that had come to our people. Though I am not informed about all of the political matters, I recall that finally, about the time of the outbreak of the Japanese war with America, Altan Khudagh was forced out of his position, largely because of the Mongolian leaders' dissatisfaction.

In discussing the war period, one tragedy comes to mind. In 1939, a great battle broke out between the Russians and the Japanese with both sides using Mongolian troops. This was near Bargha, in Hulun-buir where the Kanjurwa lineage had many followers and a large monastery. I had personally spent much time there. This conflict was known to us as the Nomunkhan Battle and to many others as the battle of Khalkha River, which was the boundary between the region dominated by the Japanese and the region dominated by the Russians. the battle was very near my Kanjur Monastery and brought great tragedy to many of our people. On both sides the big powers forced Mongolian brothers to fight and kill each other. I heard reports that during the battles, which lasted about five months, the Inner Mongolian troops trained by the Japanese finally refused to move forward to kill Outer Mongolian Khalkha men. Many young officers who had been trained in military academies in Manchukuo but who rebelled during the battle disappeared and were known to have been annihilated by the Japanese. Though there was no great damage to the Kanjur Monastery or to the lamas in that area, the fact that this was an important place in the overall region of the battle and used by the Japanese troops as a base caused us great concern. The whole situation was a nightmare.

We heard that the battle of Nomunkhan was considered by some Japanese to be a test of whether their Mongolian-trained troops would really fight for them against their countrymen, under communist rule in Outer Mongolia supported by the Russians. Certainly, the Japanese must have been disappointed in the results, for in this case blood (nationality) was thicker than indoctrination or ideology and the Inner Mongols did not fight Outer Mongols. We heard, for example, of incidents in which the Outer Mongol and Soviet troops prepared to use their artillery to shell the Japanese Inner Mongolian forces, but they spread the word by Mongolian language that the Mongols should lie low and not be killed with the Japanese. Many were saved from the barrage. In one instance, it was reported that a group of Inner Mongolian troops were isolated and had gone for a long time without food. At this point, the Outer Mongolian forces with loud speakers announced that they were preparing to attack, and that the Inner Mongolian troops should retreat and that food would then be left for them while the Outer Mongolian troops retreated, leaving the food for the Inner Mongolian brothers to eat. Such situations persuaded the Inner Mongolian troops that they should not follow the Japanese commands to slaughter the Khalkha troops.

These experiences gravely affected the morale of the Inner Mongolian troops and, after this defeat, the Japanese decided not to use Inner Mongolian troops against the Khalka Mongols. Thereafter, they were transferred to the south against Chinese lines. In 1944 and 1945, they were committed in combat against Chinese Communist guerrillas along the Great Wall and were very effective. They demonstrated that Mongol soldiers could, indeed, be valiant fighters in a just cause.

After the Nomunkhan war, a group of lamas came from the Kanjur Monastery in Hulun-buir to Badghar to visit me. As they were returning they were detained by the Japanese military intelligence group (tokumu kikan) at Pandita Gegen Monastery for quite a long time. Finally they were released but after this incident no one was allowed to travel the route through the border area, because it passed near Soyolji Mountain, in East Üjümüchin, a strategic point where Inner Mongolia, Khalkha (MPR), and Manchukuo met.

Another, less significant development during 1939 was the reorganization of the Dolonor shabinar into a formal banner organization. Dolonor, I have stressed, was a very special place to me. Here I studied and worked for many years. It was an important place not only for the Mongols but also for the Chinese and Japanese as an economic and administrative center. In the early Manchu-Ch'ing period two great imperial temples were established in Dolonor. When important incarnations were located here, they attracted many lamas who in turn attracted other

Mongols and Chinese merchants, and as population grew this area became a fairly large center of religious, business, and political activities.

Finally, because of the growing Chinese population, Peking organized an administrative office called the To-lun t'ing in the early part of the Chinese Republic, it seems in 1914. Later, as the population grew the office was reorganized into a *hsien* (or Chinese district) administration, with its operation restricted mainly to the Chinese population in the area. There was, however, a large Mongolian population here because of the two great monasteries in which were situated thirteen important incarnations, each having his own monastic quarters, *shang* (treasury), and group of disciples (*shabinar*). This Mongolian population of lamas and disciples was not under the jurisdiction of the Chinese *hsien* but was under the overall administration of the *Lama tamagha*, which during the Manchu-Ch'ing Dynasty was under the jurisdiction of the Li-fan *yüan*, as mentioned above.

The Rise of Communism and My Escape to Taiwan

The Japanese occupation was an unhappy time for the Mongols, but many times worse was the coming of the communists, both Soviet and Chinese, in the fall of 1945. This was especially so for Lamaist Buddhism. The Soviets from the north were accompanied by the Khalkha Mongols, many of whom had turned to communism earlier with the revolution and the establishment of the Mongolian People's Republic (MPR) in 1924.

Some people wonder how it was possible for the Khalkha Mongols, when they had traditionally been such devoted Buddhists, to change so quickly and espouse the evil, godless doctrine of communism. I feel that the reason was not because the people had lost their faith or rejected Buddhism, but rather because the lamas as spiritual leaders were not responsible for governmental administration, for politics and other affairs of state. One must understand that by the time of the revolution the princes, the *jasagh-noyan*'s, the real rulers of the people, had become greatly indebted to the Chinese. There were many demands on their resources but nothing to restrain them from making heavy demands on their people in various taxes. In those days the princes were very oppressive and many were very arbitrary in punishing their people with the long "black whip" (*khara tashuur*).

Also, according to the reports, it seems that in Khalkha there were too many lamas. Even worse, many of them were really only "part-time" lamas; they came to the monasteries, were ordained lamas, made their oath at the altar before the Buddha, and then departed to eat, make merry, and cause trouble. It was difficult to discipline them, and because of their misbehavior many people had a negative impression and opposition to them grew.

The lamas and faithful believers felt that they should not get involved in politics, nor organize public movements. They believed that they should support the government. Consequently, as the communists began to take over and change the old ways in Outer Mongolia, the lamas and devout Buddhists were very passive and did not organize any resistance. Even though the lamas and heads of monasteries had negative feelings about the revolutionary government from the beginning they were acquiescent. Only later, as a reaction against radical governmental oppression, did they rebel. Consequently, by the time the lamas and the people learned that dark days for the religion had come, it was too late for them to do anything. Outside people would say that they were fatalistic. Be that as it may, everything has its *chagh* (fate or time); therefore, when the time had come for Mongolia's conversion to Communism, it was accomplished and no one could turn the clock back.

The end of the war, Japan's withdrawal, and the communist incursions came in August of 1945. Earlier, in the spring of that year we held a *cham* at the Dolonor Monastery. I was thirty-one at the time. This dance-drama or ritualistic presentation commemorating the ancient victory of Buddhism over the wicked Tibeten King Landarma, was to be the last I would ever observe in Mongolia, for soon Inner Mongolia was inundated by Russian and Outer Mongolian troops from the north, and later by Chinese Nationalist and Communist troops. Thus, Inner Mongolia became a crucial site in the Chinese civil war.

Regarding the Chinese Communists at Yenan during the war it may be noted that the leaders at Badghar Monastery were only vaguely aware that based in the southern Ordos on the borders of Otogh and Üüshin (Ügüshin) Banners there was a group of Mongols attached to the Chinese Communists. They were far away and to us they lived in another world. Their radical anti-religious ideas were of no consequence to us at the time. Only later did we become aware of such leftist Mongolian leaders as Ulanfu. We never dreamed that they would change our world as they came in to take power with the collapse of Japan's empire.

We were more aware in those years of the threat from Outer Mongolia (MPR). From the reports of such famous lama refugees as the Dilowa *khutughtu* and Ochirdara (Vajra-dhara) *gegen* we knew of the terrible things that had befallen the monasteries, religion and lamas in the Khalkha areas, so in the Japanese-Russian confrontation we were more worried about military forces invading from the north. In a sense our fears were well founded, for in August of 1945 Soviet forces along with Khalkha Mongolian troops did come in and create many problems for our people.

I spent the summer of 1945 at Juu-naiman süme. Then in August the Russian troops came into Dolonor, bringing with them much suffering for our Mongolian people. In the chaos and turmoil of Japan's collapse and the communist takeover, I wandered from home to home among my believers. Finally, in the middle of September I escaped from Juu-naiman süme and the communist areas, suffering from hunger and fatigue for some eight days before I arrived in Peking.

One reason I fled was that I had learned by many reports and rumors from different places of the terrible things had happened in some monasteries. Some one hundred and twenty lamas were killed by Soviet troops at Pandita Gegen Monastery. It was the custom of the lamas at this monastery to gather together when a Japanese or Mongolian official came to make an announcement. Consequently, when the invading Soviet forces instructed the lamas to gather together, they assumed that the officers wanted to make a speech and many of them out of curiosity gathered in the courtyard of the monastery. The Soviet troops then forced them behind a heap of ashes from the monastery stoves and massacred them brutally with machine guns. After this mass murder, the same troops, as they moved southward, stopped at the Changdu Monastery where they killed more than twenty lamas for no reason. Then, after coming to the monastery at Dolonor, the Russians destroyed all the images and scriptures and looted the area. Fortunately I was absent from these places when all of this happened because I hid when the first reports of the crisis came in. As I wandered among the people, hearing reports of these terrible events, I determined that I would flee to Peking.

During my stay in Peking, this city was also in turmoil because of the end of the war and the influx of troops and refugees. In the chaos I found it impossible to work with the Nationalist generals and administrators in Peking, and in April of 1947 I even considered going to Kalgan where Fu Tso-yi had established a new base. I finally decided that I could only work with Generalissimo Chiang Kai-shek, but his own problems precluded this. In 1948 he was elected President of the Republic of China. Previous to this, in Chungking, he held only the title of Generalissimo and later Chairman of the central government.

Because the situation in northern China was very tense in the fall of 1948 due to the advancing threat of the communist troops, I made my way to Tsingtao, and here I conducted a great public prayer ceremony with thousands present hoping for a favorable change in the difficult military situation. From Tsing-tao I travelled by boat to Shanghai and Nanking, arriving in November 1948.

When I arrived in Nanking, the head of the Mongolian Tibetan Affairs Commission was Mr. Hsu Shih-ying. This man was quite famous for his earlier illustrious career when he served as Prime Minister of the ephemeral Peking regime in the 1920s, before the Northern Expedition (1928) when the Nationalist forces unified China and established the Nanking government. Later, he served as minister of Japan just before the war began with Japan's invasion in 1937. The Mongolian leaders felt that Mr. Hsu was quite sympathetic to Mongolian autonomy and opposed the harsh policies of such warlords as Fu Tso-yi who exploited and suppressed the Mongols. In Nanking Mr. Hsu graciously helped me obtain new clothing and quarters in which I could stay for a time, and extended other cordial hospitality, including a handsome picture of President Chiang Kai-shek who I met during the winter in Nanking. I went to Canton in the spring because of the threatening communist sweep from the north.

From Canton I went to Taiwan by means of a commercial boat, arriving in 1949 in company with some of my Mongolian countrymen, including Sechin Jagchid, Jirghalang and others. During our sea journey we met a dilemma in the form of a terrible typhoon. If we stayed at sea we may have been in danger when the typhoon struck; but, if we docked at some Fukien harbor we risked being captured by the communists. Finally a group of leaders on the boat decided to take the risk of making a dash for the port of Kilung in northern Taiwan. Although we succeeded in landing shortly before the typhoon hit, the boat was damaged and never sailed again, but became a floating hotel.

On the fifth day of the eighth month of 1949 I moved to the P'u-chi *ssu* (temple) near Taipei, a temple originally established by the Japanese during their occupation of Taiwan. One or two years after this, I and the Jangjia *khutughtu*, who was also then in Taipei, put the difficulties of the past behind us, established a very cordial relationship, and visited together from time to time. The Governor of Taiwan at this time was Ch'en Ch'eng, and it was through his good offices that arrangements were made for me to live at P'u-chi *ssu*, a monastic temple for Chinese priests. Later in the 1950s he served concurrently as the Premier and the Vice-president of the Republic of China (Taiwan). Under his leadership a very successful land reform was carried out.

In 1952 Premier Ch'en Ch'eng asked me during an appointment to do something for the benefit of Buddhism in Taiwan. Two Chinese monks, Tz'u-hang *fa-shih* and Lü-hang *fa-shih*, also came to the appointment. Inasmuch as the dominant population of Taiwan was Buddhist, we were asked to use our office and influence the people indirectly and explain to the people the anti-communist but favorable religious policy of the government and to urge them to lend their support. These two notable Chinese monks and I then travelled around the island in a circuit, preaching to the people. In 1953 two of my disciples and I also travelled the circuit once more for the same purpose. From 1954 to 1956 I resided at the P'u-chi ssu. In 1957 the venerable Jangjia *khutughtu* passed into *nirvana*, and I administered over the various ceremonies at his memorial service. Soon after, I was nominated First Director of the Board of the Chinese Buddhist Association.

In May 1958 as the head of a Chinese delegation, I visited Bangkok, Thailand, and Cambodia to commemorate the 2500th anniversary of the birth of Lord Buddha. Then as head of the Chinese Buddhist Association, I traveled around the island of Taiwan, preaching to the people. Until 1961 I was elected each year as the First Director of the Board of the Chinese Buddhist Association; then in 1962 I resigned the office, but continued as honorary president of the board.

The Rise of Communism and My Escape to Taiwan

In 1964 I was invited by my followers in Hong Kong to visit them and there I read Buddhist scriptures, prayed, blessed the people, and attracted many more patrons and followers. After that visit, I resided most of the time in Taipei, meditating and studying, but travelled three times to Hong Kong from 1969 to 1971, where I performed special ceremonies and blessings for my followers. On these occasions I presided over important gatherings of monks and followers and carried out various ceremonies.

In my present circumstances in Taiwan I am totally involved in spiritual affairs. I arise at four o'clock in the morning to read scripture and to pray, and my first prayer is always for peace among mankind. Following this, I take my morning tea at six o'clock. To the Mongols, tea in the morning really means breakfast, for it involves not only tea mixed with milk, but also small cakes and some meat and other milk products, or millet. The rest of my time I spend largely in reading scripture, in meditation, or with my friends when they visit from time to time. My evening meal is ordinarily from five to six o'clock, following which I devote myself to my evening religious observances.

One thing uppermost in my mind, which I will never forget, is that I am a Mongol. I am continually concerned for my fellow countrymen and greatly desire the restoration to our Mongolian people of the benefits of freedom, a good life, and the blessings of the Buddha. To me, the ideal is a well-developed Mongolia that is a Buddhist nation. We must realize that all of us are subject to, or inseparable from chagh, predestined fate. We may neither resist it, nor push it forward. I feel that I am first and last a Mongol, regardless of what my chagh or that of the Mongols may be. I can never forget or cease to be concerned about my country and my people. I am aware that what I do and say is important not only to me personally but for all Mongolians.

In addition to my obligations as a Mongol, I am also a Buddhist and am continually reminded that I must be a model Buddhist as well as a model Mongol. I read Mongolian, Tibetan, and a little Chinese. But I cannot write Chinese and thus cannot write letters to my Chinese friends. From this time on, I trust that if something important occurs I will be more careful in recording it.

In my evening meditations I continually pray not only for our Mongolian people but also for the Chinese, particularly those in Communist China. I pray that they may not be oppressed, that

[193]

they may take heart and in due time regain their freedom, and that I myself may in the future return to Mongolia and to my people. Since I was taken from Serkü Monastery many years ago as a young incarnation, I have never to this day had the joy of casting my eyes once more upon my birthplace. I am now (1979) in my sixties and often wonder what happened to my old home and family.

My thoughts naturally often turn to my home of many years, but I probably would not recognize the vicinity now of what was once Badghar Monastery; the famous old Buddhist center is now near the scene of a great industrial works. The Chinese Communists have now established an important steel center at Pao-t'ou, using the iron at Bayan-oboo of Darkhan Banner in Ulanchab League, the water of the Yellow River, and the rich coal deposits near Badghar Monastery.

Nevertheless, I have been made very comfortable in Taiwan thanks to my disciples here who built for me a small temple-residence, named Kan-chu ching-she (elegant residence of the Kanjur). Due to these unforeseen changes in my life, coming out of the steppes of Mongolia to this Chinese island, I am now preaching the Path of the Buddha mostly to the Chinese people–almost no Mongols. Outside of Taiwan I have devoted disciples in Hong Kong, Manila, and even in Canada and America. I have visited these Asian disciples and hope to visit the ones in the West.

Index

abral, 75, 117
acupuncture, 85
Aghu-yeke-onoltu *süme* (formal
  Mongolian name of Badghar
  Monastery), 27
Aghwang-lobsang-choi-dong (name of
  Jangjia *khutughtu*), 26
Aghwang-lobsang-dambi-nima (New
  temple name of Kanjurwa), 7
Aghwang-yontson (Ya *jasagh*)
  administrative assistant to
  Kanjurwa, 45
Alashan region: history of, 42
Alashan *yamun* (administrative office
  of Alashan area), 41
altan bomba (system for finding
  imperial incarnations), 16
Altan Khan, 14, 20, 45; meets with
  Third Dalai Lama of Tibet, 6
Altan Khudagh (Japanese adviser),
  185–186
Altan *oboo* (burial site for important
  lamas of Bagdhar), 138
Altan Tobchi (old record), 111
amban, 50, 126
arad (common people), 155, 164
Ar Boghda, 159
archery, 92, 107
Ariin-süme, 21, 22, 25, 27
Ariyabul (Buddhist diety), 70, 87
arja, 87
ar shang, 80
Autonomous movement in Mongolia.
  See Mongolia, independence
  movement in
Aoyama (Japanese doctor), 115–116
Ayushi Buddha, 110

Badghar *choilung* (Tibetan name for
  Badghar Monastery), 27
Badghar Monastery, 11, 165–172;
  customary meditative seclusion
  described, 72–73; customary
  vacation from, 109; founded by two
  leading incarnations, 27–28;
  instillation of incarnations at, 27;
  local diety of, 96; smallpox
  epidemic at, 137; Tibetan-style
  architecture of, 65; under political
  influence of Fu Tso-yi, 144
Badmatsereng, Kanjurwa first named,
  4
baghshi: explained, 8, 62; relationship
  to disciples, 157
Ba *jasagh*, 47, 49
baling, 72, 129
band, Chinese, 46, 54; lama, 54;
  Badghar Monastery, 63
Banner, 56, 82
Bargha area, 92, 126–130, 147
Bayan-tala League, 171
birthdays, 110–112
bodhisattva, 14, 87
boghda lama: reincarnations of, 13–14,
  17
bölkomlin khamghalakh ("collective
  security"), 140
bolsh, 53
bomba, 70
Bon religion, 85
bootees, 6
Boxer Rebellion, 43
Buddha: teachings of, 113; 2500th
  birthday of, 192